May 2015

What Should I Do with
the Rest of My Life?

Yolanda,

Whatever you decide to do - make sure it's something that makes you happy.

Enjoy!

Elizabeth

D1052887

What Should I Do with the Rest of My Life?

TRUE STORIES OF FINDING SUCCESS, PASSION, AND NEW MEANING IN THE SECOND HALF OF LIFE

BRUCE FRANKEL

AVERY

a member of

Penguin Group (USA) Inc.

New York

AVERY

Published by the Penguin Group

Penguin Group (USA) Inc., 375 Hudson Street, New York, New York 10014, USA • Penguin Group (Canada), 90 Eglinton Avenue East, Suite 700, Toronto, Ontario M4P 2Y3, Canada (a division of Pearson Penguin Canada Inc.) • Penguin Books Ltd, 80 Strand, London WC2R 0RL, England • Penguin Ireland, 25 St Stephen's Green, Dublin 2, Ireland (a division of Penguin Books Ltd) • Penguin Group (Australia), 250 Camberwell Road, Camberwell, Victoria 3124, Australia (a division of Pearson Australia Group Pty Ltd) • Penguin Books India Pvt Ltd, 11 Community Centre, Panchsheel Park, New Delhi–110 017, India • Penguin Group (NZ), 67 Apollo Drive, Rosedale, North Shore 0632, New Zealand (a division of Pearson New Zealand Ltd) • Penguin Books (South Africa) (Pty) Ltd, 24 Sturdee Avenue, Rosebank, Johannesburg 2196, South Africa

Penguin Books Ltd, Registered Offices: 80 Strand, London WC2R 0RL, England

First trade paperback edition 2011
Copyright © 2010 by Bruce Frankel

The Sex Collectors: The Secret World of Consumers, Connoisseurs, Curators, Creators, Dealers, Bibliographers, and Accumulators of "Erotica" by Geoff Nicholson. Copyright © 2006 by Geoff Nicholson (New York: Simon & Schuster, 2006).

Jane Kenyon, excerpts "Otherwise" and "American Triptych: Potluck at the Wilmot Flat Baptist Church" from Collected Poems. Copyright © 1978, 1993 by Jane Kenyon. Reprinted with the permission of Graywolf Press, Minneapolis, Minnesota, www.graywolfpress.org.
"Blue Skies" by Irving Berlin. © Copyright 1926, 1927 by Irving Berlin. © Copyright Renewed. International Copyright Secured. All Rights Reserved. Reprinted by Permission.
Iconoclast: A Neuroscientist Reveals How to Think Differently by Gregory Berns, Harvard Business Publishing, 2008.

Most Avery books are available at special quantity discounts for bulk purchase for sales promotions, premiums, fund-raising, and educational needs. Special books or book excerpts also can be created to fit specific needs. For details, write Penguin Group (USA) Inc. Special Markets, 375 Hudson Street, New York, NY 10014.

The Library of Congress has catalogued the hardcover edition as follows:

Frankel, Bruce.
What should I do with the rest of my life? : true stories of finding success, passion, and new meaning in the second half of life/Bruce Frankel.
p.   cm.
Includes bibliographical references.
ISBN 978-1-58333-365-5
1. Older people—United States—Case studies.   2. Success.   3. Self-realization.   I. Title.
HQ1064.U5F69   2010
646.7'9—dc22   2009044543

Printed in the United States of America
1   3   5   7   9   10   8   6   4   2

ISBN 978-1-58333-418-8 (paperback edition)

Book design by Meighan Cavanaugh

Some of the names and identifying characteristics of the interviewees featured in this book have been changed to protect their privacy.

For my parents, Anita and Bernie

ACKNOWLEDGMENTS

The path that leads to success, passion, and new meaning may be found intentionally or serendipitously. But the ability to follow it, to endure its tests or apprehend its lessons, comes from faculties aided and nurtured by others. I doubt that I could have ever completed this book without the consistent and selfless encouragement and collaboration of others. And I am grateful to everyone who helped me with priceless cooperation, insight, and enthusiasm. This book would not exist without their conversations and critiques.

Many people suggested subjects and leads for the book, but I would be remiss not to single out Jim Emerman of Civic Ventures, Marcie Schwarz, Nancy Emerson Lombardo of Boston University School of Medicine, Cathy Pokines and Cecelia Taylor of the U.S. Small Business Administration, Mary Gergen, who publishes The Positive Aging Newsletter, Dick Goldberg of ComingofAge.org, and Margaret Newhouse of PassionandPurpose .com. In some cases, their suggestions led directly to the inspiring people in this book; in others, their interest and the queries they sent out on their email lists on my behalf buoyed me at an important juncture.

I am profoundly grateful to Jim Jerome for his unstinting friendship and his many valuable suggestions. Susan Dalsimer's clear-sighted critique helped firm an early draft and relieve some anxiety. Thanks, too, to Pam Barr. I am grateful to Jean Brown for her speedy transcriptions when I was in a crunch. Abundant thanks to the editorial team at Avery/Penguin, including copy editor Allison Hargraves and copy chief Elizabeth Wagner, who caught my errors and fixed my prose as best they could, and to Miriam Rich, for her cheerful efficiency. It has been a delight to have Lucia Watson as my editor. She has been unfailingly gracious, upbeat, sensitive, and thoughtful. Her improvements to the manuscript were uniformly deft and clarifying.

I owe a special appreciation to Ryan Fischer-Harbage, my agent. Before he had any vested interest, he kept after me to pursue this book. From the time we met, in a workshop he gave on how to write a book proposal, he lived up to my impression of him as an ideal agent—excited about books, knowledgeable about the business, and poised to represent the author's best interest. I feel lucky to have him in my corner.

I could not have written this book without the nurturing and encouragement of friends and loved ones. I am eternally grateful to Liz Frankel, the mother of my three children, for her years of love, devotion, and support. Special thanks to Marisa Galisteo, who gave me a compass and taught me to use it. Thanks to Linda Nettekoven and Larry Wallack for putting me up in Portland; to Kevin Roche for lunch in Nashville; to Rik Kirkland for sage advice; and to my brother Geoff and sister-in-law Maria, Doug Brandt, Kathryn Grody, and Lenore Hecht for cheering me on.

I owe a huge debt to Leslie Shafer Koval, whose love lifted me when my writing got me down. She helped unknot my thoughts when they became tangled, pulled me out of my chair to dance when I sat too long, and shared her paradise with me.

Throughout, I have been fueled and humbled by the faith and confidence of my sons, Alex, Zach, and Isaiah. They can only be a fraction as proud of me as I am of each of them.

I owe supreme thanks to my parents, Anita and Bernie. Before his death in 1996, my father's business life was a roller-coaster ride. Regardless of how low its dips, he remained an exemplar of cheerful resilience who never spoke a word of envy. He delighted in knowing people and the stories of their success, the more humble their origins the better. Part of what my mother taught me is found in the introduction, but there was much she breathed into me long before she reached her eighties. In one of the earliest sound bites of childhood, I hear my mother say convincingly, "You can become anything you wish." Her resolve and her willingness to risk failure to achieve beauty when she finally began painting again was a happy beacon. But nothing was as good for me as the enjoyment she took from having me read chapters to her over the phone as I completed them.

Lastly, I offer my abiding admiration and gratitude to the astonishing people in this book, who opened their lives, homes, and souls to me. It has been my honor and privilege to watch them at work in a world they continue to enrich and illuminate with their active presence, and to tell their inspiring stories, which, I hope, will endow readers of this book with the inspiration and courage to achieve what can scarcely be imagined or foretold.

CONTENTS

What Should I Do with the Rest of My Life?

Introduction

I am now in the final year of my sixth decade. If I were a generation older, I would be anticipating the finish line of my working life and the greeting *Happy 60th!* would loom above it like an anvil waiting to drop on my surviving dreams and aspirations of youth. It was not long ago, after all, that novelist William Styron, in the grips of a depression that began on that same birthday, called sixty "that hulking milestone of mortality." Gratefully, the prospect of turning sixty has improved significantly. The age at which we imagine limitation encroaching on our abilities to perform mentally, physically, and sexually has been receding rapidly. But far too often the old beliefs cling to everyday language, attitudes, behaviors, hiring practices, and, perhaps most important, to the conversations we have with ourselves.

In recent years, neuroscientists have been providing news that is a powerful antidote to negative views of aging. In one of the most optimistic developments of our time, a scientific revolution has found that the brain is plastic and that what we do, think, and experience changes it throughout our lives. Moreover, a groundswell of research has been confirming that our brains can remain fit, like our bodies, for a quarter of a century beyond sixty and, increasingly common, longer still.

Such good news could not come at a better time.

With devastating speed, the financial crisis of 2008–2009 has destroyed hopes for early retirement entertained by many of the nation's seventy-eight million baby boomers, born between 1946 and 1964. A "once-in-a-century" economic event—as former Federal Reserve chairman Alan Greenspan called the recession—has depleted savings, devalued homes, and ravaged stock portfolios, college savings, and retirement accounts. Even if economic recovery takes place in 2010, people are likely to have to work years longer than they ever dreamed to regain lost financial ground.

This will further stoke the already growing trend of longer work lives. With average life expectancy surging beyond seventy-seven, the potential for boredom and the expense of living two or three decades of idle life were already making retirement less alluring. Even before the economic downturn, when they were feeling considerably more flush, 79 percent of boomers between fifty and fifty-nine did not intend to voluntarily retire from full-time work at the traditional age, according to a MetLife Foundation/Civic Ventures Encore Career Survey. Rather than pursue the life of leisure their parents' generation had, they intended to find meaningful employment, at least part-time. About half of those already in second careers have chosen to remain as consultants in familiar professions, while nearly a third have chosen to enter new careers in education, health, and nonprofits.

For a decade, students of successful aging have been promising that the trend of encore careers would benefit older adults and be a boon to American society. Some have been making the case for socially connected work in the second half of life as a source of individual and societal renewal. Marc Freedman, the cofounder of Civic Ventures, has built on the groundbreaking work of John Gardner, the architect of Lyndon Johnson's Great Society and the founder of Executive Corps and Common Cause, and has had a notable impact. As a result, the discussion has been shifting away from how to protect the rights of older Americans to work to how to cultivate work that enriches their lives, allows them to play vital roles in improving and strengthening their communities, and employs skills, talents, and creativity generated over a lifetime.

Considering what is being learned about the resilience of the miraculous three pounds of protoplasm we carry around in our skulls, there may be another upside to this shift. The brain does not like to be idle either, and work is one of the best ways to keep it busy. The less we demand of it and the less stimulation, novelty, and variety we provide, the more likely it is to shrink—quite literally—and stop doing the things we hope it will, like remember. The wonder is that what is required to keep the brain strong, nimble, and durable is not neurological magic so much as common sense, discipline, luck, and loving-kindness.

The full implications of these discoveries are just being explored. But they have already overturned centuries of dogma that at birth the brain is allotted its one hundred billion cells, which then die off throughout a lifetime and at an accelerating pace as we age.

The stories of the people in this book also refute that old dogma, but with an evidence not found in laboratory animals and brain scans. They offer persuasive and encouraging proof of the long-lasting human potential for physical, intellectual, and creative vitality that can be reclaimed and enlarged upon by people from their sixties to the cusp of one hundred.

. . .

This is a book of profiles of people who have succeeded after sixty. Their stories are not simply examples of successful aging, they are inspirational in the truest sense. We want to breathe the positive air they breathe, take risks and experience the energy and strength to remake ourselves as they have, be consumed by our imaginations as they are, pursue passion and purpose—at any age—as they do. They do not so much defy age as defy the limitation that our culture places on age, a culture that too often discounts, trivializes, or humors the ambitions of older adults.

Over the two years spent gathering these stories—listening to the people in this book and watching them at work—I have frequently returned home to share their accounts with family and friends. More often than not, my auditors brightened with interest, particularly if they were baby boomers. What became obvious was that they, too, were hungry for proof that there is as much possibility left in their lives as is incessantly advertised in commercials for financial services, facial products, and remedies for sexual dysfunction. Almost always, when I finished one tale or another, the listener would say something like, "I guess there's hope for me!" or "So, what should I do with the rest of my life?"

Occasionally, someone would comment, "Better late!" But the success and reward of these later-life achievers bestows more than exemption for tardiness. They have gotten the chance to savor the process of becoming something new and surprising—and recognition for what they do—in ways impossible for a young person obsessed with the next act. Their stories are, after all, more than just proof that they have succeeded. They are profiles in courage, endurance, discipline, devotion, and creativity in the third age.

Only a couple of the subjects in this book had more than modest means when they began their later-life endeavors. None, for varying reasons, had it easy. Five of the women had spent the bulk of their lives as homemakers, and the majority of the men had modest careers they were happy to leave behind when they retired. All overcame painful personal losses or adversity, including the death of children and spouses, divorce, disease, and the wreckage of a career. They have faced the biases of age, race, and gender. And none had savored before age sixty the kind of recognition, satisfaction, and fulfillment they have since.

Goal setting, challenge, and follow-through are fundamental to feelings of well-being and success. The people in this book are ardent goal setters, whether pursuing the perfection of a paragraph or bringing renewal to a desolate urban landscape. For some, goals arose spontaneously, as in the case of stone sculptor Theodore Ludwiczak, who never carved anything before pulling a rock from the Hudson River one summer day; or Naomi Wilzig, whose passion evolved only after she received a request from a son to find him a piece of erotic art. Or there's Thomas Dwyer, who retired from a career in government intelligence and claimed dance before he had taken a single lesson. Some, like Dana Dakin who flew off to Ghana, virtually without a map, were motivated by their sixtieth birthday to create a microfinance program. Runner Margie Stoll took to the road in a record-breaking way. Getting his Ph.D. at sixty conditioned Robert Iadeluca to undertake a hospital internship at seventy. In almost all cases, circumstance and chance play an important role in the unpredictable outcomes, as with Betty Reid-Soskin, who was called back to rescue a legendary family music store on a drug-infested street and ended up becoming the nation's oldest national park ranger.

This book began one day in 2006 when I was having lunch with my friend Jim, who makes his living as a ghostwriter for celebrities.

5

We were treating ourselves to the $7.50 two-roll lunch special at a neighborhood sushi joint on the Upper West Side of New York City. On the verge of celebrating his sixtieth birthday, Jim had just had a book deal he was counting on blow up. He was in a morbid state of mind. He wondered out loud about his chances of ever achieving anything approaching the success he once imagined for himself. "How exactly did this happen to me?" he asked.

Four years younger than Jim, I was beginning to wonder the same thing about myself. It was a darkly comic lunch. It ended only after the waitress had graciously poured the fourth glass of water. On my walk home, I began brainstorming book ideas. As soon as I reached my apartment, I phoned Jim and, somewhat whimsically, suggested that we work our way out of our mutual funk by collaborating on a book about people who never had much success before but, surprisingly, achieved significantly after turning sixty. I was aware of other books on late bloomers that profiled famous late achievers, such as Harry Truman, Winston Churchill, Mother Teresa, Paul Cézanne, Eubie Blake, Isak Dinesen, Harland Sanders—otherwise known as Colonel Sanders—and Julia Child. But I was interested in people who were alive and whose accomplishments before sixty were considerably more average—more, that is, like Jim's or mine.

While he was considering joining me on the project, Jim got a celebrity book deal and went on, it should be noted, to write a bestseller.

At about the same time, my then eighty-four-year-old mother was making a slow recovery from a quadruple bypass. For months she had been tied to a wound pump and was stuck in her apartment in Coral Springs, Florida. She had always been an attractive, energetic, and resourceful woman with a good sense of humor and wide interests. In addition to raising two sons, she had held a variety of jobs—naval draftsman, publicist for actor Canada Lee in the 1940s, a cosmetics counter manager at Bloomingdale's, and a country club bookkeeper. At sixty-seven she became a certified paralegal, but ended up spending the last fifteen years of her life in business as an accounts manager for a gold wholesaler in Florida. Much to her unhappiness, she was laid off at eighty-two. Now, uncharacteristically, she seemed to have given up. "What can I do about it?" was her prevailing attitude. "Whatever will be, will be."

For my mother's sake and, without admitting it, for mine, I began reading about the recent discoveries of the maturing brain. Everywhere I turned in the popular literature, there was reason for excitement. As my appetite for the newly optimistic views grew, so did my desire to see the proof of these neurological principles in life, in action. So began my quest to find the remarkable, not-so-average-anymore people who are the subjects of *What Should I Do with the Rest of My Life?*

As my mother recovered, she and I kept up near-nightly phone conversations. To motivate her, I plied her with the stories of the late bloomers I was discovering. And I implored her to return to her early passion of painting. One day, she called with news. She had signed up for an art class at a local public school. Initially, there was just the satisfaction of an amateur attempting to paint autumn scenes and girls holding cats. Then she began copying Caravaggio and reading art history and studying the Great Masters. No matter what she was working on at school, each Monday night she returned home and said, "It was okay. I learned something new."

One night, more than a year after she had returned to painting class, a man who had seen her carrying her paintings home from class the previous week stopped her on her way from her car to the entrance to her building. He wanted to know if she would consider painting a portrait of him and his two sons—for a fee—so that he could give it as a Christmas present. She hesitated. She told him she

7

would get back to him. That night, she laughed at the idea. "What would I charge him?"

Two weeks before her eighty-fifth birthday, she accepted her first commission. Since, there have been others, to paint portraits and wildlife, and she has returned to the gym three days a week. And as I slowly pushed forward with my writing, she would say, "At the rate I'm going, you're going to have to include a chapter on me in your book."

One of the first preliminary interviews I conducted was with Virginia Marsh Bell, of Lexington, Kentucky. After raising five children, she returned to school in her fifties because she believed she had nothing of value to put on a résumé other than a thirty-seven-year-old college diploma and a wallet full of children's photographs. "And I knew I couldn't sit home one more year and watch *Monday Night Football*," she said. She took a typing class. That gave her the courage to take a graduate course in social work at the University of Kentucky. At sixty, she received her MSW and began counseling families at the university's Sanders-Brown Center on Aging. On request, she developed a program to give respite to caregivers. Then she established one of the first dementia-specific day centers in the United States. And, at age seventy-four, she wrote the first of several books on her "Best Friends" approach to caregiving to people with Alzheimer's and dementia. She also began receiving invitations to deliver her message around the globe. Several states, including all of Maine, and a number of foreign countries, including all of Canada and Hungary, officially adopted her approach.

When we first spoke Virginia was eighty-five. She had recently returned from speaking in Beirut, Lebanon, was continuing to take high-impact aerobics at 6 A.M. each morning, and had begun to study string theory in math. Why string theory? I asked. "Because you've got to make the brain sweat," she said.

Her phrase became my mantra, and I had hoped to include her story in this book. But in 2008, when I was ready to head to Kentucky to spend time with her, Virginia had to beg off. She had been diagnosed with non-Hodgkin's lymphoma, and, understandably, she wanted to conserve her energy to fight the disease and continue doing her work. As I began to write this introduction, I was seized by the need to check in with Virginia and see how she was doing. When she came to the phone the relief I felt was soon surpassed by my astonishment. Not only had she successfully survived treatment and was in full remission, at eighty-six she had run the Lexington Bluegrass 10K race. "My goal was to run the six-point-two miles at a pace of at least fourteen minutes a mile. I did. I beat everyone, except one woman, from seventy up." Of course, she was still going to her high-impact aerobics class each morning and continuing to study string theory. "There is such awe and mystery in the universe," she said. "I don't mind getting old. I enjoy life to the fullest. What I hate most of all is the idea of missing the rest of this century."

No neuroscientist, gerontologist, or social scientist, I plunged into writing this book without any theories to prove, data to collect, or ax to grind. I found my subjects by scouring the Internet, from recommendations from nonprofits and government organizations, and by word of mouth. I was looking for people who had "succeeded significantly in some way," I would say. Sometimes, my inquiries met with resistance, as if I might only mean financial wealth or celebrity. Some feared it was a mistake to define success narrowly or too traditionally. Ultimately, I knew I would know what I wanted when I saw it, but I knew it would have to include some way in which a goal had been reached and had received some kind of public recognition. What I came to see in the people whom I chose was how well they fit into Henry David Thoreau's belief about how success happens: "I have learned that if one advances confidently in the direction of his dreams, and endeavors to live the life he has imagined, he will meet with a success unexpected in common hours."

Usually, it was not solely the accomplishment that attracted me to a subject, it was the whole skein of events and accidents that had brought success unexpectedly in common hours. And those tales filled me with curiosity about the worlds and families into which my subjects were born, the ways they shook off failure and overcame grief, and where they found the courage to take risks and persevere in later years in spite of the collective chorus of doubt.

As unique as each is, as a group the individuals in *What Should I Do with the Rest of My Life?* have done what the scientists tell us we should do: they maintain healthy diets, exercise regularly, challenge themselves, fill their lives with novel experiences and varied social connections. They are, for the most part, thin. They like to dance and to exercise. They tend to be more spiritual than religious. Even those who are of a more solitary nature interact and communicate daily with extensive networks of people. And despite occasional complaints about minor forgetfulness, they have exquisite memories. Listening closely to their own desires, and not to prescriptions for aging well, they have followed their own curiosity on paths of learning and discovery. And in doing so, they have fed their passions and given themselves permission to achieve success.

Many of them possess ample wisdom, a virtue long attributed to aging. Remarkably, brain studies may be providing some insight into that, too. Neuropsychologist Elkhonon Goldberg says wisdom may be the result of cognitive processes that occur in the brain as we age. In *The Wisdom Paradox*, he notes that pattern recognition is the primary means by which we learn. As we age, we accumulate templates for pattern recognition, and they, in turn, allow for relatively quick and effortless decision-making. The decision-making appears intuitive, but it is actually the result of pre-analysis, compressed and crystallized. "Aging," Goldberg writes, "is the price we must pay for accumulating wisdom patterns."

It is also striking that the many subjects in this book who suffered profound pain and loss were willing and able to revisit their traumas, even when it meant returning to moments most of us hope never to see. Remarkably—and instructively—they do not remain rooted in rumination or regret. They live their lives forward, actively attending to the present and moving optimistically toward what they hope to create. Many were motivated by generativity, the act of producing out of concern for future generations. But even more often they expressed their interest in helping to improve lives today.

From the hot summer morning when I first sat in a booth with Loretta Thayer in the Silver Leaf Diner in upstate De Kalb Junction, New York, to the moment Betty Reid Soskin, driving her sporty red BMW, dropped me off at the Oakland International Airport, I have experienced my own awakening about aging. Each of the elders in this book has challenged my thinking, not simply with the fact of their age, but with the quality and intelligence of their pursuits and the integrity of their characters. My conversations with them have altered my own time line. They have convinced me that past failing can prove as easily preparatory as predictive. Age does not of itself limit or enable us. The choice is ours.

MARGIE STOLL

The Natural

*"I don't know why running makes
me feel younger, it just does."*

Time is of the essence to Margie Stoll—not because she is running out of it, but because she runs against it. That's why at 8 A.M. one perfect May morning three days before her sixty-eighth birthday, she was on a high school track in Nashville, Tennessee, eager to begin a grueling workout that would include a warm-up mile, then four progressively quickening quarter-mile laps, and finally a series of ever speedier 800-meter runs in which she would burst into high gear for the final 200 meters of each. Her short-cut tawny hair glinted with sunlight. Her blue eyes twinkled. And though some distance runners dread speed workouts, a radiant Margie could not wait to get at it.

As she began to run, even an unschooled observer could appreciate the remarkably relaxed fluency of Margie's stride. Her upper body and thin, tan arms seemed light cargo for her long legs. Efficiency of movement took over, and age vanished. She no more wasted words than steps. "I'm afraid that I'm just not a very good storyteller," she would tell me later. "I don't know how to give expansive answers. It wouldn't be me. That's one reason I like running. I can be alone, and I don't have to talk." She prefers to let her times and records speak for her.

Here is a bit of what they say: in the eight years since she took up competitive running, Margie Stoll has racked up forty Tennessee single-age record times in track and road races, in distances from 100 meters to a half-marathon. She claimed two gold medals in the 2003 National Senior Games, four in the 2007 National Senior Games. In 2006, she was ranked the number one over-sixty-five runner in the United States in the 800-meter, 1,500-meter, and 5,000-meter distances, and as the number two runner in the 400-meter.

The following year, her top finishes earned her the honor—at sixty-seven—of being ranked among the nation's top three over-sixty-five-year-old women runners by *Running Times,* the premier American running magazine. In 2008, she was awarded the Southeast Masters District Award for the best combined age-graded 5,000- and 10,000-meter times. Not bad for someone who ran her first official race on the eve of turning sixty.

"If people who think about senior runners like Margie Stoll have this idea of a little old lady shuffling down the road, they ought to come see her run and she can educate them in about five seconds," Dallas Smith, a senior grandmaster and Tennessee ultra marathoner, said. "She's one of the best senior distance runners in the world. She's certainly dominant in this area. She has the heart of a great runner. When the gun fires and the race starts, she just pours her heart and muscles and bones into winning that race. Her effort and determination and willingness to fight are as fierce as any linebacker on the Tennessee Titans football team."

Margie's life as a competitive runner began one spring day in 2001 after a game of tennis. She noticed a sign-up sheet for the district trials of the National Senior Games. She was close enough to her sixtieth birthday to compete in the 60–64 age group. "So, I asked my doubles partner if she wanted to sign up for the doubles competition with me. She had other plans, so I signed up for singles myself. Then I noticed they had other events. I just signed up for all the track events: the one-hundred meter, the two hundred, four hundred, eight hundred and fifteen hundred. They were all on one morning, one after the other. I didn't know any better. I just knew that I was turning sixty and I wanted to prove that I could still do something," she said.

Margie knew no one at the district trials at Middle Tennessee University in Murfreesboro, and had no idea what to expect. When the official called the 100-meter runners, she went to the line. "I got into the crouch but had to ask if the toe could be on the line or needed to be behind it," she recalled. As she waited for the start gun to fire, she asked herself what she had gotten herself into. She reminded herself that no one else cared whether she ran or not. Only she would be disappointed if she didn't.

"In other words, I got myself into this, so it's up to me to do it. More positively, I was saying to myself, *Hey, this is what you've been wanting to do since you were a kid . . . a real track, a real official, a real race, and even a real gun start*," she said. "Running, unlike some sports, does not let you procrastinate. You have to follow the official's instructions. You don't have a choice when to start. When the gun goes off, it's then or never."

It was then.

Admittedly no sprinter, Margie ran hard from the start, but when she swept across the finish line she had no idea who in the bunch that crossed with her had won. A couple of minutes later, someone congratulated her on her victory.

She was trying to wrap her mind around that when she was called to the starting line for the 200-meter race. She finished first in it as well, and then in the 400-meter and the 800-meter races. Between each race, Margie sat by herself, in her own world. After the 800-meter race, a man came up to her and said, "You know, you're pretty good." When he discovered that she was a beginner, he offered her the name of a book on how to train. She was flattered and intrigued. But she did not have time to talk. She had the 1,500-meter race to run.

Margie took off at her own pace. Another athlete surged ahead. Margie remained composed and decided not to try to do more than she could. She settled into her stride. And then, lap by lap, she ate up ground between her and the lead runner. On the final lap, Margie, with energy to spare, kicked up the pace and easily overtook the lead runner, garnering her fifth gold medal of the day. After the meet, an impressed head official, a track coach at Middle Tennessee State University, encouraged Margie to take running seriously. "That's when I said to myself, *What is going on here? Am I really that good a runner?*"

A few weeks later, Margie—an ardent Chicago White Sox baseball fan—invited some friends and family to Comiskey Park to celebrate her sixtieth birthday watching a Sox game in her native city. During the game, she announced that she was going to take up competitive running. Those who were present remember her glee over the fact that as the youngest runner in the 60–64 age group, she would have a competitive advantage.

Her new ambition came as a surprise, even to her husband and three children. After all, the prior extent of her running was jogging occasionally—often in her jeans—around her Nashville suburb of Green Hills. Beyond that it can only be said that she regularly read the track and road racing results published in the *Tennessean*.

"We used to jog together sometimes, and I thought that was all she wanted," her husband, Hans Stoll, a professor of finance at the Owen School of Business at Vanderbilt University, told me. "I was delighted, but, to be honest, I didn't think she was that good." (He had not gone to the district finals. Margie would not have wanted him to. "This is my world," she said, unequivocally.)

Five days after her sixtieth birthday, she ran her first distance road race, the Memorial Day 5K Dash at the City Cemetery in Nashville. "I figured that if I didn't survive it, they could just dig a hole and throw me in it," she told Jeanine Renfro, a contributor to *Tennessee Running* magazine. There was no need to worry. Her earlier victories were not flukes.

Running from the outfield warning track at Herschel Greer Stadium, Nashville's minor league baseball field, up to Fort Negley, the site of the Union's biggest Civil War fortress west of Washington, D.C., and down through a maze of paths through the city's cemetery, Margie took first place for her age group. Her time was a respectable 26:41. She averaged 8:36 minutes per mile.

Three months later she cut that time by one minute and forty-three seconds in the state Senior Olympics. She not only took a gold medal in the 5,000-meter run, she also claimed gold in the 400-meter and the 1,500-meter races. Pleased as she was, it was beginning to dawn on Margie that to compete at a national level she needed to improve. "I didn't have very good form at all," she said, examining a photograph of one of her early first-place finishes. "Do you see how I'm bent at the waist? That's what happens when you get tired, the core collapses."

Not long after, an acquaintance of her husband, impressed by Margie's times, recommended that she ask Bob Lunsford, Nashville's guru of running, to coach her. She laughs at the memory of how nervous she was to approach him at the Green Hills YMCA of Middle Tennessee, where he was director of the Wellness Center. He was not taking on new runners, he said, but after hearing her out, he suggested they go out to the track and see what she could do.

She started out well, but about a hundred meters shy of completing a 1,600-meter run, she stopped running. "That was good, but why'd you stop?" Lunsford asked.

"I got tired," Margie said.

With a gently self-deprecating laugh that often accompanies her thoughts, Margie says Lunsford only agreed to coach her because he wanted the challenge. He designed a simple program aimed at strengthening Margie's core, increasing her endurance, and making her leaner, as measured in muscle-to-fat ratio, not weight. The unvarying schedule he created for her included a four-mile run on Mondays; cross-training (fifteen-minute warm-up on an elliptical runner, twenty minutes on an exercise bike, and thirty minutes running in the pool) on Tuesdays; four laps of 1,600 meters at a 7:20-a-mile pace, resting five minutes between laps on Wednesdays; two days rest before a run and one day off after. Lunsford was particularly concerned that at her age Margie got lots of time to recover.

Five foot five and a half inches tall, she lost five pounds in the first two months and another five pounds over the next six months, dropping to 109 pounds. "I've kept the same weight ever since. And yes, I went down a size in jeans. My hips got narrower, and I definitely feel stronger and more energetic. I notice my increased strength in my legs and upper body when I play tennis. When I get to the ball, I can do more with it. My increased upper-body strength comes in handy, too, when I carry one of my three grandchildren upstairs to bed."

As important as the physical conditioning, Lunsford also gave Margie her reason for running competitively: "Go for the glory," he told her. She made the phrase her mantra and began a remarkable transformation as a runner. "I had a very clear sense that I was improving. My times were coming down at each race. It almost seemed too easy," she said. "I guess there is such a thing as a natural."

In October 2002, just sixteen months after her first road race, she notched her first single-age state record, running the Oktoberfest 5K in Lebanon, Tennessee, in 22:46, cutting nearly four minutes off her first 5K race time with a 7:27-mile pace. Setting the record was no accident. Margie had looked it up online before the race. "Near the beginning of the race was a steep downhill. Since it was raining and slick, some people slowed down, but I told myself to take quick short steps and to keep going. I don't think of anything else when I race," she said. "The important thing is to focus and not waste any steps."

Nine months later, she posted two of her most satisfying victories at the 2003 National Senior Games in Hampton Roads, Virginia. She took first place in the 5K, with a time of 23:39. She won the 10K with a time of 49:57, one minute thirty-three seconds ahead of the silver medalist. The highlight came when she learned the official results. "It was like being on Miss America," she said, of the countdown from eighth place to first. "After they called second place, and I knew I'd won, that was really something." She began crying as soon as she stepped up to the winner's podium to receive her gold medal.

Margie's early triumphs and having a coach were as exciting and validating as they were redemptive for a woman whose dreams and opportunities as a potential athlete had never gotten the chance they deserved. Born May 23, 1941, Margie was the third daughter of Agnes Louise and John Christie Shaw. Her mother was an unflappable Midwesterner, her father a Scottish immigrant who worked as a purchasing agent of materials for the pioneering footwear company that made Dr. Scholl's. With two daughters already, Shaw badly wanted a son. But he would make the most of having another daughter, doting on Margie and sharing his enthusiasm for sports with her, regularly taking her out to play catch. Margie loved spending that time with him.

And though she was an extremely shy girl, as she grew up Margie reveled in getting picked to play baseball with the boys in the close-knit, pre–World War II suburb of Lombard, Illinois. She was faster, anyway, than most of them. Only a boy named Phillip could keep up with her.

"But I grew up before Title IX, and when I got to junior high school all that stopped," she said, referring to the 1972 federal act that for the first time guaranteed girls equal educational opportunities in federally funded schools and opened the way to girls' sports programs. The girls had no sports teams in her school. "And gym class was mostly a social thing for girls. We were happy to just watch the boys. But oh, how I envied those boys their real uniforms, real schedules of games, and real coaches to help develop their skills."

When she was thirteen, her father suffered a fatal heart attack. He was fifty-three. It happened one night after her parents had a small party. Margie, frozen with fear, listened from her bed as she heard her father's sudden, violent coughing. Recalling his death more than half a century later still renders her speechless. "I just can't talk about it," she told me one day at a picnic table outside the Y.

Though her older sister Joan Williams remembers Margie as innately competitive, Margie says that her father's death was what instilled a powerful work ethic in her. Her mother—from whom she says she inherited the calm, relaxed quality that enhances her running—went to work full-time in a bank without any apparent complaint. Margie believed that if she didn't work hard and get the best grades possible, she would never win a scholarship to a good college. She worked relentlessly, her sister says, at everything, including winning the first seat for the flute in the school band.

She was awarded a half-scholarship to Washington University in St. Louis, where she majored in French. She played no sports there either, though there were a couple for women. "But I was too much of a coward to go out for them," she said. She received a full scholarship to a new master's in teaching program at the University of Chicago, where she met her husband, Hans. Paired with others, they met on a blind triple date. But he was a tall, smart, and skeptical Ph.D. candidate studying with Nobel Prize–winning supply-side economist Milton Friedman. More to the point, he wore an attractive hat. "I thought *that* was interesting," she said. Margie was a beautiful, sophisticated-looking young woman—with a sparkle in her eyes and an easy laugh, which Hans says is what captured him. The morning after they met, he called her to go play Frisbee.

Margie began running when the couple moved to the capital after they were married in 1967. Several days a week, she jogged around the Washington Monument and in Arlington National Cemetery. Later, after three children—Andy, Erica, and Kevin—were born and the family was living in Pennsylvania, Margie ran whenever she could. "I would take the kids and put them in the middle of a soccer field at Swarthmore College and try to get in four laps before I was needed. I guess I always wanted to run and was trying to find a way to do it," she said.

In 1982, two years after moving to Nashville, life swerved off course. One morning while showering, Margie discovered a lump in one of her breasts. She immediately called her doctor. His assurance that it was probably nothing proved baseless. She had a malignancy. "Kevin was only five. And my first thought was, *I'm not going to see my children grow up.* I called a cousin who was a doctor and asked what I should do. Radiation was just coming into style and he said, 'Just have the mastectomy and the chemotherapy and get it over with.' I did and I'm glad. In those days, I didn't have many friends here that I could talk to. And even if I had, you didn't talk about cancer, especially breast cancer. So Hans and I had to handle it on our own." Hans still regrets how clueless he was during that traumatic time of hair loss, mastectomy, and six months of chemotherapy. "I didn't do my part. I assumed that because the tumor was small, the risk and possible consequences were small."

Margie counts her survival a matter of early detection, quick treatment, and good luck. She discounts all other possibilities, including divine intervention. "It was very small and we caught it early. I was lucky. I don't like it when people refer to survivors as heroes, as if the other people, those who died, didn't fight," she said. "I just did what the doctors told me to do. I even ran during that."

For two decades after her recovery, Margie lived a life mostly devoted to fostering her husband and her children's successes, as Hans and her children each attested with unsolicited gratitude. They also uniformly noted that Margie had an irrepressible competitive streak. "She was always a tough-minded and competitive person, from the smallest thing," said Andy, himself a former state tennis champion. "She was always organizing family competitions. Parents in other families might watch their children play, but we were a family that loved to play sports together—basketball in the driveway, tennis, soccer. She was always encouraging us to play pick-up games."

Margie still organizes family activities around competitions. On a night I had dinner with the Stolls, we had to move from the patio of their handsome, three-story brick house to the family room in time to watch the 2009 finals of *American Idol* on a big-screen television. Margie was not interested in the performances, really. She favored the talented theatrical singer Adam Lambert, but she was betting objectively—and, as it turned out, correctly—in the family balloting that Americans would favor the good-looking underdog rock singer Kris Allen.

Less than a year after Margie set her first Tennessee record, Lunsford, a non-practicing physician who gave up medicine to concentrate on biking and running, died of a heart attack. He was fifty-three, the same age at which Margie's father died. Margie keeps several of her first coach's notes to her. "I love your style, grace, and tenacity," he wrote in one. In another, he said, "I am having so much fun watching you being the best that you can be."

His death was a blow to Margie. When she first returned to training at the Y, "I had to tell myself to stop looking for Bob," she said. Still, she never faltered in her ambition. In 2004, she began working with Dave Milner, another Tennessee running coach, to plot the races Margie would undertake and to create a more elaborate workout schedule for her to use in her ceaseless, solitary training. Her times continued to improve and, almost casually, she ascended in the ranks of the nation's elite runners.

More than one advanced male runner has fallen behind Margie's efficient stride. Peter Pressman, the president of the Nashville Striders Running Club, met Margie not long after she began running competitively. For the first few years, Margie and Pressman, a veteran runner four years younger than her, regularly flip-flopped in finishes. "She's a deceptive runner. There's no waste of motion or energy in her stride. It almost looks as if she could continue at her pace forever. I enjoyed our little battles, but from the time I met her she made considerable progress. After a while I was just pleased to keep up with her. We both got older, but I got slower and Margie got faster."

To understand how impressive Margie's times have been, consider the results of a race—the Shelby Bottoms Boogie 15K in 2005—that, at sixty-four, she finished in one hour and twelve minutes. "You want to know how good that is?" Dallas Smith said. "Compare it with men in the thirty-to-thirty-four age group, when men are supposed to peak in endurance running. She would have finished in front of half the men in that age group."

Margie is quietly proud of her growing list of accomplishments, including the highlight of taking four gold medals at the 2007

National Senior Games in Louisville, in the 800-meter, 1,500-meter, 5K, and 10K events. But she vigilantly guards against overstating her prowess and is quick to emphasize that the fastest woman distance runner over sixty-five is Marie-Louise Michelsohn, a mathematics professor at the State University of New York, Stony Brook, and a leading authority in the field of complex geometry.

Michelsohn has been setting American age-group and world age-group records ever since she took up running in 1995, at fifty-three. She began running after her daughter suffered a massive cerebral hemorrhage at the age of twenty-four. "The rehab process was arduous and frightening both to her and to me," Michelsohn told *Running Times* writer Mike Tymn. Running was suggested as a way to control the stress. She began running a mile a day and gradually built up her distance. Three weeks after her first run, Michelsohn entered a five-mile race. "I did it, I loved it, took third in my age group, and was hooked." Her running steadily improved in her sixties, an accomplishment she dismissed in an e-mail, writing tersely: "Challenges are invigorating." She ran her fastest 5K on a track a month before she turned sixty-four and her fastest 800m a few days later. On May 24, 2009, at sixty-seven, she broke the American age-group record for the 10K by two minutes when she was clocked at 44:47:58 during the USATF Pacific Association Open in San Mateo, California. That added to the seventeen American records she already held in the 60–64 and 65–69 age groups and the eight world records she holds in the 60–64 age group. "Marie-Louise is in a class by herself," Margie said. "Her records will stand for a long time."

Margie calls running "a greedy sport," meaning that her ego and health may benefit from it, but she cannot quite see how her running benefits anyone else. Still, she has regularly volunteered as a runner to help others gain self-esteem, lose weight, and acquire good habits. "I don't think she is aware of the impact she has on other people," said

Diana Bibeau, a reading specialist and Nashville distance runner. "She is always encouraging and cheering others on," including, Bribeau said, mostly overweight women who joined walking groups to work toward becoming runners. Margie was among the first and most consistent volunteer leaders. Margie has also mentored preteen girls in the local chapter of Girls On the Run, an international nonprofit prevention program that encourages girls to develop self-respect and healthy lifestyles through running.

In the program's crowning event the girls run a 5K. During training for it, Margie says there is often more chatter than she would prefer. "They talk about everything: their pets, what happened in school, their vacations. I sometimes begin to think that they must not have enough opportunity to talk at home. Sometimes, I have even suggested that we be quiet for a certain distance. Of course, maybe they are the normal ones and I am abnormal in not liking to talk."

Before they run in their 5K race, Margie instructs "her" girls to tie their laces, take a deep breath, and have fun. When others start off too quickly and pass them, Margie says, "Don't worry about them." If her girls want to walk, she suggests they slow down instead. "I'm a purist. A runner does not walk," she said. "Near the final one hundred meters, I always tell the girls to give it all they've got. For me, that last one hundred meters is what the whole program is about. I'm not sure that the fun and games they are asked to play to get them to think positively about themselves will stick with them, but the effort of those last one hundred meters will—especially if they throw up at the end."

Margie also runs each year in the Susan G. Komen Race for the Cure in Nashville, one of 120 5K runs and fitness walks around the globe to raise funds and awareness for the fight against breast cancer, to celebrate survivorship, and to memorialize those who have died of the disease. In 2008, Margie not only finished first in her age group, with a time of 23:55, she was the first survivor to cross the finish line, first in her age group for the sixth straight year.

One of her favorite runs is a bit unusual. Unfailingly, twice a year, Margie drives to the Charles Bass Correctional Facility, a minimum-security state prison in West Nashville, to compete in races with the inmates. "Except for a few bad choices, many of the young men could be my sons," she said on the way there for the spring 2009 Striders and Stripers 5K. After being cleared through security, she and two dozen Nashville Striders entered into the prison yard. A large, hand-painted sign announcing "The Jaunt in the Joint" greeted them. Despite her earlier affliction of shyness, Margie made her way without hesitation to a knot of inmates—including some three times her size and some old acquaintances—to begin catching up and talking, with warmth, ease, and grace. "There was a time when I couldn't have done this," she said. "I still have to force myself, but I do it because I know it's the right thing. My religion is simple: Be nice to others."

Many of the prisoners knew of Margie's stature as an elite runner and were anxious to see her compete. She ran, as I did, in the second heat of the 5K. It required running nine laps, each one-third of a mile, on a path of mowed grass inside barbed-wire-topped fencing. Margie started with her long, low, and seemingly effortless strides. She has, in runner's parlance, good biomechanics: her footstrike is flat-footed, her stride neutral, and her motion consistently forward, as opposed to bobbing up and down, allowing her to cover as much ground as possible.

By the end of the first lap, she had caught up to and then moved past the runners who started quickly. With each succeeding lap, she stretched her lead over men one-third her age. Margie lapped me the first time on her fifth lap. Having tried part of Margie's track workout earlier in the day, I (Excuses! Excuses!) was fighting off a biting tightness in my hamstrings, being out of shape in the late afternoon Tennessee sun, and the possibility of humiliating myself by collapsing in front of the inmates.

As I began to falter, some chanted encouragement—"Come on, Blue." Then, as she glided past as if on roller skates, in a sweet but firm voice, I heard her say, "You have to finish, Bruce. It would be a bad precedent for the inmates if you didn't. You can do it."

Though she had trained for my benefit for an hour and a half in the morning, Margie made no excuses (she disdains excuses) for not having one of her best runs. Still she crossed the finish line to a burst of applause with a time better than all but a couple of twenty-something men. Soon, she was sitting under a tent, steering conversation onto their efforts and encouraging them to keep training. "She's amazing. I hope I'm in that kind of shape when I'm half her age," a twenty-four-year-old inmate serving time for auto theft said.

On the drive back to Nashville, Margie spotted some oak leaf hydrangeas and became practically loquacious, rattling off the names of varieties of hydrangeas, including Annabelle hydrangeas, French hydrangeas (an old friend said that Margie once reacted with uncharacteristic displeasure when she criticized the brilliantly blue French hydrangea as gaudy), climbing hydrangeas, and peegee hydrangeas. She began growing the flowering plant in the 1980s when she and Hans bought a lake house in Mount Juliet with a couple of Annabelle hydrangea bushes. After an older neighbor gave her a little education, Margie became an aficionado. She was soon propagating them with abandon.

She opened her own business, Hydrangeas of Braid Cove, in 1993, and began selling dried hydrangeas to event and wedding planners in addition to selling as many as 1,500 stems a summer—for $1.50 each—to area florists. Most of all, she delighted in giving cuttings to friends, relatives, neighbors, or virtually anyone who had a garden. "'The Johnny Appleseed of Hydrangeas!' That's what I really want on my gravestone," she laughed.

The comment was pure jest. Margie Stoll, who runs about thirty miles a week, is not planning on going anywhere soon except to more races. Her current trainer, Sarah Fisher, met Margie while competing against her and began working with her in 2007. "I was initially struck by Margie's composure and her unique quality of combining desire to win, pride in her achievements, knowledge of her abilities, and modesty. I have never met anyone quite like her. I have never heard her utter a bad word about anyone. But Margie's impeccable manner hides a will of steel," Fisher said. "She never, ever fails to do the very best she can on the day, in the conditions, against the competition. She is class personified."

Recently, Fisher had been focusing on improving Margie's form and giving her the kind of hands-on coaching she never had before. With small adjustments, Fisher, an acutely observant former banking executive with an MBA from Harvard, hoped to shave a few more seconds off Margie's times. On the track, Fisher ran behind Margie, repeating reminders to her to start properly, to fall forward as she runs, and to look her way around the curves—that is, to look at least twenty-five yards ahead, so that her body turns under her head and forces the head to follow, naturally. Otherwise, the head, which is heavy, tilts, weights the body, and slows a runner down. She also reminded her to bring her elbows closer to her body as she kicks into higher gear for the final two hundred yards in her 800-meter runs. "She thinks, she accepts, she adapts, and then these little tweaks become habit—and she improves," Fisher said.

To push Margie during her kicks, Fisher had brought along Nathan Hamilton, a twenty-six-year-old runner. Margie got a bit of a head start. ("It's my birthday," she said when Hamilton complained.) She otherwise conceded nothing. "Every time we came out of the turn into the last two hundred and I would start to catch her, you could just feel her kicking it up," Hamilton said. "She is such a tough competitor." When the running portion of the practice ended, Margie had enough energy left to lead everyone—laughing—in skipping, hopping, high-kneeing, and heel-to-butt kicking exercises up and down the field four times. Then, Nathan spontaneously offered to take her out for her birthday and dance her socks off. Margie looked a bit surprised, but when he grabbed her hand, she gamely did an impromptu swing dance with him on the field.

Despite the intensity of her training and weekend running schedule, Margie is no prima donna, according to Hans, who says he enjoys watching her go off to a race at 4 A.M. filled with good humor. "Then she'll come home and cook breakfast for me and go work in the garden for the rest of the day," he said. "She doesn't just lie around on the couch for the rest of the day."

There is little likelihood that Margie will ever again improve on any of her absolute personal bests, though it seems impossible to discount anything with her. "Now it's just about not losing time. As you get older, you start to lose time. That's the big problem. And that's why it's so important to do weights, not to lose muscle mass. Everybody, no matter how good you are, is going to get slower. The idea is not to get hurt and to slow down as little as possible. I'm just hoping that I'll outlast everyone else."

While running may not precisely be a Fountain of Youth, there is good evidence that regular running slows the effects of aging. A study from the Stanford University School of Medicine that tracked five hundred runners for twenty years found, as reported in 2008 in the *Archives of Internal Medicine,* that elderly runners had fewer disabilities, a longer span of active life, and are half as likely as non-runners to die an early death. The study, undertaken at the start of the running craze in 1984, focused on concerns expressed at the time by many researchers that vigorous exercise would do older adults more harm than good and, long-term, would increase their chances of injury. The study, however, confirmed speculation by its senior author, Dr. James Fries, that keeping the body moving might not extend longevity, but it would compress the period of time at the end of life when people were unable to carry out their daily activities. "If you had to pick one thing to make people healthier as they age," he said, "it would be aerobic exercise."

To celebrate her seventieth birthday and a decade of competitive running, Margie is planning to run in the Boston Marathon in 2012, so that she will be able to take advantage of being among the youngest runners in the seventy-to-seventy-five age bracket." She is also aiming to win her way back among the top three women runners in her age group, as ranked by *Running Times* and to continue to earn standing as an elite runner. (That designation is given to runners who rank above the ninetieth percentile in an age group, as compared to the performances of those in different age groups.) She faced her first major hurdle in accomplishing that goal in when she raced in the 1,500-meter race in August at the 2009 National Senior Games, where she was one of 10,000 athletes competing at Stanford University in Palo Alto.

As she warmed up on the track and tried to focus on her goal pace, she found herself hopelessly distracted, wondering when Marie-Louise Michelsohn would appear on the track and eclipse her dream of the gold. When she went to the stand to wait for her race to be called, she asked Hans, "Have you seen Marie-Louise?" He had not. No sooner had he shaken his head than an announcer called Marie-Louise to the check-in table. Margie speculated that her nemesis had not yet initialed her name on the sign-in sheet. When her age group was finally called to the starting corral, Margie continued to scan the faces of eighteen other runners for a Marie-Louise. Then, suddenly, a race official arrived to give last-minute instructions and she heard her name announced, but not that of Marie-Louise. She was a no-show.

But now Margie had only time to stretch her arms and take a couple of deep breaths before the starting gun sounded. She was lined up third from the inside of the track and needed to get by just two runners to get to the inside lane. "That was accomplished pretty easily, so I didn't have to worry about trying to pass on the first curve," Margie wrote in her own post-race recap. "Approaching the stadium side of the track, I heard the announcement, 'In first place is Margie Stoll from Tennessee.' Nothing could have sounded sweeter. I just needed to hear that sentence three more times. I would not let myself slow down. If somebody caught up to me, kudos to her, but I would not help her by slowing down." She was ahead of pace at 300 meters, then at 400 meters. She began hearing her coach's voice in her head: "Light feet, focal points, and relaxed shoulders . . ." She mentally checked to make sure of each. And as she did, she heard a group of male voices chanting, "Go Tennessee!" Not that she needed it, but the cheer gave her a shot of adrenaline. Soon enough, she heard it again and then, loudly, one last time before she heard the announcer bellow, "Crossing the finish line in first place is Margie Stoll." She glanced up at the scoreboard and saw her name at the top with a time of 6:33:84. "It was official. I had lived my fantasy," Margie said. Over the next few days, she also took gold in the 800-meter finals, with a time of 3:13:47, as well as two silver medals, in the 5K and the 10K, behind the road racer ranked #1 by Running Times.

Her competitive streak is hardly quenched. Margie is now nursing a whimsical hope that her high school class will stage a one-mile race when it holds its fiftieth reunion in Chicago. She already counts winning a virtual race in 2008 against the men of her class's cross country team among her sweetest victories. She had learned from an old boyfriend that the team planned to stage the race by documenting runs on their various hometown tracks. Margie asked for the race to be expanded to women so that, unlike in high school, she could compete. Then, she looked up all the men's times. She knew she could beat everyone except one classmate who was still running a 7:11 mile. "So, Sarah and I really started practicing hard," not only in training on the track but by having Margie regularly compete in all-comer one-mile races every weekend. "Then, on July fifteenth, I went to the track. I had my son Andy come and pace me. Sarah was out there yelling what to do. Hans was taking pictures. And I had a couple of friends cheering me on. I did the mile in six:fifty-seven," she said, laughing heartily. She finished thirty-one seconds ahead of her toughest challenger.

In explaining her passion for running, Margie says she likes everything about running except the necessity to rise early and running when it is cold. She subscribes to the belief that one runs to her own beat, compelled by nothing but herself, responsible to no one but herself, and free to reap all the rewards of running for herself, too. "Running must have some magic," she said. "It's not just the occasional and appreciated compliment that makes me feel younger. The running itself makes me feel like a kid again.

HARRY BERNSTEIN

Ruby of a Writer

"These have been the most productive years of my life."

Some days Harry Bernstein shakes his head at how long it took him to embrace the first commandment of writing: *Write what you know.* By the time he did, he was no neophyte. After all, his first short story was published when he was seventeen, in 1928. That was the year Mickey Mouse debuted in movie theaters, the old Boston Garden opened, and Herbert Hoover was elected president, months before the stock market crash ignited the Great Depression. In the 1930s, Harry's stories appeared in some of the best American "little magazines," such small literary journals as *The Anvil, Story,* and *Literary America* that were devoted to serious if noncommercial writing. His work was published alongside such celebrated writers as William Carlos Williams, Richard Wright, Gertrude Stein, and Nelson Algren. Harry was poised for literary success. One of the nation's most acclaimed editors of the era even asked him to write a novel. But things did not go Harry's way. Instead, he suffered seven decades of literary frustration, rejection, and failure.

Yet for fifty-five years—through ten years of low-paid and ungratifying work as a reader for Hollywood studios, fifteen years as the editor of a construction trade magazine, and another thirty years of "retirement"—he kept his fingers moving on the typewriter. Fueled by resistant hope and habit, he wrote about forty unpublished novels. He does not know how many exactly because he lost track. If he thought they were good he showed them to agents or publishers. Usually, he heard nothing back. Or worse. And with each fresh disappointment, he lost a little more faith. "I figured if they didn't like them then they probably weren't any good so I threw them in the trash," he said.

He was ninety-three when he decided to once again devote himself fully to writing, turning this time to the memories of his childhood instead of to his imagination. He submerged himself in writing about life before World War I on a cobblestone street in a poor Lancashire mill town called Stockport in the north of England. He reimagined his life as a working-class kid coming to terms with the grievous mysteries of that small universe, a street divided by an invisible line, with Christians on one side and Jews like himself on the other. To get started, he didn't do any research. He didn't have to. He just pushed everything else out of his mind and wrote.

When his debut memoir, *The Invisible Wall,* was published in 2007, he was weeks away from turning ninety-seven. The book was greeted—first in Britain, then in the United States—as an affecting memoir, not just as the exceptional feat of a nonagenarian. William Grimes wrote in the *New York Times* that the "heart-wrenching memoir" evoked a world of pain and prejudice "in spare, restrained prose that brilliantly illuminates a time, a place and a family struggling valiantly to beat impossible odds." The setting, Grimes added, was so beautifully rendered that the writing recalled early D. H. Lawrence. Other reviewers praised the book's "dancing prose," which transported the reader to a street-level view of a world that might otherwise have been lost. "An exceptional book," wrote a reviewer for the British *Guardian. Publishers Weekly* lauded Harry for writing a "coming-of-age story" that provides enduring lessons while taking on the "heft of a historical novel with stirring success." More than one reviewer compared *The Invisible Wall* to *Angela's Ashes,* Frank McCourt's 1996 bestseller about his childhood in the slums of Limerick, Ireland. Harry's publisher in Sweden compared him to Nobel laureate Isaac Bashevis Singer.

"The reviews made my head swim," Harry said. "I never allowed myself to aspire to such literary heights. The praise meant a great deal to me after all those years."

When he said it, the phrase "all those years" did not glide by me in the cloak of a cliché. I considered how difficult it was to pursue any regimen—diet, exercise, worship, or meditation—day after day, year after year. Then I did the calculations of Harry's unrequited literary efforts: spanning eighty years, the time between the publication of his first short story and *The Invisible Wall* exceeded the average American's life expectancy.

"What drove me?" he asked, echoing my question. He paused, seemingly puzzled, as if he had never before considered that he had a choice in the matter. "I suppose it was ego. I always saw myself as a writer, and I always hoped I would get a book published and find a means to make a living. So I never stopped writing. I'd go down in the basement and pound away. I used to sit down and write blindly. I'd have an idea and say to myself, *Let's see what's going to happen.* There weren't any rewards in it, but it didn't make any difference to me. I didn't talk much about the writing, not even to Ruby," he said, referring to his wife of sixty-seven years. "I didn't want to burden her with my hopes, and she respected my privacy. She never once asked me what I was writing. The worst thing anyone could ever say to me was, 'How's the writing going?'"

The writing was going well the day I met Harry and he welcomed me into his retirement bungalow in Brick, New Jersey, not far from the shore at Point Pleasant. A lunch of tuna, cold cuts, and potato salad, prepared by his homecare aide, was on the kitchen table, awaiting my arrival. As Harry showed me through the living room, decorated in earth tones and vintage Danish modern furniture, I was struck by how imposing, even a couple of years away from the century mark, Harry appeared and by the natural authority of his sonorous voice. His impassive expression gathered weight behind oversize glasses resting on the bridge of his hooked nose. I was reminded that the French writer Georges Simenon swore, "Writing is not a profession but a vocation of unhappiness." Between the misery of Harry's early life and the years of his blighted writing ambitions, I did not expect him to exude the cheeriness of a lottery winner, but I wondered out loud about his sober response to success. "Remember, there were circumstances of writing that book I would rather never have happened," he said. "It would have made all the difference for Ruby to be here."

Bracing himself on a walker, Harry rose to his full height of six feet, retrieved a photograph from a shelf, and handed it to me. In the picture, a tan, oval-faced woman with deep brown eyes and hair that was still mostly dark was smiling an irresistible smile. It was one of those smiles that melts age out of a face no matter how lined. Although already in her eighties in the photograph, she was still fit and lithe-looking, dressed in a black leotard. The picture had been snapped just before she went off to teach her weekly yoga class. She possessed an aura of irrepressible joy. When I looked up from the photograph and back at Harry, his eyes were damp with love and loss.

"I've never known anyone whose name was more fitting than hers," he said, speaking slowly and with a deep tone that gathered each word into the faintest of English accents. "She was a gem. She was so beautiful in my eyes, but not just to look at her. It was her whole manner. She wanted me to be a writer, too. She would willingly have me stay home and write while she went to work. It was a remarkable marriage. I can't remember one dull or one boring moment. Even when we didn't talk, it was good to be with her. She was always smiling. She was always optimistic, never brooding or gloomy about anything. After she died, I think I died, too."

Harry did not die, but he sank into a grave depression after Ruby's death from leukemia on May 3, 2002, ten days after she was diagnosed. For months afterward Harry was punished by a brutal loneliness. Living alone for the first time, he considered suicide and gave serious thought to the ways and means of committing it. Nearly a year after Ruby's death, his daughter, Adraenne, a nurse practitioner, shook him out of paralyzing self-pity, saying, "Dad, you have lost a wife, but we have lost a mother, and you are the only one left us and we need you."

Soon Harry sat down to write again. He knocked out a first-person essay that asked how, at ninety-four and without the possibility of future romance, he was supposed to move on with his life without his friend, companion, lover, and soul mate. He submitted the piece to *Newsweek*, which—much to his surprise—published it as a "My Turn" column in October 2003. It provoked an unusually large and emotional response, including at least a couple of marriage proposals from younger women. It also restored Harry's confidence in his writing.

Emboldened but still depressed, he sat down at the small typewriter stand across from his bed and began to pound out words on the IBM Selectric typewriter that Adraenne had recently given to him. "I turned to writing because I wanted to fill the void. At first, writing was a sort of therapy. When you're old, it can seem as if you have no place to go. It seems as if you have no future. But I soon found that reliving the past made the present more tolerable because

I could immerse myself completely in it and just forget everything." Even more, he felt gladness in returning to the memories. "It gave me a feeling that I was closer to Ruby than I had been able to feel. You know, when someone dies, they seem to go so far away. Death is so remote. Suddenly, she had disappeared. But by bringing back the particulars, I had the feeling of being close to her and it helped me."

It helped his writing, too. It came easily. He began without notes or outline, and effortlessly unearthed the vivid details of his past—the color of a dress, the smell of rotting fruit, the expression of a face, Mrs. Turnbull's bitter voice. Often, at night, he would lie in bed sleeplessly, recalling and dwelling in a scene until it was completely formed in his memory. Then, and only then, would he rise at whatever hour and start typing, as if the words were dictated. Memory and imagination merged. "Can anyone remember every word that was said? Is that possible? No. I must confess there is a certain amount of what I call embroidery. I do not remember exactly what was said. I remember certain phrases, like when a bully taunted from across the street, 'Bloody Jews who killed Christ!'"

Harry easily recalled the working-class neighborhood where he grew up in the town of Stockport, with its sad rows of soot-blackened houses, their stubby chimneys "jutting out of slate roofs into murky skies." He recalled, too, the quickening staccato rhythms in the evening of men with empty dinner pails and women wearing striped petticoats returning home and the doors shutting behind them on the strictly divided street.

Besides their poverty, the two sides of the street had little in common. There were the summer nights the residents of the street brought out chairs and sat in front of their houses to share the music coming from the only gramophone. And there was the shared fear of the landlord. "If you couldn't pay the rent, you would be put out in short order or sent to the workhouse. It was very Dickensian," Harry recalled. "The landlord would always come on Sunday, carrying a notebook and a sharp pencil, because he knew the Christians would be home and so would the Jews. When they heard the first rapping at the door, panic spread through the street as families began frantically searching for a few coppers. I think our rent was about a shilling a month. Once, my mother ran to the mantel and looked under the oilcloth for some coins but found nothing. So she told me to run to my friend Philly's house to borrow money from his mother. I ran as fast as I could. About halfway, I ran into Philly, who was running the other way. We looked at each other. I said, 'Where are you going?' He said, 'I'm going to your house to borrow some money for the rent from your mother.' I said, 'I'm going to your house for the same thing.' I don't think we understood quite because we said, 'Well, I'll see you later, ta-ta.' And off he went to my mother and I to his. They say great comedy comes of great tragedy, but I assure you there wasn't anything funny about it."

Born in 1910 (his birthday was celebrated on April 17, but his birth certificate reads May 30), Harry was the fifth of six children whose parents emigrated from Poland. His father, Yankel, was a tailor in a local sweatshop. In his book, Harry portrays his father unflinchingly as a gambler, a drunk, and a bully—one who dragged Harry's older sister down the street to work in the sweatshop instead of allowing her to accept a scholarship to a prestigious school. There was no mystery to what lay behind his father's temperament. Sent to work when he was five and abused by his various masters, he was a monstrously violent drunk by age twelve. According to family lore, one day after Yankel left for work, his parents stripped their house of its furnishings, fled from their son, and moved to England.

On discovering that his family had abandoned him, Yankel bashed his head against a wall until he needed to be hospitalized. After he was released, he worked his way across Europe and tracked down his family in Stockport. When he banged on the door in the middle of the night and demanded to be let in, his mother, Sarah, dumped a latrine bucket on his head. Yankel caused such a disturbance that the family eventually did let him in and soon he was terrorizing them once again. At about the same time, an innocent sixteen-year-old orphan named Ada arrived from Poland to stay with a family friend. It immediately occurred to Sarah Bernstein that she was *the* solution to the problem with Yankel. She bamboozled Ada, filling her with lies about a suitor and inveigling a match that placed Ada in the clutches of misery for the rest of her life. The rest of the Bernsteins promptly disembarked for Chicago, leaving Yankel and his new wife behind.

Harry's family lived a penurious existence, surviving for many years on pocket change his father doled out to his mother on Saturday nights before he left for the pub. Meanwhile, Ada sowed her children's heads with dreams: new shoes to ensure Harry's admission to a fine school, the marriage of her daughter to a rabbi, tickets for all to go to America. She also promised that one day they would turn the empty front room into a real parlor, with plush furniture and a piano. But time and again poverty would crush her hopes. Desperate to earn extra money to feed and clothe her five children, she crawled under a fruit seller's stand one day, as Harry watched, to retrieve fallen fruit. "When she crawled back out, she had the slime of rotten fruit smeared all over her clothes and even her lovely head," he told me. The vendor refused to take more than a few shillings for the bruised fruit Ada had retrieved. And with that bit of produce, she set up a small shop in the front room of the family's home, reneging on her frequent promise that the family would turn it into a proper parlor room one day. "We never forgave her for it, not realizing that her fruit business was the only thing that stood between us and starvation," Harry said.

Soon, World War I announced itself to the street. "The telegram girl would come and bring with her this dreadful envelope with black borders that the War Department sent. She would come whistling a merry song. People would come out and stand with hands on their hearts. Everyone, Jew and Christian, would rush to comfort the unlucky one," he said.

Romance occasionally flowered despite the invisible wall, and on two occasions Harry played the role of innocent go-between. The first time, he carried notes between a neighboring Jewish girl and a Christian boy. When they were found out, the girl's father beat her and banished her to Australia. The second affair was a scandal for Harry's family and provides the sad climax of *The Invisible Wall*. Harry keeps secret the relationship between his brilliant older sister Lily and Arthur Foreshaw, the intelligent, idealistic Christian boy from across the street. Arthur had helped prepare Lily for a scholarship exam and, on occasion, saved Harry and his siblings from anti-Semitic bullies who tormented the Jewish children as they walked home from school. When Arthur survived World War I and returned, the first thing he did was walk across the street to call on Lily. Blinded by religion, Harry's mother sent Arthur away. Doing so, however, did little to stop the young lovers.

Defying her family, Lily married Arthur in a civil ceremony and brought Harry along as the family's sole witness. When Harry reported the event at home, his mother declared her daughter dead and the family went into mourning, sitting *shiva* and mumbling prayers for seven days in a darkened room. Reconciliation would only come after Lily gave birth to a son. For Harry, who refused to have a bar mitzvah, the episode was the end of Judaism. "I think religion has done more damage and destruction to the world than any war," he said.

It took a year for Harry to complete *The Invisible Wall*. He did not show it to anyone before he began sending it out to publishers in New York. He was cautiously hopeful. One after another, they returned their verdicts: "It's too quiet." The critique mystified Harry. "Too quiet? I still wonder, what the hell did they mean? What's quiet about it?" He had almost given up hope when he read a newspaper article about the memoir of an English girl who had lived in Israel. He sent his book to the publisher, Random House U.K. For a year, it sat unread in a slush pile of unsolicited manuscripts. "I wrote a couple of times, 'Are you still interested?' The editor who received it just scribbled back on my letter, 'Yes, still interested. Unfortunately, it's still on the pile.' Still on the pile. Well, I knew what that meant," Harry said.

Impatient with the months of indecision, Harry hired an agent in England to get a definitive answer. Not long afterward, the agent reported back that the editor liked Harry's book, just not enough to publish it. Instead, she was passing it along to a colleague, Kate Elton, publishing director at Arrow, a Random House imprint. Since the book arrived without a cover letter from an agent, "it had none of the overhyped pitch that you sometimes get with these things," Elton told Motoko Rich of the *New York Times*. "I read it without knowing what I was getting at all."

Elton read the manuscript in an afternoon in February 2006. She phoned Harry the next day and told him that she was about to make an offer. She wanted to know only whether to make it to him or to his agent. Elton offered five thousand pounds—about nine thousand dollars at the time. "It was almost embarrassingly small, but I was happy to have a serious publisher. So, it all started," he said.

Praise for *The Invisible Wall* was immediate. As encouragement poured in, Harry felt impelled to begin a second volume, *The Dream*. "Until then I had no intention of writing ever again. I was encouraged by people who got hold of me on the telephone. They all wanted to know what happened to this family," Harry said. Once again, the writing went swiftly as he adhered to advice he had gotten long before: make it as simple as possible, say just what was in his mind, avoid flowery words and phrases, and let the characters speak for themselves. "The way I describe them, that's the way they are."

Harry's interest in writing may have begun when he was nine or ten and his mother asked him to write letters to America for her. As she dictated, Harry penned pleas to Yankel's relatives asking for money for passage to the United States. Over the years, Harry's grandmother replied only once. "What do you think I am, the Bank of England? Or do you think I took the crown jewels with me when I left from England?" she asked, Harry wrote in *The Dream*. Still, the family attended each delivery of the mail filled with hope. They were shocked and then jubilant when the postman handed Harry a thick envelope, sent anonymously and containing tickets for the entire family aboard the S.S. *Regina* in 1922. His mother, who would later discover that Yankel's father had sent the tickets, sat transfixed, holding her dream in her hands, as Harry and his siblings rejoiced. Their raucous celebration woke their father from a nap. He greeted the news with disdain, roaring, "Who the bloody hell wants to go to America?" And he swore that he would not go.

But to Harry's bitter and everlasting disappointment, Yankel journeyed with the rest of the family, via Quebec, to the West Side of Chicago. He so dreaded his father's brutish ways, Harry prayed his father would remain in England. His misgivings increased when the Bernsteins moved into an urban landscape that bore little resemblance to the imagined world of mansions, manicured lawns, and swimming pools he had seen in magazines. The discrepancy between the stirring visions of life in America that his relatives had described in their letters and the reality was not lost on Yankel either. After a brief respite, he renewed his cruel behavior, needling relatives with derogatory nicknames and provoking Harry's grandmother, with whom his family was staying, to send them packing. Harry acted out the scene for me, raising an arm high in the air and mimicking his grandmother's imperious voice, "That's enough! Leave!"

After a year in which the family tasted poverty in Chicago and learned shattering truths about their relatives' lives in America, the Bernsteins' circumstances improved temporarily. Harry was again employed as the family's letter writer. This time, however, in letters going *to* England, he transcribed his mother's boasting about life in America. His brothers and sister were prospering, he wrote, and they were living in an airy apartment where they enjoyed having a toilet, electric lights, a telephone, and even a piano. "Harry is now going to high school and studying to be an architect," Ada reported and Harry scribbled, proud to be using his new Waterman pen.

But the good times were short-lived. By 1927, Harry's older siblings had left home—one to marry, one to hop freight cars west, and one to be a speaker for the Communist Party. To make matters worse, Harry's father, after a brief respite of sobriety, was returning home drunk and abusive again, having spent his earnings on alcohol. Faced with his father's hostility to them, Harry scrapped his plans to go to college.

Instead, he took the civil-service exam and got hired as a clerk in the grim fortress of the Chicago post office on Dearborn Street. He hoped his income would help ease things for his mother and allow him to save money for college tuition. The night soon came, however, when Harry lost patience with his father's tyranny. When Yankel demanded that he hand over his bankbook, Harry finally let loose. He smashed his father in the nose and sent his blood flying. Amid the mayhem that ensued, Ada discovered that her husband had already stolen her savings from under her mattress. She took Harry and his younger brother Sidney and fled to New York on a bus. Harry's savings kept them fed and housed in Brooklyn for a while until he could find work.

In 1930, he lost his job and decided to finally go to college. With help from a foundation grant, Harry began taking courses at Columbia University and got a job working in the library, at first as a page who fetched books from the stacks. "Then I got a nice, cushy job for a while. All I had to do was check cards of people who wanted to go into the stacks. That lasted until I got in an altercation with a professor over a girl he was dating. I was beginning to horn in on him," he recalled. One day, the professor accosted Harry and told him to stay away from the girl, that she did not want anything to do with him. "I knew otherwise, and I threw a punch. That did it. I got canned. Good thing, too. Otherwise, I'd probably still be there," Harry said.

Actually, it was not such a good thing. By then, the Depression was in full swing, and Harry joined the legions of job seekers, desperate for work, marching past the employment agencies on Sixth Avenue in Manhattan. It took weeks, but he was elated when a cigar-smoking character at the West Side Garage Association hired him to stake out a garage on West Forty-ninth Street. The job was simple. For four hours during the middle of the night and four during the day, he jotted down the license-plate numbers of every car that went in or out of two midtown garages. He never asked why. Getting paid seventeen dollars a week was all that mattered. That is, until one summer night when he was concentrating on taking down the license plate of a big black Packard and someone snatched his pencil and pad. He looked up to find four or five goons surrounding him. One told Harry they were going to give him something to help him remember his very last license number. They proceeded to beat and kick him, breaking his nose, jaw, ribs, and one leg and nearly knocking out an eyeball. "To this day, I don't know what it was all about," he said.

He had time to wonder as he spent months recuperating in a hospital on Wards Island. It was then, at twenty-two, that Harry began writing short stories and sketches in earnest.

To Harry's dismay, while he was recovering in the hospital, his father found his way to New York, and Ada, who had once pledged to Yankel that she would never abandon him the way his mother had, took him back. During the years that followed, the family moved from one apartment to the next, ever in search of something cheaper. Soon, the Bernsteins were living in a musty basement apartment in the Bronx and surviving on a few dollars that Yankel contributed and what little Harry occasionally earned writing magazine articles. Harry even wrote some scripts for comics for ten dollars apiece, but the publisher went out of business owing him fifty. Daily, the family's fear of eviction grew along with the prospect that they would find themselves huddled with their belongings on a street corner like so many others.

It wasn't long before Harry cooked up an article about being a bodyguard for a mobster. He made it up based on photographs of gangland figures, and submitted it to *Popular Mechanics*. A month later, the landlady knocked on the door. Instead of proffering a scowl and an eviction notice, she was full of apologies for opening his mail by "accident" and quickly handed Harry an envelope and the check it contained. Knowing the family was from Chicago and seeing the title of Harry's article—*The Profession of Bodyguarding*—printed on the check, she assumed Harry worked for the Mob. To her, Harry must have seemed delighted that the "boys" back in Chicago had paid him for some protection work. She never suspected that he was floating on air because he had just risen a rung as a professional writer.

The series of stories he started writing during his months in the hospital were published in the early 1930s and marked him as a promising young writer. That several of his stories were selected for publication in *The Anvil* by its editor, the proletarian novelist Jack Conroy, was particularly impressive. Conroy, who would become a friend, had helped to launch the careers of writers Richard Wright, Erskine

Caldwell, and Nelson Algren. Whatever pride Harry may have once attached to his publication in the good little journals of his day faded over the years. When I asked to see them, Harry directed me to the garage of his New Jersey home, where I found brittle copies jammed, in no particular order, into a small cardboard box.

"I became one of the great army of writers who dreamed of becoming famous," Harry told me. "I wrote and sent out much, but my work was often returned to me with polite rejection slips."

Still, one of his "hospital stories" drew an admiring letter from Clifton Fadiman, then the editor of Simon & Schuster and one of the most powerful literary presences in publishing. He invited Harry to submit a novel, and Harry started writing.

The turning point in Harry's life came in 1935 when, instead of attending a lecture, Harry went to a dance for the League Against War and Fascism at the legendary Webster Hall. When his eyes fixed on a beautiful girl in an orange dress, Harry overcame his awkwardness and asked her to dance. He learned that Ruby Umflat was a Polish immigrant who worked at Brentano's bookstore, and the two spent the rest of the night talking about writers—Steinbeck, Hemingway, and Sinclair Lewis—and fell madly in love. "Before meeting her, everything in my life had been gloom and misery. There was always some little fly in the ointment, but for the most part after meeting her everything after was joy and laughter."

They met regularly all summer after Ruby finished work at Brentano's and spent their nights walking around the city and attending concerts in Central Park. One moonlit night, they grew restless listening to the orchestra play Mozart and snuck away to walk around the lake until they came to a billowing golden willow tree. "We went inside its canopy and it was like a room with a high ceiling, like a cathedral, and that is where we made love for the first time," Harry told me, his voice trailing to a modest whisper. It was not long before

47

they began to discuss marriage, but Harry worried about leaving his mother alone with his father and about how he would support a wife. One day, Ruby countered his concerns. "Listen, Mr. Gloom, I have a job and I have saved two thousand dollars in the bank." She said she would support them and his mother.

Ruby also reminded Harry that Clifton Fadiman had continued to encourage him in weekly letters as he waited for him to finish his novel and that Edward J. O'Brien had selected Harry for inclusion in his prestigious annual list of contemporary American short-story writers. O'Brien's selections were then a closely watched source of notable new talent. Harry was not budged by Ruby's argument. But the sight of her tears when she sobbed to Harry that the only thing stopping him from marrying her was that he did not love her enough changed his mind.

They were married on May 3, 1935, and moved into a room in a brownstone on West Sixty-eighth Street. Their rent was seven dollars a week, half of Ruby's salary. "We had a three-day honeymoon in Central Park, and then she went back to work at Brentano's and I sat home and wrote my novel. That upside-down arrangement was common in those days. It was the Depression."

Eventually, Harry completed his novel, *Hard Times and White Collars,* and submitted it to Fadiman at Simon & Schuster. "I didn't hear from him for a while. Then, after a month of waiting, I got a letter from him in which he said he'd like to see me. Well, that shouted right to heaven! That meant he was going to publish it, otherwise why would he want to see me?" That night, Harry and Ruby toasted his success with a budget-busting four-dollar bottle of wine. They were so ecstatic they could hardly sleep. The next day, Harry donned a clean shirt, a carefully matched tie, and well-shined shoes. Filled with excitement, he set off for the publisher's office. Fadiman greeted Harry warmly and his hopes soared. "He told me how good the book was and how much he liked it. From the way he was talking I was certain he was about to offer me a contract. I could feel myself swelling with pride. Then he said the book would not fit his list. At that moment, it was over for me. I was through. There I was with nothing to show for my work but a pat on the back."

On his way out the door, Harry asked Fadiman if he could help him find work. "Are you looking for a job?" the surprised editor said, then asked Harry if he liked to read. "Does a duck swim?" Harry responded. Fadiman picked up the phone and called his brother, Robert, who was a story editor at Metro Goldwyn Mayer studios. Harry soon had a job reading novels and scripts for the movies. MGM paid him five dollars for a novel, five for a play, and two for a short story. "I read some awful things," he recalled. "The first was tripe, something to do with a spoiled heiress who was wangling for a handsome architect, who in turn loved a shopgirl."

When he turned in his first synopsis, the story editor was amused by Harry's negative critique. He had already asked someone else to read the book, and that reader thought it would make a good movie so the editor planned to recommend it to the studio. He suggested that in the future, if he received another book to read, Harry should write a longer synopsis. The next one Harry wrote was ten pages. The editor was not entirely satisfied and told Harry some readers commonly wrote fifteen- or twenty-page synopses. From then on, Harry wrote that much and more. "They took up more of my time than I expected. In fact, I was not getting any time to write my book. But I thought, What the hell. As soon as I break in I'll be able to ease off. My book would wait, my epic." Harry read his "guts out"—novels, romances, mysteries, short stories, travelogues, even books on the Canarsie Canal. Assignments usually had a twenty-four-hour deadline, and he would frequently have to read until midnight and then write twenty to thirty pages. He rarely made more than twenty-five dollars a week.

One story editor gave Harry a lesson in analysis: "Don't look for Shakespeare. A piece might be literary crap, but it can make a first-rate picture," he wrote in *The Dream*. None of the plays he read ever made it to the screen, but a few novels did, including Steinbeck's *Grapes of Wrath,* Richard Wright's *Native Son,* and the autobiography by Margaret Landon upon which *The King and I* was based. Over time he met other movie readers, and many, he said, were, like him, "failed writers who hadn't yet given up and were just in the reading job as a stopgap until they finally made it." Back then, he said, sardonically, he was going to write a novel entitled *Books of Wrath* that would deal with migratory manuscript readers in America. "The work as a reader for the movies held me back and hurt me a great deal as a writer," he said. Despite the incessant demand to read and report on books, Harry still found time to work on his own fiction. But the material was creatively toxic to his imagination. "It's like trying to speak in a room with a lot of other voices. There's only so much room in a human being's mind. I would have accomplished much more if I had not become bogged down in reading all those worn-out movie plots."

When Harry's son, Charles, was born in 1940, the Bernsteins moved from Manhattan to Laurelton, an emerging neighborhood being developed from farmland at the far end of Queens. Harry was rejected from the army for service in World War II because he had suffered from rheumatic fever as a child. Meanwhile, Ruby took a job as a school secretary and continued to earn the family's steadiest paycheck. "Ruby liked her job. She liked her home. She liked taking care of the kids. I never heard one word of complaint," Harry said. And, of course, she never stopped being supportive of Harry's writing.

His children had to be, too. "My bedroom was his office during the day, and all day you'd hear the typewriter booming," Charles recalled. Money was usually tight, but the family managed. Harry had a car, though mostly he kept it up on blocks in the garage because he couldn't afford to use it. Adraenne, who was born in 1945 and would eventually go on to major in English at Vassar, also remembers the endless clacking of the typewriter and how, at night, she had to climb around hanging laundry in the basement to a nook where her father continued to write when Charles was in his room. No one dared go near Harry's desk. "I never showed my writing to anyone. In fact, I was so terrified that anyone would see what I was working on that I would go into fits if anyone came near my desk," he said.

In the mid-1950s Harry took his first regular job as an editor of the building trades magazine *Home of Tomorrow.* For the next eighteen years he commuted from Long Island to the publisher's offices in New Rochelle. "It was easy work. I had my own hours and my own office," he said. He continued to write novels and send them to agents and publishers, and have them rejected one after the other. "Writing became secondary to me. It was something I did in my spare time, if there was spare time. I occupied myself making a living and with my family. They went very swiftly, the years." When he was forced out, at age sixty, in 1970, his salary had reached the fantastic sum of two hundred dollars a week. He started a data-processing trade magazine and sold it for $50,000 in 1973, when Ruby finally retired from her job as a school secretary.

With the sale of their small house in Queens and the sale of Harry's trade magazine, Ruby and Harry were able to buy a two-bedroom bungalow for $33,000 in an adult community called Greenbriar. One of its attractions was that the streets were all named after writers. Their house was at the intersection of Whitman and Dickinson, two giants of American poetry. "Too bad we're the only ones here who know who they are," Harry said ruefully one day when I raised the pleasant coincidence of his intersection. "We thought we were moving into a community of intellectuals." He laughed a deep, muffled laugh.

In retirement, Ruby, who had studied dance with Martha Graham in Greenwich Village in the 1930s and stayed fit throughout her life, began teaching yoga at Greenbriar while Harry continued to write. They followed the same pattern when they vacationed three months a year in the arts community of San Miguel de Allende, Mexico. In addition to fiction, Harry began a newly busy life in journalism, writing articles for local publications such as the *Asbury Park Press* and *Staten Island Advance.* ("When I was younger, I always wanted to be a newspaper reporter, but no one would ever give me a job," Harry said.) He also wrote a number of pieces for the New York *Daily News* Sunday magazine.

By then Harry had little reason to hope for literary success. His novels had been rejected one after the other. In the 1950s he wrote one about the violent anti-communist riots in Peekskill, New York, in 1949, that followed the announcement of a concert by the protean black singer, actor, and civil-rights advocate Paul Robeson. The most prominent African-American from the 1920s to the 1950s, Robeson was as celebrated for his rich baritone voice, his skill in bringing the plays of Eugene O'Neill to life, and fighting for labor rights and an end to the color barrier in professional sports as he was reviled at the start of the Cold War by anti-communists for his outspoken admiration for what the Soviet Union had done to recognize the full humanity of blacks. Robeson was red-listed. Anything sympathetic to him was doomed. Whatever merit Harry's novel had, publishers would not touch it.

He wrote *Oliver's Story,* a novel about a writer's workshop Harry had attended in his youth on Fifty-seventh Street, then a hotbed of the arts and modernism. An agent discouraged him from submitting it anywhere, telling him readers were not interested in stories about writers. "I regret now having thrown it and the others away. I believe it could have made a good satirical novel. I listened to the wrong advice," Harry said glumly.

At seventy, in 1981, he finally got one of his novels published—more or less. *The Smile* tells the story of the rise and fall of Miss Torrington, Connecticut, who briefly enjoyed celebrity as a fashion model. Harry considered it a good psychological study of a woman without much intelligence but who had great looks and style. In the afterword Harry's old editor Jack Conroy comments that he was tempted to compare Harry's "exposure of the shallow and unsubstantial standards of the commercial world that often betray those who live by them" to Theodore Dreiser's. "But Bernstein is his own man, with his own conceptions and style," he wrote. Unfortunately, Harry never got the chance to see if the book would sell. "My luck," he said. "The publisher went broke before it was distributed."

It was a monumental disappointment. But even that did not douse Harry's drive to write fiction. He continued to plug away. Harry's greatest hopes were for a novel he wrote in which the main character was a fictionalized version of John Hinckley Jr., the twenty-five-year-old who attempted to assassinate Ronald Reagan outside the Washington Hilton Hotel in March 1981 to win actress Jodie Foster's heart. "I thought I had a pretty good book," Harry said, "but it was turned down by mostly everyone."

And that is where Harry's story might have ended were it not for his need to escape the grief that followed Ruby's death. "As I began to write the memoir, I realized that the best fiction I had ever written I wrote by turning my own experiences into fiction. I discovered that I had a natural ability to write about myself. Finally accepting that made all the difference," Harry said.

Between the publication of *The Invisible Wall* and *The Dream*, shortly before his ninety-eighth birthday, requests for interviews and talks poured in from around the globe as well as from local libraries and reading clubs. Harry turned down a request to appear on Jay Leno's *Tonight Show,* but accepted an invitation to speak at the 92nd

Street Y, a cultural mecca in New York. He gave a charmingly bittersweet recap of his life to a mostly gray-haired audience interested in the art of the memoir. Dressed in a blue jacket and a dress shirt without a tie, Harry spoke with the skill, confidence, and sense of humor of a practiced author. A woman a couple of rows behind me whispered to a friend, "Isn't he something?"

In addition to winning readers and good reviews, Harry's first books soon brought prestigious grants and awards.

The Guggenheim Foundation gave him a $40,000 grant to work on his third book, making him one of the oldest recipients of the prestigious artists' fund. And the Christopher Award honored him at a formal ceremony, along with other writers and filmmakers, for "affirming the highest values of the human heart" and fulfilling the Christopher credo that "it is better to light one candle than to curse the darkness." When the citation was read for Harry, the audience erupted with a standing ovation. Harry remained seated in a wheelchair and raised one hand in acknowledgment. He was visibly moved at the improbable moment as a Catholic priest handed him his Christopher medallion of honor. "The thought flashed through my mind of how that little street in England would have reacted had they been able to know what was happening then. The world has come a long way since those early days, for a Catholic organization to be honoring a Jew."

It was easy to imagine the gratification his mother and Ruby would have felt seeing Harry rewarded at last. For as much as Harry's is a story of heroic perseverance, it is ultimately a love story. No matter how the rest of the world perceived what he did, Ruby possessed and never surrendered the true vision of his talent. And as much as any story of late-blooming success, Harry's illustrates how much the faith and love of others, demonstrated in countless, unnoticed daily acts, matters. Harry himself had noted as much when he dedicated

The Invisible Wall to his mother ("Ma, who gave up so much and received so little. Can this book make up for it? Can anything?") and *The Dream* to Ruby ("whose love made the dream come true"). A few weeks after the Christopher ceremonies, Harry had a willow tree planted next to a man-made lake across from his house to honor the love that he and Ruby shared and first consummated under the willow in Central Park.

By the beginning of summer Harry finished a third book, *The Golden Willow*. In it, he tells about his unforeseen adventures after turning ninety. Like the previous two books, it took him less than a year to write—remarkable considering that he claims to be a lazy writer. Part of what allowed him to work quickly, he said, was that he no longer felt any pressure when he wrote. "I spent so many years when I had to write thirty or forty pages in a day, writing treatments for the movie studios. So if I don't feel like writing now, I don't. I have only one luxury when I write: I write when I damn well feel like it." He had also honed his method of writing. "I won't sit down to write unless I have a hunk of material—a chapter's worth or as much as a short story. If the raw material is good, I won't make any mistakes. Never sit down to write anything unless you can hold the story in your hand like a ball. And whatever you do, be sure you finish what you have started. It's like building a house. Don't stop until you can put a chimney on it."

Disconcertingly, Harry struggled to put the final bricks in place for *The Golden Willow*'s chimney. For a while, he was nagged by the fear that he would have to rewrite a chunk of the book and that he had perhaps run out of things to say. Still, he was not about to add pages just to make the brief book longer. "One thing I don't do, I don't pad."

After suffering a few anxious weeks, his agent notified him that Ballantine Books had accepted his manuscript and agreed to pay a $175,000 advance. *The Golden Willow* was published during the same week that Harry celebrated his ninety-ninth birthday. By then, because he had received so many letters asking him what ever happened to her, he was sketching out a fourth book based on the character of his sister Rose, who once had fancied herself royalty.

In late October 2008, Harry was set to undergo surgery to clean out a severely blocked carotid artery, an operation that, at his age, carried a significant risk. But without surgery, his risk of having a fatal stroke was very high. The day before the operation, he was supposed to take a limousine from New Jersey and meet his daughter at NYU Langone Medical Center. Late in the day she phoned him from the hospital to see where he was. She informed him that his bed was ready and that the staff was waiting to get preoperative testing under way. Harry was a little peeved by the call. He was in the midst of work for his publisher, he told Adraenne, and as far as he was concerned, it couldn't wait. The hospital bed could.

"I'm supposed to be getting ready to die," he told me that night, when I visited him at the hospital. "But these have been the most productive years of my life. You live in a sort of dream most of your life. Your dreams are wishful thinking of what you want to be and want to have. It's not until you face the harsh reality of yourself that you can do or say anything intelligent. Write what you know, they say. Well, it sure took me a long time to get that, didn't it?" A week later, Harry was back at his desk, pounding out some more of what he knows.

One Woman, Two Villages

"This is the kind of love I want."

It might have been otherwise for Dana Dakin if her romance with a multimillionaire had worked out. But then if the romance had worked out, Dana would not have moved to Wilmot Flat, New Hampshire. And if she had never moved to Wilmot Flat, she might never have ventured to Pokuase—and it would then have also been otherwise for thousands of women in Ghana.

For twenty-five years, Dana, a tall, vibrant woman whose stature and styled white hair often make her look like an advertisement for an Eileen Fisher store, had been running her own consulting business for institutional investment firms. As she turned sixty, after moving to Wilmot Flat and discovering something of the power a community working together can have, she felt an intense need to mark a new stage in her life and to incorporate the lessons of her New Hampshire village into whatever she pursued. "I became determined to greet the youth of old age by giving back," Dana said. As it turned out, she would decide to launch a micro-finance program to help women living in poverty and without opportunity in a village in Ghana she had never seen.

In the six years since her initial visit to Pokuase, WomensTrust, the nonprofit she founded, had distributed a total of $182,000 in more than two thousand uncollateralized micro-loans to stimulate entrepreneurship and economic development.

The loans have already brought important, if sometimes subtle, changes to the village. Not only have they altered the lives of women who had earned little more than subsistence from makeshift businesses—selling bread, cassavas, charcoal, fabrics, footwear, and pots and pans—they have seeded other potentially far-reaching changes, too. "Women's lives are improving. They are dressing better. Women who were selling goods off their heads have gotten the confidence and the money to get a table to sell off of. Women who were selling off tables have taken bigger loans and opened little kiosks. Women who bake and manufacture goods have hired more people and gotten bigger ovens or whatever they needed to produce more. And sometimes one of them says, 'We're all going to town to buy stuff from wholesalers. Why don't we become a wholesaler?' They diversify and take action on their business ideas. It's amazing."

The benefits appear to be social as well as economic. Husbands, for instance, are treating spouses with more respect. "Everything is pride and shame, and in a place where husbands often can't get a job, women now are able to help a family out of poverty. Maybe the men don't feel as trapped," she said. Physical abuse of wives has until recently been a significant and widespread problem in Pokuase as in the rest of Ghana, where a UN study in 2008 found that 34 percent of all women still consider violence against them by husbands justifiable. "Whatever the explanation," Dana said, "the local public nurse in Pokuase says that wife beating has gone way down since WomensTrust started giving out loans."

Pokuase's problems have hardly disappeared. Referred to as an urban village, to some it is just a slum town an hour north of Ghana's capital, Accra, by public transportation. It sits directly off a highway being built by the Chinese. The streets are red, dusty, and littered with plastic bags and garbage. The best homes are made of cement, the rest of scrap metal. Latrines remain highly unsanitary. Too few clean wells and too frequent use of bacteria-ridden river water remain constant threats to public health. Maternal mortality rates, anemia from iron-poor nutrition, and hypertension remain epidemically high.

Girls still struggle with family pressure to leave school young and work for their families. But it is also true that since Dana began WomensTrust in the village, more girls are staying in school beyond sixth grade. When she arrived, families commonly believed that it was not worth the investment of their meager resources to educate girls. The number now finishing ninth grade is rising rapidly.

Now, more conventional measures of Dana and WomensTrust's success have begun to accumulate. In 2006, the nonprofit was awarded a $10,000 "Stand for a Better World" award by Mannington Mills. Then the United Nations African Mothers Association gave the organization $10,000 to start an entrepreneurs' club. And Dana was selected as a 2008 Purpose Prize fellow, an award that recognizes people over sixty who defy societal expectations by using their creativity and talent to address critical social problems. In the spring of 2009, at age sixty-six, she was invited to serve as the Lois Langland Alumna-in-Residence at Scripps College in Claremont, California, and to teach undergraduate women about international development, investment philanthropy, and empowering poor women.

Dana grew up in an emotionally rigid home in Orinda, California, the daughter of Dana and William Cook, a housewife who enjoyed flower arranging and a successful San Francisco insurance broker. "Everything in our house was about living the American dream. It looked like *Leave It to Beaver* on the outside, but it wasn't fun. My parents believed in achievement, discipline, and narcissism," Dana said. She worked hard to meet her father's demanding expectations, got straight A's in high school, but barely socialized. Two weeks after Dana turned nineteen, during her sophomore year at Scripps College, her ten-year-old brother, Billy, was accidentally shot to death by a friend playing with a shotgun. "It says a lot that our parents didn't call us to tell us that Billy was killed," recalled Dana's younger sister, Connie. "A neighbor met us when we came home. And that was the whole flavor of our childhood. We were never really allowed to grieve. And I think Billy's death went very deep and silent in both of us. Dana learned very young that she was in this life alone and had to make whatever happened her own."

After her brother's death, Dana's parents asked her to leave college and return home. Instead, alarmed by the prospect of losing recently gained freedom, she married Harold T. Couch, the doctoral student she was dating. Less than a year later, Couch confessed that he was still in love with a former girlfriend. Dana left the marriage and finished her degree in international relations. After graduating, she moved to San Francisco, secured a divorce, and—hoping to eschew typically underpaid women's careers—found herself working in a succession of short-lived secretarial jobs. She often pretended to take shorthand as she rewrote her bosses' letters. "I was so frustrated. I didn't know how to get ahead. There was no opportunity for a woman, which is why I really identify with African women. I just know how frustrated they must be," Dana said.

Her situation was made worse by the bias she faced as a divorcée in the 1960s. When her first husband asked her to remarry, she agreed.

But the second try fared no better than the first. Dana soon met and, after her second divorce, in 1968, married John M. Boyle, an ambitious Harvard MBA. They moved to New York, where she was assigned by her company to work on a project at the New York Stock Exchange that she turned into the opportunity for which she had been waiting. The project, a transformative Wall Street study that led to the end of fixed-rate brokerage commissions, gave Dana cutting-edge tools to become an early investment measurement analyst, an expert on why some money managers succeed better than others.

By 1974, she had moved back to San Francisco, divorced Doyle, and was an analyst for Callan Associates, one of the nation's biggest institutional investment consulting firms. It didn't help her income. She earned $15,000 a year, one-sixth of her male counterparts who sold her research. When asked for a chance to do the same, she was told, "You're a woman. Our clients will not accept that."

She had had enough of such chauvinistic discrimination. After marrying stockbroker John H. Dakin, she struck out on her own. She founded Dakin Partners in the late 1970s and carved an innovative career as a marketing consultant to institutional investment firms interested in wooing pension funds. Initially, many of the firms feared that in marketing themselves they would lose the veneer of refinement that comforted institutions placing pension funds in their hands. "But Dana was able to convince these people that it was important to market themselves, that the world was changing and they needed to publicize themselves in an authentic way," said Maureen Oddone, a fellow marketing consultant and friend. Dana's creative agency pioneered packaging entrepreneurial spin-offs of traditional banks and insurance companies. In a business world dominated by men, she achieved a reputation for asking about what wasn't obvious, quick synthesis of complex issues, and creative flair. Her client list included major companies with serious financial muscle, including SEI Investments (a leading global investment firm that administers $420 billion in mutual fund and pooled assets), Mellon Institutional Asset Management, and Dreyfus International Investors.

Still, her business had never become self-sustaining. By the early 1990s, Dana was questioning how much longer she wanted to push on with her business. At about that moment, Dean LeBaron, an iconoclastic quantitative investor, entered the picture. Dana and Dean had often run into each other in the rarefied world of high finance and flirted with having a relationship, but the timing was never right. Finally, she and LeBaron were simultaneously free, ready, and interested. After a life of romantic disappointments, Dana was optimistic that at last she had found a relationship with an intellectually compelling soul mate. She hoped they would spend the rest of their lives together. "Spending thirty minutes talking to Dean is like spending weeks talking to somebody else," she said.

In 1993, Dana took a radical step. She left her home in Mill Valley, California, and moved to Lake Sunapee, New Hampshire, to live with LeBaron. He was in the process of selling his privately held firm, Batterymarch Financial Management of Boston, for a reported $120 million. Two years later, the romance was over. LeBaron, as it turned out, had other interests, and Dana was left heartbroken, depressed, and in disarray.

Waiting was never Dana's strength. Instead, she did what she usually does in times of distress. She went to the nearest bookstore. Inside, she stopped to read a newspaper article from the *Concord Monitor* that was perched on a store display. It told the story of the remarkable romance of two poets, Jane Kenyon and Donald Hall. Kenyon had been the poet laureate of New Hampshire when she died of leukemia at forty-seven in 1995 in Hall's old family farmhouse in Wilmot. The poets had shared a life that inspired Kenyon to write her most famous poem, "Otherwise." It concludes with an unforgettable stanza on love and mortality:

> At noon I lay down
> with my mate. It might
> have been otherwise.
> We ate dinner together
> at a table with silver
> candlesticks. It might
> have been otherwise.
> I slept in a bed
> in a room with paintings
> on the walls, and
> planned another day
> just like this day.
> But one day, I know
> it will be otherwise.

That's the kind of love I want! I'm moving to Wilmot Flat! Dana told herself.

And like that, Dana, at fifty-two, went off to find a house there. Her budget was under $100,000. Not long after she began looking, she bid on a mountainside ranch house. But she lost out to a higher bidder. "I thought maybe it was a sign that I just wasn't meant to live in Wilmot. But then I became determined. I would not accept that outcome. So I hired the realtor who represented the buyer who outbid me." She began, as she likes to say, to look at lots of little houses with no potential. One day, six months later, when she was house hunting, the realtor drove past Wilmot Flat's dilapidated former fire station. Dana asked about it, and he tried to put her off: "You don't want to look at that."

But she did want to. She had a gut feeling about it. "And besides, it was so sad. I could see it needed to be fixed. It was forlorn. And it needed to be rescued. That's me, isn't it, romantic and to the rescue?" she said, laughing her best full-throated laugh at her own foible.

When she bought the wood-framed firehouse, it needed a lot of help. By 1997, after camping out inside it for two years, Dana had saved enough money to begin renovations that took two years to complete. Local workers installed new windows, demolished a dropped ceiling to reveal beautiful original wood rafters, jackhammered the grimy floor and replaced it with a new wood floor over radiant heat, and installed an open kitchen. Stained clapboard went up on the walls of the front fire engine bay, turning it into a large sunroom that now doubles as a plant-filled office.

The more time Dana spent in Wilmot Flat renovating the fire station, the more she craved time to be there. The first year of renovations, she stayed in Wilmot for four months. The next, six months.

Dana may not have found a love like Kenyon and Hall's, but she had found the love of a place—a community of 1,369 residents, neighbors more bound by traditional New England values than by property values or shopping venues.

Wilmot Flat might have no retail stores and only one restaurant, but during the summer it has a farmer's market on the green where a couple of dozen vendors sell produce and goods and neighbors mingle and talk. It has a communal character, and its character seized Dana's affection. That and a spirit seen in another of Kenyon's poems, "Potluck at the Wilmot Flat Baptist Church," in which she describes a visit to the church for a reading, and, on entering catching the smell of coffee and seeing the speaker's table "decorated with red, white and blue streamers and framed *Time* and *Newsweek* covers of the President, just elected." She felt, she wrote, the presence of people "trying to live ordered lives," and "was struck again with love of the Republic."

"I fell in love with those same real folk, who try to make things as pretty as they can, and do so with resourcefulness and incredible joy," Dana said.

It took a little longer for the village to embrace Dana. Her renovation of the firehouse and her unpredictable comings and goings gave rise to suspicions. By traditional New England standards, she seemed too mercurial and rootless. Some had even heard her talking about letting people use her house for yoga classes when she wasn't there. Then word got out that the United States Postal Service planned to abandon the current post office, which it rents, and build a modern facility elsewhere.

Dana went ballistic in its defense.

"I said, 'Uh-oh! If we don't fight this, we're going to end up with a town with no center, like the ones I grew up in in California.' The post office and the community center were shoring up the center of town. The town came together at the post office during the week and at the community center on weekends," she said. She held a small organizing fund-raiser at the fire station and immersed herself in village affairs. The community mounted a successful campaign to keep the post office where it was.

Meanwhile, a two-year study determined that the old community center, which doubled as the village's preschool, needed to be condemned and replaced. Dana took up the cause. She courted the newer, more affluent residents of Wilmot like herself to contribute to building a new community center. She donated a piece of her own adjacent land to allow for a building to be sited better. Folks in Wilmot Flat began to warm to Dana and her motivating enthusiasm. Her attachment to the village grew still greater, along with her astonishment at how the tiny community came together and built the new center. "I couldn't believe so few people could get so much done," she said as we sat at her country kitchen table.

For all the calm and community Dana found in Wilmot Flat, her own life continued to feel fragmented and unsatisfying. The nature of her consulting business was changing and stirring uncertainty. As financial institutions began to employ ever more abstract and speculative strategies, imaginative clients seemed harder to find. Meanwhile, a nagging desire to do something meaningful to celebrate her sixtieth birthday, which she had been nursing for a decade, kept growing more insistent.

It had begun when a business partner introduced Dana to Olga Murray in Sausalito. For thirty-seven years, Murray had worked as a staff lawyer for justices of the California Supreme Court. For most of those years, she worked directly for the chief justices, helping to write landmark opinions on civil rights, women's rights, and environmental policy. But what captivated Dana was when Murray told her the story of how she had celebrated her sixtieth birthday five years earlier. She had gone trekking in the Himalayas and fell in love with Nepal. She also fell in love with its children, who desperately wanted to go to school. Though poorly nourished and clothed in rags, the children's capacity for joy was breathtaking, Murray told Dana. When she returned to California after her first visit, Murray began to tell everyone who would listen that for the price of a good haircut in the United States, she knew she could make a difference in the lives of the children. In 1985, Murray began giving college scholarships to four children.

At the time Dana met her in 1990, Murray was on her way back to Kathmandu to found the Nepalese Youth Opportunity Foundation.

In the two decades since, it has aided more than 225,000 destitute children and opened orphanages, schools, and nine rehabilitation homes for severely malnourished children. It has also saved more than 4,300 girls, as young as six, from being sold as domestic slaves by trading pigs and goats for their freedom.

As she herself turned sixty, Dana turned to Murray's inspiring example and to the adage that life is lived in thirds—first to learn, then to earn, and last to return. It became her mantra. Although she had not made a fortune by Wall Street standards, she had succeeded well enough to want to give back something to the world. Only she still had no idea what that "something" might be. She got into the habit of asking everyone she met if they had an idea for her.

In 2002, Dana met another woman who had precisely the idea she needed. After bumping into her at a crafts fair, Dana told Martha Virden Cunningham, founding executive director of the Women's Fund of New Hampshire, about her search for a mission to celebrate the start of her seventh decade. Cunningham had just finished David Bornstein's book *The Price of a Dream,* and recommended to Dana that she read the story of Nobel peace laureate Muhammad Yunus. Possessed by the dream of eradicating poverty in the world, Yunus challenged conventional banking by establishing Grameen, a bank dedicated to giving the poorest Bangladeshis minuscule loans. Acting on his belief that credit is a basic human right, not just a privilege of the rich, and that even the poorest of people are entrepreneurial, Yunus and his bank have loaned more than two and a half billion dollars to more than two million families in Bangladesh. About 97 percent of the bank's clients are women. "Compared to men, who spent money freely, women benefited their families much more," he explained to *Time* magazine in 2008. His efforts have spawned hundreds of programs worldwide such as Dana's WomensTrust. They, in turn, have made loans to some one hundred million people.

Exhilarated by the simplicity, potential, and power of the micro-finance model, Dana overturned a small library of literature. For six months, she read everything that she could, including Yunus's autobiography *Banker to the Poor*. She networked everywhere possible and quizzed everyone she met. *I can do this!* she told herself. She had made her decision. She would go to Ghana and focus her efforts on women. Neither part of her decision was chance.

Back in the early 1960s, when Dana was a star student at Scripps College, the selective all-women's college at Claremont, California, she wrote her honors thesis on Pan-Africanism as espoused by the first president of independent Ghana, Kwame Nkrumah. Dana believes that her interest in Africa originated with the worldwide attention focused on the Swiss philosopher physician Albert Schweitzer, who won the Nobel Peace Prize in 1952. He was lionized for dedicating his long life to the practice of medicine in Labarene, French Equatorial Africa, now Gabon, and magazines frequently ran stories on the hospital he built and how he used the money he received for the Peace Prize to add a leper colony to it. As an undergraduate, Dana's interest allowed her to cobble together a major with courses examining the social, economic, and cultural issues at the moment that African nationalists were revolting against colonial rule and achieving independence.

Researching Africa anew forty years later, Dana was emboldened to go to Ghana when she learned that it was relatively safe for travel and that English remained the official language of the former British colony. No small thing for Dana, who is not adept in languages. Then, too, her friend Tetteh Tawiah had been raised in Accra, Ghana's capital, and might be a good resource.

When she told Tetteh that she was planning to go to Ghana to establish a program, he was alarmed. He was worried for Dana's safety and tried to dissuade her. "She was going to stick out like a sore thumb—an older white woman traveling alone. Even I would be cautious traveling alone in an unfamiliar African country," he told me over coffee in a Starbucks in the Citicorp Building in Manhattan.

Dana was undeterred. She convinced Tetteh to call his father, Hope Tawiah, a semiretired construction project manager in Accra, and ask him if he would give her some guidance when she arrived in Ghana.

Contrary to plans, Tetteh's father was not waiting for Dana when she arrived at Kotoka International Airport. Nor was anyone else there. Fortunately, Dana had foreseen the possibility of a mix-up and had made reservations at a hotel in Accra. She spent the day after her arrival shopping and pondering her next move. "The one thing I knew was that there was no turning back. I didn't want to go home and say it didn't work out. There was something inside me that insisted I do this," she said. She finally reached Tetteh's father by phone, and the following morning he appeared in her hotel lobby accompanied by a bearded man wearing a white caftan and carrying a wooden staff, a fetish priest from the village of Pokuase. They had arranged to take Dana there and for her to stay at Topido, an inn run by the only white person in the village.

After a twenty-mile ride north, they arrived on the outskirts of Pokuase, where Tetteh's father had a good relationship with the village chief, Nii Otto Kwame III, with whom he had been in business. Dana's bags were taken to her room and she was whisked off to meet Kwame. He was holding court on the screened veranda of his house when she arrived. He wore a West African dinkra fabric over his shoulders and, surrounded by a translator and several young assistants, he spoke with solemnity.

Dana explained her idea to start a micro-finance project in Ghana. The chief said Pokuase would welcome it. Though everyone was cordial, she left the meeting without making any promises except that she would return to inform the chief of any decision she made.

Back at Topido, the innkeeper, who was Dutch, quizzed Dana about the purpose of her visit. "How are you going to start this thing?"

"Good point. I guess I have got to meet some women," she answered vaguely. "But how am I going to do that? I can't just go walk down the street."

"I know what you have to do," he said, and laid out his plan.

On Sunday, he marched Dana into one of the village's many small churches and up to its altar. He persuaded the minister to hand over the microphone to her and prompted Dana to explain her mission. Without nervousness and trusting her vision, she spoke through an interpreter. "I wanted them to understand me so much that I lost all self-consciousness. I just wanted to make it as clear as possible what I wanted to do and exactly how they could participate," she said. When she concluded twenty minutes later, she encouraged any woman interested to come see her at the inn. To her relief, several showed up the next day. Excited that her dream was actually taking shape, Dana kept her word and returned to the village chief to inform him that she had decided to launch her program in Pokuase. He told her that he was delighted. He then informed her that she would have to work through him.

"Oh no, this is woman to woman, but I will keep you informed," Dana said emphatically. Though slightly astonished by her brash response, he assented.

Her confidence stoked, Dana made appointments and met with high-level Ghanian government officials, members of Parliament, agency directors, and the minister of Women and Children's Affairs. But the meetings were of little help. Stymied, she fell back on her self-described talents as social chairman, a form of overcompensation for what she claims is her congenital shyness. She decided to throw a party at Topido. But she needed a caterer. The innkeeper suggested she speak with the recently retired couple next door: Agnes Badoe, a former regional school administrator and an excellent chef, and her husband, George, the former treasurer of a sugar plantation who had been blinded by an overdose of malaria medication. They put the party together and Dana was impressed by Agnes's organizational skills. She spent the remainder of her first visit to Pokuase discussing micro-lending with the Badoes and recruited them as her program administrators.

On her return to Wilmot Flat, Dana focused on teaching her adopted New Hampshire village about her newly adopted village in Ghana and what she intended to do with her new organization. Eager audiences of friends spread the word of her adventure. She began making presentations to any group that would have her, including church groups, women's groups, gardening clubs, schools, and the Rotary. As exciting as it was that people began to send small donations, Dana knew she would need a large infusion of capital to launch the program.

She looked around at her options. She owned a late-model Volvo sedan and an old Volkswagen bus. As a single woman, she didn't need both. She sold the Volvo for $18,000 and committed $5,000 as start-up funds for WomensTrust.

When she returned to Pokuase in October 2003, she carried her bed linens, an umbrella, micro-finance procedure manuals, a video camera, and her seed money. She also brought something profoundly heartening: the support of Wilmot Flat and a sense that the two villages were about to become bound to each other.

In Ghana, George Badoe had studied the micro-lending manuals Dana had left behind. He had readied a system of journals and ledgers to track loans and repayments. Agnes had designed an application for borrowers, which, working from Yunus's model, required women to form groups of four to six to apply. While each member of a group would receive an individual loan, none would be eligible for another loan until the entire group's loan had been repaid. That was something Yunus had discovered encouraged high repayment rates. Dana and the Badoes drafted a constitution, opened the necessary bank accounts, and registered the new entity with the national government in Accra. Dana also received her first unpleasant lessons about the unspoken costs of transacting government business in Ghana. Bureaucrats wanted to be paid, too.

In November, seventy-three excited women showed up at Topido, formed groups, and signed up for four-month loans, ranging from twenty-two to thirty dollars. A total of $2,022 was loaned, at an interest rate of 15 percent. The first-time borrowers had their pictures taken for the bank passbooks they received. For many, it was the first photo ID they had ever had. Two-thirds of the women signed for their loans with thumbprints.

The Badoes were doing such an efficient job that Dana believed, naively, that she could make a two-week visit every six months and return to the business of earning a living while furthering awareness of her project. At home, her hope that her village in New Hampshire would take an active interest in helping Pokuase was affirmed. One night in mid-January 2004, she spoke at the Wilmot Public Library. Though it was the coldest night of the year, with wind chill temperatures approaching forty below zero, local residents packed the library to hear about Dana's adventurous projects.

During her next visit to Africa, she was introduced to the plight of the elderly in Pokuase. To illustrate what she encountered, she returned with photographs of an elderly woman breaking stones in a quarry for a living. The woman's only tool was a small hammer. She placed the product of her effort in a basket and, at the end of her workday, received no more than a couple of dollars. But most elderly in Pokuase have no work and survive on as little as a dollar a day, often provided by relatives. Dana committed WomensTrust to remittances of five dollars a month to twenty-two men and women, ranging in age from 85 to 115. The amount has since increased to ten dollars a month.

On that trip, Dana also discovered why so many young girls were not in school during the day: only 20 percent made it to sixth grade. *This is terrible. The loan program will never work unless we keep girls in school,* Dana told herself. Shortly after she returned to the United States, she read a report issued by the Council on Foreign Relations titled "What Works in Girls' Education" that validated her fears. The report, introduced by Hillary Rodham Clinton, a longtime advocate for expanding girls' access to education around the world, cited extensive evidence of the beneficial impact of educating girls in developing countries. "I was shocked," Dana said. "When you educate girls, every indicator—economic, nutrition, birthrate—improved. Why hasn't our country put money into this simple act? Why did the World Bank come in years ago and say to the countries, 'You're going bankrupt, you're going to have to charge for schools,' leading to girls being pulled out of schools by their families? It was too much. I had to do something."

On her next trip to Pokuase, she walked unannounced into an elementary school she frequently passed and ran into a senior teacher named Emma Eshun. She led Dana to the head administrator's office and then stayed to listen as Dana explained her concern. She told the administrator she would like to start a scholarship program to retain promising girls at risk of being taken out of school by their families. By the time school started the next fall, Eshun had been made the school's principal, and WomensTrust gave its first scholarships to eleven girls. In keeping with WomensTrust's insistence on accountability, students must maintain a minimum of a 2.5 grade point average. By 2009, 120 primary and secondary students were receiving scholarships. And one scholarship recipient had graduated from high school, a spectacular accomplishment, and gone on to receive training as a birthing expert. "She is a total success story," Dana said enthusiastically.

As her organization reached its second anniversary, Dana was struggling to balance her work and her nonprofit. She hired Susan Kraeger, a fifty-nine-year-old local woman with a strong background in fund-raising, to become her executive director. They traveled together to Ghana and began to analyze what was happening with the program. They found that repayment rates were falling and that the number of loans being approved had dropped by half. There were two reasons: the Badoes had abandoned the all-important group-loan protocol, and, as Dana recognized, it was critically important to have a native of Pokuase, whose life was woven into the fabric of the community, administering the loans. Dana fired the Badoes, who lived apart from the village, and hired Gertrude Ankrah, a former bank clerk, shopkeeper, and women's organizer, who had grown up in Pokuase. She had post–secondary school education and political ambitions, and her mother owned a bakery in town.

As a result, the number of women recruited to participate in the micro-lending program increased tenfold and the rate of repayment has soared to 85 percent. Many in Pokuase still don't understand Dana's purpose in coming to the village, and some believe because she is white and used to stay at the Topido, she must be the Dutch innkeeper's wife. Gertrude herself did not fully appreciate Dana's commitment until she made the daylong flight across the Atlantic Ocean from Accra to Boston to attend a micro-finance conference. "You really must have the passion to help to travel like this and do it again and again. It showed me Dana really meant what she said," Gertrude said.

. . .

Collaboration is the bedrock of Dana's work in Pokuase. She has a formidable but welcoming persona. But her greatest asset may be that she knows how to interest, excite, and invite others to share in her experiment. She has learned, by listening to the women in Pokuase, that it will take more than credit to make WomensTrust's loans sustaining. It will take education and health care programs that address the root causes of poverty and an innovative model that provides a way for other Americans to bring their commitment to Pokuase.

In the summer of 2008, forty volunteers, student interns from Dartmouth College, teachers, artists, and retirees headed to Ghana, under the auspices of WomensTrust, to bring their skills to Pokuase. "We like to call it the *overground railway,*" she said.

"Dana's gift is as the visionary who empowers people to make connections, get things done, and let it go where it wants from there," said Lisah Carpenter, the executive director of the Nurse Practitioners Association of New Hampshire. After hearing a luncheon presentation on WomensTrust in Wilmot, she asked her organization to consider how it might help. Before she knew it, the group's president, Linda Messenger, was en route to Pokuase to do a health-needs assessment that focused on the village's high maternal mortality rate. There, she met Victoria, a nurse who is the sole care provider for the village's twenty thousand residents, responsible for everything from acute care to infant checkups and home visits to the elderly. Because of the high rate of anemia, caused by pregnancy-related iron deficiency, one in twenty women in Pokuase dies during childbearing years. (Strictly speaking, maternal mortality refers to a mother's death within six weeks of childbirth. In Ghana, that rate is 550 per 100,000. The rate in the U.S. is 14.2.) Messenger, with the help of two nurses from the University of Massachusetts graduate school in nursing at Worcester and a nursing student at Colby-Sawyer College in Andover, New Hampshire, screened 150 babies and 750 women in 2008 and dispensed a six-month supply of iron-infused vitamins. Of course, that is hardly the only health-related issue. The village is also plagued by poor sanitary conditions (because the hard-packed ground makes it difficult to dig proper pits), a lack of clean drinking water, and a high incidence of hypertension.

Sometimes even Dana is surprised by the responses her talks generate. After she spoke to students at the Tuck School of Business at Dartmouth, several students secured funding to visit WomensTrust in Pokuase. Virginia native Desmond Ang returned after graduation in 2008 and was drafted into the position of "interim chief operating officer" in Ghana. An informal talk Dana gave at a church in New York resulted in a $10,000 grant from the United Nations African Mothers Association. But when Dana and former executive director Kraeger finished speaking before Country Squires, a group of highly successful men based in Andover, New Hampshire, the response was not promising: "What about the men?" one of the Country Squires asked.

"We're doing nothing for the men except improve the lives of the women," Dana shot back.

WomensTrust received only two contributions totaling seventy-five dollars, and Dana was discouraged. But the next day, Bo Grove, one of the group's members and a seventy-one-year-old retired U.S. Air Force general, called to volunteer to help Pokuase's women learn business planning. Grove created a curriculum to teach semiliterate women the basics of income, expenses, and profit, and flew to Pokuase to teach it. Seventy men and women attended his classes. On his next trip, after seeing firsthand that most had difficulty with basic math, he added classes on arithmetic and using a calculator. "It's impressive how much can be accomplished by one person with the will and motivation to start and sustain a program like this," he said of Dana. "It's impressive that someone would decide I need to do this and go out and do it."

Others have been similarly inspired and brought their ideas and skills to Pokuase. Exhorting, *"Kami ami!* [Keep it loose!]," Jackie Abrams, a basket artist from Brattleboro, Vermont, taught a group of women how to make stylish wallets and handbags (from recycled black plastic bags that litter Ghana). The women formed the Kami-Ami Women's Cooperative and have fulfilled its first order contract from a Ghanaian crafts shop in Accra.

WomensTrust also facilitated a program created by Hannah Davis, a twenty-year-old junior at New York University, who started the Ghana Literacy Project in Pokuase in 2007 to teach critical thinking skills to junior high school students. Its first project, funded by Davis's grandfather and his Rotary club in Rhode Island and called the Girls Exploration and Empowerment Club (GEEC), supplements the rote-style education of the public school system with Saturday morning programs of self-exploration, science experiments, computer and writing skills, and a theater program. "The heartbeat of WomensTrust is education, and if we were to invest in one area for maximum impact, it would be to keep girls in school," Dana says.

WomensTrust's success stories are amazing. One woman, Theresa Appia Amponosh, started out with a $55 loan and, by 2008, worked her way up to a $3,000 loan, the largest given so far to an individual, from WomensTrust's Entrepreneurs Club. Amponosh, who worked hammering stone in the local quarry for a couple of dollars a day in earlier years, founded the private Celestial Light School. Her students pay forty pasewas, or about forty cents, a day for school and lunch. The loans from WomensTrust have allowed her to purchase rice, oil, fish, and other foodstuff in bulk so that she no longer has to shop at the market each day to make meals for the children.

"Until WomensTrust, if you go to the bank, nobody give you a loan," she said by phone. "If you go to the moneylender, nobody give you a loan. But WomensTrust gives us help so we can help yourself and do something for our families. WomensTrust helps us raise our level in society."

At Dana's request, Amponosh has agreed to serve as one of three Ghanaian members of WomensTrust's board of directors, an important step WomensTrust is taking. It is a move, along with an ongoing effort to shift program management from Wilmot Flat to Pokuase, Dana hopes will improve the WomensTrust's sustainability. Amponosh said she agreed to serve on the board, after consulting with her husband, because WomensTrust is not a political organization and because of Dana. "She is a friend to Pokuase and well loved. She's not here for herself. She could stay in America and enjoy her life, but she chooses to come here. If we had five women like her in every district, we would have no poverty in Ghana. She is a very hardworking, dynamic, and unique woman. She is white, but she is one of us!"

It is just that hands-on, bottom-up, on-the-ground approach that has led William Easterly, one of the toughest United States critics of foreign aid to sing Dana's praises. A former World Bank economist and the author of *The White Man's Burden: Why the West's Efforts to Aid the Rest Have Done So Much Ill and So Little Good,* Easterly says that throwing $2.3 trillion of Western aid at African poverty over fifty years, between 1955 and 2005, achieved virtually no economic growth. The West's assumptions about what was needed were key to the failure to help. "It's like a Greek tragedy of hubris and arrogance. We thought we knew the answers to Africa's problems in advance," he said at a WomensTrust fund-raiser in Manhattan in September 2009. "We might be better off doing what Dana did in Pokuase. You go and you get to know the people. You gain their trust, not for paternalistic purposes. You go with the intention of finding out how we can help. That's why Women'sTrust is probably the best project I have seen in Africa." Not long before her sixty-sixth birthday, Dana wandered through the farmer's market in Wilmot Flat one morning. She luxuriated in the first crisp hints of autumn air and lingered in pleasant conversations at the farm stands long enough to make her a little late for an appointment. There were women selling hand-spun yarn, hand-crafted satchels, beeswax candles, jars of jelly, jewelry, and heirloom vegetables. At once she felt her now secure connection to her adopted New England village and the importance of the bridge she had built between it and the village of Pokuase with its increasing ranks of entrepreneurial women.

"It was always in the back of my mind, I suppose. I knew if you could take this idea that I saw in Wilmot of people caring about people, if you could integrate what we have and what we know with what they have and what they know and what they need . . . oh my God! This isn't science. It's just good business practice. The whole trick of what we are doing is that we keep going back. We keep going back. And guess what happened? It has worked. It has worked because we give resources, we keep promises, and we keep coming back."

The three stages of life may not have proven as precisely sequential as Dana imagined when she recited her mantra approaching sixty and began her journey to Ghana, but that may be for the better. "Here I am, still learning and earning—respect and experience—and returning. Every day I work to make WomensTrust a little better. It takes a great deal of perseverance, but I am getting the satisfaction of 'return.' If that Reaper tapped me on the shoulder today, I'd say, 'Fine, but could I just take care of a few things?'"

ROBERT IADELUCA

Doctor of Substance

"Let the shadows fall behind."

Robert Iadeluca's license plate is his credo: ALL-OK. More than a few motorists in recent recessionary times may have felt provoked by its cheery boast to shout, "Yeah, what's so okay?" That would have suited the loquacious, bushy-browed, eighty-nine-year-old psychologist just fine. "Think about it for a moment," he instructed me, straightening his six-foot-two-inch frame before he proceeded with his signature Socratic probing. "Does it say everything going on in my life is okay?" He waited—long enough for the question to fill the spare office where he treats his patients atop Hospital Hill in Warrenton, Virginia. "No, it just says all okay. That's just my attitude toward life."

A few biographical facts dispel any doubt about the truth of his assertion and prove his right to proclaim it on his license plate even in the most difficult times. He has, after all, known such times as well. In 1972, he lost his job as assistant director of public relations for the New York State commissioner amid a state fiscal crisis that forced massive budget cuts. Having worked for the state for only two years, he got bumped early. Gone, through no fault of his own, were a good salary, the security of a government job, health benefits, a pension plan, and any prospect of a comfortable retirement. He was fifty-two and had no savings to fall back on.

Faced with the daunting challenge of finding a new job in an era when employers looked even less kindly on older workers than they do today, Robby, or Dr. Robby as he is now known by patients, colleagues, friends, and fans, dared to do something that must have then seemed ludicrous for a man his age. He enrolled in graduate school. Seven years later, at fifty-nine, he received his Ph.D. and then began a new career as a research psychologist. A decade later, he upped the ante. He volunteered for a hospital internship, earned state certification to treat patients for alcoholism and substance abuse, and, at seventy-two, became a full-time therapist. Over the next seventeen years he earned the respect of colleagues and community alike for his clinical work. In the process, he also became something of a poster boy for eternal youth.

One day shortly before we met, Robby, a veteran toastmaster, spoke by popular demand at a Warrenton Chamber of Commerce luncheon. When he finished his talk the one hundred or so chamber members present rose and gave him a long ovation. "I have never seen anyone else get an ovation like that here," Karen Henderson, the chamber's director, told me. "Robby exudes the positive and reminds us that the mind runs the body. And he is revered in this community for it."

His daily routine illustrates just how encompassing his "ALL-OK" is. He rises at 5 A.M. each morning in his white Cape Cod house on Lee Highway in pastoral Amissville, in the midst of Rappahannock County horse country, just east of the Blue Ridge. Because, in winter, he keeps the thermostat set at fifty-five at night, he quickly dons his white terrycloth bathrobe and nudges the thermostat up as soon as he gets out of bed in the morning. He feeds his twelve-year-old black-and-white cat Cookie and has a short conversation with him. Then, with a cup of hot chocolate, he heads upstairs, with the sociable cat trailing. He sits down in his straight-backed chair at his metal-topped desk, turns on his custom-built computer, and begins to probe the minds of others and to take on civilization. That is not as metaphorical as it sounds. For the last seven years, beginning when he was about eighty-two, he has been typing out virtually every word of Will and Ariel Durant's eleven-volume opus, *The Story of Civilization,* and leading an international online discussion group. Robby's group has so far made it through seven volumes of the landmark work.

When he started this group, now on Seniorlearn.com, he had already facilitated discussions on Studs Terkel's *The Good War* and Darwin's *On the Origin of Species,* among other works. He headed the discussion of *Civilization*: "Where do we come from? Where are we now? Where are we headed?" It is, he says, his interest in those questions—his unquenchable interest in people or, as he might say, everything—that drives him.

Each morning before he undertakes the deconstruction of the history of civilization, Robby reads about its most recent events in four online newspapers—the *New York Times,* the *Washington Post,* the *Washington Times,* and the *Wall Street Journal.* Then he reads and answers a trove of daily e-mails, showers, dresses, gulps down a handful of vitamins, and hustles on his way. Three days a week, he drives his red 1998 Toyota Camry fifteen miles north from his white, two-story Cape Cod, to an 8 A.M. Chamber of Commerce breakfast meeting, where he participates in old-fashioned networking. Five days a week, he arrives at his office by 9 A.M. With rare exception, he sees a patient every hour until evening. Except, that is, for time he allots for his daily two-mile walk or an hour at the hospital gym and to grab a salad for lunch in the state-of-the-art, glass-enclosed hospital cafeteria. (Robby has kept a mostly vegetarian diet since he was in his fifties.) He usually devotes Saturdays to doing paperwork in the office. And that's it, except for the nights he goes dancing or the weekends when he volunteers at some community event, such as ushering at the community theater, or when he needs time to write his monthly column for *Warrenton Lifestyle* magazine. "I'm slowing down. I'm finally beginning to understand the saying the spirit is willing, but the body isn't," Robby declared earnestly after reviewing his schedule with me.

For all of his compassion for others, he admits to feeling impatient when he hears an able-bodied person use the excuse of age to resign from doing what he says he wished he could. Too often defeat and laziness creep into a person's belief system, he says. "They say, 'Oh well, I can't do that' or 'Pretty soon I'm going to be sixty-five and then I won't be able to do very much anyway.' So they don't bother to take care of themselves because there's no point in it. They're going to rot away anyway, they think. Whereas me, I'm going to love to be one hundred. How do I know this? Barring an unfortunate accident, I know this because I keep going until all of a sudden it's nine o'clock at night and I've got to get ready for bed. I don't have time for this garbage of 'I'm too old.'"

From time to time, he worries about whether he should mention his age to prospective clients. Few, if any, would guess it correctly. He stands erect. He moves with fluidity and strength. His hair remains dark, his attitudes liberal, his mind relentlessly curious. "People get caught up in stereotypes. Occasionally—rarely—a person hears how old I am and they don't want me to treat them because they assume I'm too old and won't know what I'm doing." But he takes no offense. He pushes aside such judgments with a favorite phrase: "That's their problem."

After all, he added, "I know who I am. I know why I am. And when you get right down to it, that's what I try to teach my patients to learn about themselves. If they don't know themselves, they can't respect themselves. If they don't respect themselves, they can't care for themselves. I build a tool kit with them, and one of the tools I use is teaching them that if you believe it will happen, it will. By the same token, if you believe it won't happen, it won't."

It is little understood, he explained, that therapeutic talk and learning stimulates important changes in brain chemistry. "It's not just functional. New synapses are being created. When someone walks out of here, their brain won't be the same brain as when they walked in. They call it talk therapy. So someone might say, 'Why do I have to talk with you? I can go talk with my grandmother.' Well, sometimes that may be good. On the other hand, when you go to a professionally trained therapist, he or she may know what to say and when to say it, and how to say it as well as when not to say it. In the tone of your voice, a therapist may have latched on to things about you, and in the process, he is changing your brain exactly as a medicine changes your brain. There's no difference. New neurotransmitters hit receptors. But in the case of medication, there's a side effect."

Those in the community who have used Robby as a therapist are legion. A number of community figures I interviewed offered spontaneously to testify to the ways Robby had helped them in therapy with addictions of one kind or another. A couple of years ago, a former client was moved to reveal her own story publicly. Some time after she had stopped seeing him, she ran into Robby on a bus transporting contestants to the starting line for the annual Fodderstack 10K, a point-to-point runners' race that begins in Flint Hill, a community just east of the Shenandoah National Park. Robby was already eighty-four, and she was concerned. On the bus ride, he confessed to her that he had decided to participate in the race on a whim and had not trained for it at all. He just figured that if he walked two miles every day, he should be able to walk the six miles to the finish line in the town of Little Washington. "About an hour and forty-five minutes later, Dr. Iadeluca comes strolling into Washington, walking strong beside a thirty-something-year-old, talking and having a great time. Of course, I had worried for naught," Ginny Hughes wrote in the *Fauquier Times-Democrat*. Her commentary ended in a celebration of Robby as an example of living life to its fullest. Summing up, she offered an even more compelling salute: "Twelve years ago, he saved my life from alcohol addiction. If it weren't for him, I would not be running the Fodderstack 10K. He is an inspiration."

Liliana Anaya, a twenty-eight-year-old who worked for a local restorative justice program, met Robby when he applied as a volunteer to help work with addict offenders and their victims. She saw his credentials and was impressed. A couple of months later she sought his help when she was suffering from a bout of depression. As a young Colombian woman, with a couple of graduate degrees, she was struggling with feeling culturally isolated in the homogenous Virginia suburb. While in college in Florida, she had converted to Islam and began dressing according to the religion's code. In rural Virginia, her decision tested her. But where other therapists in her experience got stuck on religious issues, Robby cut through them. "He learned about my culture and the way I practiced my religion so that he could understand my personal patterns and treat me from that perspective, not from his perspective. The first thing he asks is, 'How can I help you?' He asked questions to understand where I was coming from. That is what makes him a great therapist."

Indeed, there is nothing novel or magical about Robby's therapeutic approach. He says he wants to learn everything he can about his patient. "I want to know what you had for breakfast, how you're getting along with your wife, how you slept last night, what medications you're taking, how many milligrams, and for what purpose. I want to know about your educational background and your sex life." Part of his job as a psychotherapist, he believes, is to model a way of thinking. "Why do you think you do this?" he often asks an addict about some destructive behavior. Just as often addicts will answer, "Because it brings me happiness." Robby then points out that nothing in the patient's description of his substance abuse sounds much like happiness. "I try to help them learn to think for themselves so that they don't look back and say they're doing something because some old guy told them to. When their behaviors change I say, 'Now you're using that good brain of yours and you're much stronger than you were.'"

From the start of the economic tsunami in 2008, as the value of homes and stocks plunged and Americans lost their jobs in record numbers, the demand for Robby's services soared. "The recession has had a very definite effect on my work. Anxiety is up. Clinical depression is up. Use of alcohol and drugs is up. I am working later. I used to say to prospective patients: 'I have an opening this Thursday.' Now, I say, 'I think I can see you in two or three weeks.'"

Robby also found himself illustrating his philosophy more frequently than ever with the story of his life, his transition to a new career, and his late-life success:

The roots of Robby's unremitting drive to improve himself were scripted in his heart by his mother, Lottie, a literate, civically active woman of Swedish and Dutch ancestry who loved music and wrote poetry. She also wrote articles about the plight of World War I veterans abandoned by the government, like Robby's father, Casto Iadeluca, who returned from the Great War paralyzed on his right side, suffering from "shell shock," and unable to ever work again.

Lottie invested her energy and ambitions in her son, Robert Banker Iadeluca. He was born in New York City on September 25,

1920. When he was six, the family moved to a small house in the then rural town of Islip, Long Island, not far from the Great South Bay, where he would spend the rest of his childhood reveling in nature, enjoying scouting, and raising homing pigeons. While the house, bought for $2,500, had little in the way of modern conveniences, Robby's mother made sure he had violin, trumpet, and piano lessons and that he sang in church choirs of various denominations. The motto inscribed on the façade of Islip High School, which Robby says he read almost every day he entered school, underscored Lottie's instruction at home: "Enter to Learn; Go Forth to Serve."

More painfully etched in Robby's memory is the February night he saw his mother sit up in bed and begin to convulse as she was signing his sixth-grade report card. After school the next day, he visited his mother in the hospital. "Always be good, Bobby. Do what is right," she told him as he left her. Those were the last words he heard her speak.

When Robby graduated from high school in 1937, his grades were not quite high enough to make him valedictorian or salutatorian. But his English teacher, Miss Goodrich, was determined to make use of his well-honed writing and speaking skills. She asked Robby to read one of his essays, titled "On the Desirability of Being Oneself," at graduation. When he arrived at graduation without a copy in hand, Miss Goodrich nearly fainted from anxiety. Unflustered, Robby stepped to the podium and recited the essay flawlessly from memory, displaying a skill that would serve him well the rest of his life.

For his first jobs, he traveled into New York City, working first as a lunchtime delivery boy for the Ritz Shoppe on Forty-seventh Street, and then in the mailroom of Madison Avenue advertising giant Batten, Barton, Durstine & Osborn (BBD&O). Despite his low station, the eighteen-year-old went to work wearing a velvet-collared Chesterfield coat and a Homburg hat, and sporting a walking cane. "I felt spiffy, and the girls took note. What else mattered?" he recalled. Perhaps more important, he continued to nurture his penchant for self-improvement on the long train commute, making the Long Island Rail Road his university on wheels. Over a span of four years, he read an estimated 240 books.

World War II soon interrupted those studies. Six months after the bombing of Pearl Harbor on December 8, 1941, Robby enlisted in the army. He was kept in the States as a training sergeant until shortly after Allied troops stormed Normandy in 1944. After a few weeks in Brittany, he was on a train transporting the 29th Division north, to chase the German army out of Holland, when Robby had one of the most pivotal and romantic moments of his life.

When the train stopped at a station in Rennes, France, Robby—who was in charge of a few of the cars—decided on a whim to duck into the station waiting room. There, he saw a petite, sultry, and curvaceous woman working behind the counter whose name, he learned, was Fernande Allaurant. She was a champion gymnast whom friends called Bijou. Using his two years of high school French, Robby quickly struck up a conversation with her, exchanged names and addresses, and, as in some classic wartime movie, reboarded the train, headed to fierce combat in the Western Front, but ecstatically happy. He kept up a constant correspondence with Bijou during months of fighting in Holland, Belgium, Germany, and France, including the Battle of the Bulge, and in Germany after the armistice was signed on May 8, 1945.

After Robby inveigled his way into a French language and civilization course at the Sorbonne in Paris, the two got even better acquainted. He returned to New York in February 1946. And with the promise of a job at BBD&O after he had a bachelor's degree, he took advantage of the G.I Bill and enrolled at Hofstra University on Long Island. Though he had spent a total of only eighteen days with her, he also wrote to Bijou to propose. He instructed her that a one-word response would suffice. "I waited on tenterhooks," he said, transported by the memory. "And suddenly, it came—a telegram with one word: *Oui!*"

Three years later, after graduating from Hofstra as a psychology major, he returned to BBD&O and began doing consumer research, until it "dawned on me that my interest in life wasn't to get people to buy a particular product like Lucky Strikes cigarettes." Unsure of what to do next, he hearkened back to a boyhood love of scouting and applied for a job as a district Boy Scout executive, recruiting scoutmasters and establishing troops. Over the next thirteen years, he headed several district councils throughout New York State and New Jersey before becoming the public relations director for the five Boy Scout councils of New York City. He then took a job doing public relations for the East Islip school district, headquartered a mile from the house in which he grew up.

His career hit a roadblock in 1966 when his marriage to Bijou fell apart too publicly for a school official in a small community. Though the head of the school board would later serve as a character witness on Robby's behalf in divorce and custody proceedings over the couple's two sons, Robby chose to resign from his position. He went to work instead for the now-defunct *Long Island Advance,* where he became a prize-winning reporter. He returned to public relations in 1968, working first for the New York City Board of Education and then running a prototype of an open-circuit TV experiment to teach courses at the City University of New York.

As his marriage to Bijou was ending, Robby ventured to build a new life for himself by returning to an old haunt, Roseland Ballroom on West Fifty-second Street in New York. He had learned to dance there before World War II when he first worked in New York as a teenager. He had taken a few dance lessons and discovered an aptitude for the fox-trot, rumba, jitterbug, and waltz—and for picking up girls. In the early years, he had reveled in the pleasures of listening to the big bands of Glenn Miller, Charlie Barnet, Tommy Dorsey, and others. When Robby returned to the ballroom in the late 1960s, the world had changed. But Roseland remained a haven to him and a place to meet women. It was there, in fact, that he met his second wife, Betsy, whom he married shortly after his divorce was final.

Not long after, Robby was recruited to work in public affairs for the New York State education office in Albany.

He had always intended to continue his own education and get a graduate degree in psychology. But, as he likes to say, "a little thing called life intervened." Year after year, he had put off graduate school during his first marriage, what with two sons, a mortgage, and an itinerant career as a scout executive. After that, starting a new marriage and the new job in the state capital got in the way.

But the idea of going to graduate school was never completely out of mind. Then, one day, after he had been notified that his job with the state would be eliminated, he was crossing the Hudson River Bridge to the state offices in Albany when it hit him. "I heard myself say out loud, 'Why not?' At that instant I knew, rather than continuing to look for a new job I was going to get my doctorate."

At work, he asked some colleagues about the likelihood he could get admitted to a graduate studies program in psychology at the State University of New York at Albany at his age. The response was encouraging, and Robby moved swiftly. "I didn't know how I was going to do it. I didn't know how long it was going to take. I didn't know the details. But I knew it was going to happen. I didn't say I hope it's going to happen. It will happen," he said.

It helped that the state education commissioner to whom he had been reporting was Ewald Nyquist, a pioneering advocate of nontraditional education. Nyquist gave Robby his blessings. Not long after, Robby was granted free tuition and a $70-a-week stipend to serve as a staff writer for the SUNY alumni office. "I was on my way," he would write years later in an article, "Grandpa Goes to School." In it, he recounted some of the sillier obstacles he faced. Before he was officially admitted to graduate studies, for example, a woman working in the registrar's office insisted that he answer every question on a registration form, including one that asked, "Do you declare emancipation from your parents?"

He would have welcomed the prospect of additional support if he had anywhere to claim it. But at fifty-three, with nothing to fall back on, going ahead with his plan would mean "no more fine dining, no more expensive clothes, no more movies. Instant gratification had to give way to long-term gratification. Money was spent on food and time was spent on studying. I had no idea how many years it would take. I knew only the destination, not the mileage." Robby told Betsy, who had two teenage daughters Robby helped to raise, of his bold, new plans and the austere budget that would come with it. According to Robby, she was fully supportive. "We were poor as church mice, but we found ways to have fun on little money," he said.

After he had been taking courses and doing well in them, Robby applied for admission to the Ph.D. program in psychology at SUNY Albany. His first application got no response. When he applied a second time, he was rejected. "This time word came back to me that I was refused because I was too old. They felt I couldn't handle it. This got me mad, so I sat down with a catalog and listed all the universities across the nation that had a good graduate program in life-span psychology. I sent applications to all of them." As a result, Syracuse University invited Robby to visit and meet with the heads of the developmental psychology program and the All University Gerontology Center. They took him to lunch, and "as the discussion progressed, I realized they were interviewing me. I was exactly the person they were looking for—older in years and yet capable of obtaining a doctorate."

Robby was given a scholarship, a stipend, and an assistantship at the Gerontology Center and "was off and running" toward his doctorate. It was an exciting moment in the field. Developmental psychology was then just beginning to look beyond childhood and adolescent development into social and psychological development across the life span. Robby's sometimes-lonely experiences as a rare older adult on campus in the 1970s led him toward gerontology. "I was the only one out there in those days. I was not only studying how people develop throughout their lives, I was an example."

In May 1979, wearing cap and gown and the dark blue colors of a Ph.D. in Psychology at Syracuse, Robby marched to receive his diploma. "I always knew I was going to get my doctorate. I could have kept doing what I was doing for the rest of my life, but in the back of my mind, I always heard, *Don't stop here! Go on!* My mother always told me I would. If I have accomplished anything in this life, it is because of her."

The bliss of that moment did not last long. A few days after his graduation ceremony, his second marriage blew up, and he and Betsy separated for good. Now, he was broke, unemployed, in debt, facing another divorce, and fifty-nine. Moreover, though he was allowed to march in the graduation, he still had a semester of doctoral work to finish up. During that time, he lived in poverty. One month, he survived on a diet of free tomatoes given to him by a friendly farmer. To support himself, he took whatever work he could get, including as a house painter and a medical typist. "That was not a time for false pride," he said.

The following May, at an age when others were retiring, Robby was hired by the U.S. Army Research Institute (ARI) in Arlington, Virginia, to use his communication skills and make the institute's research intelligible to generals and other officials at the Pentagon. At the time, the army was deeply concerned about how families adjusted to military life because of the effect that domestic issues had on soldiers' performance in training, combat, and in positions of leadership. As he interviewed military families, it became increasingly clear to Robby how the inherent contest of loyalty between the army and a soldier's spouse—each claimed ownership of the soldier—contributed to stress, and frequently it led to alcohol and drug abuse. The experience stimulated Robby's interest in substance abuse.

Meanwhile, Robby, who had sworn off marriage after his second one collapsed, placed a personal ad in the *Washingtonian Magazine*. He was still interested in female companionship, after all. "Who would like to taste life with me?" he queried. He received 235 responses. One was from Lois Rodney, a forty-five-year-old registered nurse. In addition to personal chemistry, they shared an interest in the treatment of alcoholism, a subject they jointly pursued during an on-again off-again marriage that lasted fifteen years.

To learn more about the disease, Robby attended lectures at the Naval Hospital in Bethesda, Maryland, where he became a clinical lecturer. Over a five-year period, he gave 350 hours of talks to recovering patients of all ranks, including generals, from all main branches of the military. By the time he retired from ARI in May 1989, he was chief of the institute's bureau of communication and was turning seventy.

But Robby's retirement lasted only two months. First, he took a course to become a state-certified substance abuse counselor. Then, restless for more, Robby applied and was accepted into a fifteen-month internship in a substance abuse treatment center at Blue Ridge Hospital in Charlottesville. There, "Robby distinguished himself in the classroom with his rich understanding of psychology and his pointed philosophical questions," Dr. R. J. Canterbury, a senior dean for medical education at the University of Virginia Health System, said.

Working two days of double shifts in a row and practically living at the hospital, Robby squeezed a forty-hour week into three days and more than two thousand hours of clinical training into eighteen months. He studied street drugs, sexual abuse, suicide intervention, eating disorders, brain injuries, genetics, and liver transplantation for alcoholics, among other subjects. "He immersed himself in the field. He proved a very thoughtful and methodical person who approaches things with an open, questioning mind," Canterbury said. "He had good interpersonal skills and developed solid individual and group therapy skills. People liked him. But he also knew how to maintain appropriate boundaries." As a result, Robby was appointed an assistant professor of behavioral medicine and psychiatry.

In 1991, at seventy-two, Robby decided to start his own therapy practice in Warrenton. But because his Ph.D. was in life-span psychology, he had no license to practice as either a psychologist or a clinical psychologist in the state of Virginia. He feared that unless he had state licensing his patients would not qualify for medical insurance reimbursements, and it would be tough to make a go of it. So Robby went to the state capital in Richmond and took the state exam for psychologists. "By mistake, the monitor gave me the exam in clinical psychology, just as she gave to the hundred other people in the hall," he said. Robby passed anyway, but he was notified that he was ineligible for licensing because he did not have a degree in clinical psychology. Though he returned and passed the correct exam and an oral exam on medications, state rules continued to bedevil his licensing. Still, he practiced and all went well, "That is, until I decided to apply for payment from Medicare. Back it comes, rejected because I'm not a licensed clinical psychologist. I blew my top," he said.

In 1996, after he hired a lawyer who filed an appeal with the state, Robby—at age seventy-six—was called before the state examining board where his case was presented. When it was done, they asked Robby and his lawyer to leave the room. "Then after ten minutes of deliberation, they call me back in, and the head of the committee says, 'Dr. Iadeluca, you are now a clinical psychologist.' I had tears in my eyes. In that instant, they were telling me what I'd known all along. Moreover, they said I was a clinical psychologist retroactively, to 1992."

As an educational pilgrim, Robby was still not done with his progress. Next, he tackled psychopharmacology because it so intertwined with the treatment of addiction. Between 1995 and 1999, he took seventeen workshops, covering such subjects as psychoactive medications, gene expression, neurotransmitters, mood disorders, drug interactions, and the biological bases of mental symptoms. He also passed lengthy examinations after each workshop and then was awarded a diplomate from the International College of Prescribing Psychologists. In his quest to achieve surpassing expertise, Robby attended more than one thousand twelve-step meetings. Most were Alcoholics Anonymous meetings, but they also included Narcotics Anonymous, Cocaine Anonymous, Nicotine Anonymous, and Overeaters Anonymous. To add to his understanding of addicts, he also spent weekends riding around in a squad car overnight with Prince William, Virginia, police so that he could observe the behavior of people from their time of arrest for driving while under the influence, through booking at a station house to blood tests at the hospital. "Then I would go see these people who were arrested the next morning in jail," he said. "Very often, they wouldn't remember what they had done the night before. So I got a tremendous education in addiction."

Knowledge, of course, has not protected Robby from heartache. In speaking with me, Robby resisted disclosing painful memories detailing the dissolution of his twenty-three-year marriage to Bijou, who died many years ago, or the reasons why his decade-long marriage to Betsy and his fifteen-year union with Lois ended. Even in vague outline, the sense of loss and disappointment was clear, but so was his wish not to inflict unnecessary pain by revealing private information or rehash what had happened. And that was instructive, for like many other later life achievers in this book, Robby chose not to dwell in regret or bitterness. Indeed, over the time I came to know him, his adherence to that aspect of his "ALL-OK" attitude seemed as essential to his drive to forge new successes as was his enthusiasm for education.

As with much else, he attributed it to his mother, recalling a sampler she kept on a wall of the house in Islip: *Keep your face to the sunshine, and the shadows will fall behind.* "It was up there so long I didn't read it anymore, I just absorbed it," he told me. "It did not say there were no shadows. They're there. I just accept them as part of my life's experience."

One of those shadows was the death of his son Roland at the age of fifty-three from a brain tumor in 2006. (Another, which he declined to detail, was an estrangement dating almost to his divorce from Bijou from his son Laurent, fifty-nine, who lives in France and could not be reached.) "Roland was the exact opposite of me. More than once he told me he didn't want to live his life sitting in an office or a classroom," Robby said, proudly recalling his son's individualist attitude. For years, he worked as a gasoline truck driver and security guard in Alaska. "I have many fond memories of him," including, Robby said, many visits with Roland in New Port Richey, Florida, during his final year in hospice care. "He spent the end of his life in dignity. The compassion exhibited by the hospice was unbelievable. That was the sunshine."

In therapy sessions, Robby—linking his forward-facing stoicism with lessons from his own life and his study of addiction—often uses the metaphor of an open door to explain sobriety to patients. He tells them that sobriety does not mean *not* being drunk. Holding his right hand in front of him and moving it back and forth, he defines sobriety, instead, as an open door of the heart, which allows one to face and enjoy the love of others while also facing and managing the pain that exists on the other side. "Sobriety is not about being 'clean' or 'dry,' or refraining from the use of alcohol or other drugs. Sobriety is embracing life in its entirety, tasting life to its fullest, working, playing, laughing, crying, building, destroying, feeling, thinking, searching. There are people who have never ingested any drug of any sort during their lifetime but who are not sober. They keep their heart's door shut and thus block out the pain. But their life is dull and numb without the full life that love can bring."

At eighty-nine, Robby continues to keep his dance card filled. Not quite as full as it was before his close friend Nancy Walbridge, an attractive blond fifty-five-year-old hospice community relations director, got married in 2008 and they stopped spending one night a week at a dance studio in Arlington before dining out. Guys would come up to Robby and say, "Hey, how do you get to be out dancing with such a beautiful chick?" And he would fire back, "Well, some guys have it and some guys don't."

He had met Walbridge at a Chamber of Commerce dinner. He did not seem remotely his age. "We connected immediately on lots of levels. Robby can talk about anything and he's comfortable with anyone. He is a true romantic. If there hadn't been the age difference, who knows?" she said. You can tell it pains him a little that the fantasy of youth is no longer his. But he has only himself to blame for Nancy's marriage. After she and her boyfriend split up a couple of years ago, it was Robby who, using his therapeutic skills, helped them to work through their issues.

"I'm not going to be sitting around with a pity pot," Robby told me one day, reminding me of his license plate. To help make things all okay, he has been spending a lot of time visiting Nancy's daughter, Rebekah, and is becoming very involved writing a series of stories he plans to record for her toddler, Avery, and has taken up bridge. When he wanted a date for an auction fund-raiser, he called his friend Martha Hartke, who is six months his senior and the widow of Indiana senator Vance Hartke. "I've got my tux ready. Have you got a formal dress to wear?" he said. They agreed to drive separately and meet at the country club where it was held. Unhappy with the noise of the auction, Robby decided to leave early. The next day, Hartke left him an impish message: "It's the morning after. I wanted you to know I had a good time and that I've taken my pill."

About the only time Robby seems dumbfounded is when someone asks him why he continues to work so many hours *at his age*. It is the question, not the answer, that stumps him. He simply does not think of himself as old. He thinks about what he has to do and what he wants to do next. In answer to why he works so many hours, he reflects on all the young people who have come to him in trouble, addicted to drugs and alcohol, and sometimes suicidal. "I've lost track of how many came in here thinking they were failures, whose families told them they were useless. And I've seen them go on and sign up for college a year later and get jobs. That's why this is the best job I've ever had. It's impossible for me to talk about the work I do without enthusiasm. Yeah, sure, at the end of the day I'm tired. But it's been a great day, I feel good about what I'm doing, and I like to think I've done some good. I go to bed and I feel terrific about it."

ALIDRA SOLDAY

Going the Distance with Granny D

"Once I faced my mortality, I was driven to do something."

For her, it was a jackhammer decade of betrayals, disease, and death. Having her brother perish in a plane crash years earlier, she needed no more lessons in impermanence. But the veteran New York City psychotherapist got them anyway in the 1990s in something of this order: breast cancer, a lover's infidelity and abandonment after she was diagnosed, her mother's dementia, her father's death, and a recurrence of cancer and surgery. It seems little wonder that she cast off her old name, Linda Brown, and took an invented one, Alidra Solday.

But what changed her life and set her on a formidable eight-year journey to become a filmmaker and make the award-winning documentary *Granny D Goes to Washington* was as simple as a vacation in California with a box of pastels and a camera.

She was exploring the rugged coastline and secluded beaches of the Mendocino headlands in 1998, during her first real vacation in years, when "it hit me. I so loved the landscapes I was seeing and so loved using my camera that I thought, *You've got to do something with this.* It made sense to put my love into shooting along with my interest in people and with my experience interviewing them in my practice as a psychotherapist. When I came back to New York, I said, *I want to be a filmmaker.* Then I thought, *Oh, that's impossible. I can't do that.*

A full-time program in film school was out of the question. For one thing, Alidra told herself, she was too old. She was nearly fifty-eight. For another, the cost of a graduate school degree was prohibitively expensive and, given the cost of living in New York, she needed to work. Still, she nudged herself and signed up for a six-week class at Film Video Arts, a nonprofit film school in Manhattan. It was a small but important first step. Despite her apprehension about dealing with technical gadgetry and video cameras, she managed to fulfill the course's requirement, completing a video interview. Hers was a straightforward one with a Korean man who spoke little English. It was that basic, but Alidra was proud: "I actually figured out what buttons to push on the camera."

Emboldened, when she heard about an undergraduate course at New York University's Tisch School of the Arts taught by legendary documentary filmmaker George Stoney, she phoned him and asked permission to audit his class. Stoney, the director of more than forty documentaries on social change and the Paulette Goddard Professor of Film at NYU, is considered the father of public access television. After they met and she explained herself to him, he said, "Sure, sure, come to the class."

The following semester Stoney went to Ireland, and his class was taken over by filmmaker Sam Pollard. In addition to editing several of Spike Lee's feature films, including *Jungle Fever,* Pollard was an Emmy-winning film producer/director and video editor. He produced *Eyes on the Prize II: America at the Racial Crossroads* for PBS and received an Academy Award nomination for *Four Little Girls,* a feature documentary by Spike Lee on the 1965 Birmingham church bombings. The following year, Alidra repeated both Stoney and Pollard's classes while continuing to see a full load of psychotherapy clients in her office near Columbus Circle in Manhattan. She also squeezed in a bunch of courses in editing, cinematography, lighting, television directing, and proposal writing at NYU School of Professional Studies and elsewhere. She took to saying, "In my next life, I want to be a filmmaker."

About the same time, as part of her continuing effort to heal herself emotionally, spiritually, and physically from her decade of trauma, she joined a group that was spending a year following Stephen Levine's book *A Year to Live: How to Live This Year as If It Were Your Last*. The book, based on Levine's own experiment with doing just that, was inspired by a comment the Dalai Lama made about living fully by preparing for death. In his book, Levine also drew on his twenty years of work with the terminally ill. He had often heard the dying express regret about how they had left so many parts of their lives for "later." As a result, he concluded, the dying often felt "fragmented about unsatisfying work, unfinished business, and compromised lifestyles." He proposed to his readers that they spend a year living as consciously as possible, to catch up with their lives, to investigate death, and to cultivate joy. As Alidra worked with the book, her mind-set began to change. *There may not be a next life. I'm going to be a filmmaker in this life,* she told herself. "Once I faced my mortality, I was driven to do something."

When I caught up with Alidra in Portland, Oregon, where she moved in 2008, I was taken slightly aback by her youthful appearance when she greeted me at the door of the rented house where she was living temporarily. She was slim and wearing tight jeans and a blue cable-knit sweater. Her movements were supple, like a dancer's. Her face was virtually unlined, her brown hair's bob carefree, her voice alternately gentle and inflected with something of her affluent upbringing in Princeton, New Jersey, and theatrically high-pitched. At sixty-seven, she had recently relocated to Portland to train and work in a clinic that specializes in dialectical behavioral therapy, a treatment that has proved effective for people suffering from borderline personality disorders.

Sitting at a table in the middle of the small, vintage, salmon-colored kitchen, surrounded by blue-green cabinets, Alidra talked animatedly about her first conscious step toward a commitment to filmmaking. In May 2000, she bought a professional-grade camcorder, a Sony VX2000. She paid $2,600 for it, a bargain at the time. "It started my love affair with equipment. As soon as I had my camera in my hands, I needed to go out and use it. I had had other cameras, but they were not *this* camera. *This* was my most professional camera."

She began to consider doing a documentary about passionate elders in their eighties and nineties with vital careers and consuming interests. Filmmaker Stoney was eighty-four, and his continuing commitment to social documentary had inspired her. She also contemplated focusing on Angeles Arrien, a cultural anthropologist with whom she took a six-day workshop on transition and change in Arizona's high desert. Alidra's interest in the subject was bound up with the complex tides of her family history.

"In the end, I think my own parents felt pretty disappointed with their lives," she said. Her father, Charles H. Brown, was a self-made man who worked as a patent lawyer for RCA until he was sixty-five. But he had wanted to be a doctor. He even applied to medical school in his seventies but was rejected. "He had put a lot into my brother, Richard, who fulfilled that fantasy by going to Columbia [University] medical school and becoming an ophthalmologist." Tragically,

Richard, a married thirty-eight-year-old husband and father of three with a medical practice in Atlanta, was killed in 1979 when his light plane crashed into a line of trees during a short trial takeoff and landing with a prospective buyer. "My father lost a lot with my brother's death," she said.

Alidra's own response to her brother's death was complicated by a decade of estrangement from her brother. Its origin was her refusal to accede to their father's wishes that she not go into theater.

A man of the 1950s, Charles Brown had few expectations that his daughter might achieve any professional success. "In his view, I should go to a good college and become a teacher, nurse, or secretary. He didn't have any way to relate to my artistic gifts. And I think because of my parents' marriage, where I felt my mother gave up her soul to be a wife and was subject to my father's erratic, explosive temper, I didn't want to be married. I couldn't conceive of a different marriage, one in which one party wasn't trying to control the other."

Alidra excelled in and out of school. She showed talent in tennis, ice skating, dance, and art. After high school, she fulfilled her father's wishes and went to Smith College, in Northampton, Massachusetts. But having spent her adolescence living in Princeton, and having seen her brother go through the university there, there was little mystique left for her in attending an Ivy League college. By her junior year, she wanted to quit college, apply to the Juilliard School in New York, and launch a career in music and theater. To assuage her father's heated opposition, she transferred to Barnard College. She would, she reasoned, at least be close to the world of the arts. She majored in musicology and began auditioning for Off-Broadway shows. After graduation, she continued voice lessons, sang in dinner clubs, and appeared in the lead role of an opera workshop performance of Francis Poulenc's opéra bouffe *Les Mamelles de Tirésias (The Breasts of Tirésias)*, which received rave reviews. Using the stage name of Linda Barrie Brown, she then spent eighteen months in a small part in the musical company of *Oliver*.

That role, along with her career in theater, ended one day during rehearsals. She was singing and suddenly heard the director yelling that he couldn't hear her voice. "I had always had a strong voice. But all of a sudden, it wasn't there. I wasn't seeing a voice coach at the time and didn't go to a therapist for help. Now, I think it must have been some kind of stage fright. I had always had side jobs, and so I just went to work at something else." She never returned to theater. Instead, she pursued a series of jobs in real estate sales, textbook acquisition, and public relations before getting a master's in expressive art therapy. She worked briefly as an art therapist at Bronx State Hospital, then a hotbed of therapeutic innovations. Inspired and envisioning a more stable income, she took a master of social work degree from Hunter College and started a private psychotherapy practice.

It took twenty years, and recovery from breast cancer, for Alidra to reassert her creativity. She was about to begin interviewing potential subjects for the film on passionate elders when a friend mentioned seeing an article about Doris Haddock. At ninety, the woman known as "Granny D" had recently completed a walk across the continental United States to draw attention to the need for campaign finance reform.

Doris had set out on January 1, 1999, from the Rose Bowl Parade in Pasadena, California. She spent the next fourteen months crossing 3,200 miles, thirteen states, and a couple of deserts on foot. Along the way, she wore out four pairs of shoes and overcame searing heat, a hospitalization for dehydration and pneumonia, emphysema, and arthritic aches of all kinds. By the end, she had transformed herself into a serious-minded, if minor, national folk hero and a media darling.

Alidra and Doris met in Florida in late 2000 when Alidra was visiting her mother and Doris, the youngest of five children, was visiting an older sister. "May I just use my camera right now to sort of hear your conversation?" Alidra asked as they began to talk. Doris was agreeable, and Alidra quickly adapted to her new role as interviewer. "I always felt comfortable interviewing people because I have interviewed people in my therapy practice for such a long time," she said.

Alidra was captivated by Doris's passionate articulation of her beliefs and her determination to make a difference in the lives of others. "Doris had such tenaciousness. Her philosophy was something like, If you don't like something, then do something about it. She doesn't complain. That's very Yankee. She just says, Do something about it!" In a telling moment, Doris explained, "As a child I was always small for my age and so I learned to fight for what I wanted."

It was during that first interview that Alidra decided to focus a documentary on Doris alone. "Are you open to that?" she asked.

Doris welcomed the idea, but warned Alidra that she would need to clear it with her literary agent. After all, she had a book coming out, she explained. The agent, it turned out, was not encouraging. "But my mind was made up. I knew she couldn't stop me. I called Doris and said, 'I'm coming up to interview you.'"

In early February, Alidra drove to New Hampshire. With the help of a woman she had met in one of the film workshops, she began filming Doris in her daily rounds, playing Scrabble with friends, talking politics, and in one of her film's most spontaneous moments, dancing around a living room with a group of older women, known as the Tuesday Morning Academy and who met weekly to keep their minds and bodies fit. "Once I started filming, I was in a state of utter joy," Alidra said.

Doris explained that she became interested in campaign finance reform around 1996. She had seen a small article in the *Boston Globe* about a bill being sent to President Clinton for his signature. It reported that, in the middle of the night, two senators had slipped an amendment requesting a $50 billion subsidy for the tobacco industry into the bill. Doris smelled corruption and brought the issue to the Tuesday Morning Academy for collaborative study. Pretty soon the women began asking people to sign petitions and they wrote to their senators, urging them to enact campaign finance reform. "We got reassuring letters, each of us, from our senators, saying, 'Dear little old ladies, don't worry about this, we're taking care of it,'" Doris said.

Taking on government felt hopeless. But on a fishing trip with her son, Jim, to the Florida Everglades, Doris saw a man walking on the road between two towns and a light went off. She instantly announced that she would walk across the country to spur reform. She explained her motivation to Alidra: "If you look at your life, you will see your life is made up of acts. And this is my last act. I would like to make some news of my life."

Alidra began to collect archival footage from the dozens of news programs that had covered Doris's ten-mile-a-day, six-days-a-week march across America. From these news clips, Alidra would eventually cull and stitch together a swift and seamless narrative of the diminutive pilgrim's long odyssey and its undulating moods of seriousness, zaniness, courage, and occasional drama. In town after town, parades, politicians, and reform-minded people of all ages greeted Doris. In snippets, she is seen speaking from bandstands and from the steps of town halls, over front-yard fences and along roadways. Captured, too, are the children, college students, and ordinary citizens who cheer her on as she tries to rouse Americans to take back their government from special interest groups and private industry by restricting political donations.

Along the way, Granny D is also seen collapsing into unfamiliar beds in houses where she was taken in for the night. And in a climactic and mesmerizing act of determination, as snow threatens to postpone her arrival at the capital, Doris cross-country skis the last one hundred miles along the old C&O Canal, from West Virginia to Washington, D.C. A host of senators and a throng of two thousand supporters are waiting for her when she arrives.

In March 2001, Doris flew to Washington to apply renewed pressure as the Senate took up debate on the bipartisan campaign finance reform bill. This time, Alidra and her camera were with Doris practically every step of the way. "I literally went on the plane with her, shot her coming on and off, being picked up, meeting senators, and doing her walk around the Capitol." Doris hoped to remind the nation's senators as they began debate of a bill sponsored by Republican Senator John McCain, of Arizona, and Democratic Senator Russell Feingold, of Wisconsin, that American voters wanted change and were watching. As Alidra discovered, Doris was engaged in a strenuously physical battle, not just a photo opportunity. To force senators to deal with her, Doris walked around the Capitol for a week. During the three days the bill was actually debated, she walked around the clock, stopping only for meals and brief catnaps. For much of that time, Alidra videotaped Doris's peripatetic vigil from every possible angle.

As exhilarating as it was for Alidra to be in on the action, she soon found herself struggling with resistance from Dennis Burke, then the director of Arizona Common Cause and the coauthor of Doris's book. Burke had befriended Doris after she collapsed in the desert. As her collaborator, he was suspicious of Alidra and began to run interference between her and Doris. Alidra had, after all, arrived without any background as a filmmaker or a journalist, he reasoned. She did not behave the way other filmmakers in Burke's experience would have. That is, he said, "She did not fade into the background."

He worried that rather than being a legitimate documentarian, she might be one of the odd sycophants, people of all stripes, whom he had watched try to latch on to Doris.

Alidra was acutely aware of Burke's discomfort with her. "I can understand that he was asking himself, *Who is this woman who doesn't have a track record as a filmmaker coming with her camera to do all this stuff?* But he prevented me from going to certain meetings. There were a bunch of people who were strategizing with Granny D around how to lobby and approach some of these congressmen and senators, and I wanted to be in on that meeting and shoot it. Dennis just stopped me. He wouldn't let me near it. But I just kept trucking on."

Doris's example, after all, had become her motivation. She revered her dogged refusal to quit what many considered a purely quixotic campaign and her readiness to sacrifice herself, body and soul, to her goal. As Doris barnstormed around the country to promote campaign finance reform and her book, *Granny D: You're Never Too Old to Raise a Little Hell,* Alidra became her ubiquitous shadow. She, or crews she hired, filmed Doris speaking at conferences, colleges, bookstores, and in radio stations during live call-in shows, where some of Granny D's most animated moments were filmed. "Sometimes, you'd think you were way the hell out in nowhere and far away from the press and far away from the next photo or the next message opportunity for this campaign, and then, all of a sudden, there's Alidra with a cameraman," Burke said.

To get more of Doris's personal story, Alidra returned to New Hampshire in October 2001 and early 2002. On a couple of those occasions, she brought along Chandler Griffin, a talented young filmmaker. They shot Doris walking along snowy roads—to illustrate her long, solitary preparation for walking ten miles a day during her cross-country pilgrimage; baking cookies and doing her laundry—to show what an exhausted Granny D did after her long walk ended and she returned from Washington the first time; and visiting Laconia, New Hampshire, where she was born and where her family is buried. Shots of her leaving the cemetery there provided evocative illustration of Doris's life with Jim, her late husband. "Granny was wonderful. You come into her house and she puts you up. She was very available. She's also pretty camera savvy. She learned how to give her sound bites. I tried very hard in the course of my interviews to catch moments of vulnerability. But she's a Yankee. She doesn't exactly emote vulnerability," Alidra said. "As she told me, Granny D is more poetic than Doris. But Doris has more street smarts and is tougher than Granny D. Either way, she really does believe in kindness and caring, and that you are your brother's keeper."

Thanks to the Enron scandal, the nation's ire over political contributions was finally aroused. And in February 2002, Congress revisited the bipartisan campaign finance reform bill nearly a year after the House of Representatives had buried it in a committee. And once again Doris headed to Washington. This time Alidra followed the crusading nonagenarian into representatives' offices where Doris delivered valentines and her message. Alidra captured Doris using all the celebrity, charm, and bluntness that made her an irresistible lobbyist.

Meanwhile, Alidra also interviewed Senator McCain on camera. He was happy to praise Doris and her walk across America. "It's one of the most remarkable feats of political history," he said. The interview went well enough, though Alidra recalled that the future Republican presidential nominee appeared at once adrenalized and uptight. "Did you get what you need?" he asked repeatedly.

To an exhausted Doris's delight, the House of Representatives approved the campaign finance bill on Valentine's Day. A month later, the Senate passed a final version and President George W. Bush signed it into law.

The bill's passage proved a pivotal moment for Alidra. She had been using up her own modest savings to make the documentary. She had already spent $135,000 (and would eventually spend still more) on travel, freelance crews, equipment, logging footage, and editing it. It was money that Alidra had once hoped would pay for housing when she retired someday. She had cut deeply into her remaining assets and desperately needed an infusion of cash.

In the hope of enlisting a public broadcast station and of raising donations to support her work, Alidra put together a five-minute trailer. She showed it to Doris and her son, Jim Haddock, to persuade them to share the "Granny D" donor list. Jim loved the trailer. And soon the three were excitedly making a list of people to whom the trailer might be sent to encourage contributions for the film. Bubbling with optimism, Alidra returned home to New York.

"Then I get a call from Jim. He says something like, 'I feel like, excuse me for saying this, I'm cutting off your balls. But we sent the trailer to Dennis. And he believes—and we have decided—that our energy would be better put into direct action rather than doing a film,'" Alidra said.

Burke and the Haddocks told me they figured that because Alidra was a psychotherapist in New York City, she did not have to worry about money for what they believed was only an avocation. They had no idea how much of her own resources Alidra had already risked or how important that money was to her.

When Alidra learned of their decision not to help her get funds for her film, she was crushed. She had no idea where she would get the money to finish the film. Deeply hurt, she was not sure she wanted to finish it. To get her bearings, she decided to go to the Green Gulch Farm Zen Center, north of San Francisco in Marin County, where she did a two-week stint as a volunteer worker and struggled with feelings of desolation. She returned to New York and within six weeks, Alidra sold her country house in Copake, New York, gave up her office in Manhattan, and referred her patients to other therapists. Then she drove cross-country. "I didn't know if I would ever do the film. I knew that I needed to save my life and I needed to make big changes," she said.

In fairness, she says, she was already struggling with traumatic emotions stirred by 9/11 and volunteer work doing therapy with some of the five hundred thousand New Yorkers it was estimated were suffering from post-traumatic stress disorder after the terrorist attacks. "Certainly for me it kicked up the old losses I had experienced and some of the unresolved trauma of my own," she said. "I went into a period of mourning and felt like I continued to grieve for a year. It was in this context that the disappointment with the Haddocks took on the force of another blow. It felt like doors were closing on my life."

Alidra returned to Green Gulch and submitted to the practice there. She rose, along with the other participants, at 4:30 A.M. every day and went to a small, dark, unadorned zendo, or meditation hall, and meditated for thirty minutes. Afterward, they did chores, such as cleaning bathrooms or gardening. Work was punctuated by simple meals and another meditation. "The training is in being nobody. The practice is that you're ignored," she said. The teachings focused on impermanence. And Alidra began to come to terms with the expectations of others that made her vulnerable to pain in an unpredictable world. "It was a lesson in life that I had somehow never learned. The question was, what was I going to make of it?" she said.

Alidra stayed at the center for seven months, paying $650 a month for the privilege. After a while, the routine began to feel oppressive and she transferred to Green Gulch's sister center in San Francisco. But she found the atmosphere there just as stultifying, and signed up for a painting class at the Center for Creative Exploration. There, instead of trying to edit out their "mistakes" as they painted, students were urged to add more paint and color to their work and paint through them. As she painted, this metaphoric activity had a striking effect on Alidra. She began to feel as if she was painting herself out of the monochromatic world of depression. Painting "introduced me back into a world of color," she said. It also spurred her to leave the Zen center, move to Marin, take a short course to activate her license to practice therapy in California, and to start a therapy practice in San Francisco. She also started looking at her footage of Granny D again.

As she did, she recovered her faith in her project. She stickered her room with Post-its that read: *This is not about me!* She told herself that the work deserved the respect of being completed. One day, on a hike in the Marin Headlands with her old friend and colleague Frances McGoohan, Alidra confessed her sadness at not finishing the film. But, she admitted, she was scared to contact Doris, fearful that her own words would sabotage her goal of returning to work on the film. She had aborted several letters. Her friend offered to help Alidra write one. It took several drafts, but finally she sent Doris a letter updating her on her life and telling her that she wanted to complete the documentary because it was important. Doris was receptive. Why not? She was by then ninety-four, the subject of a second film project—*Run Granny Run,* directed by Marla Poiras for HBO (a project to which Burke gave his blessings)—and preparing to run for the U.S. Senate.

Alidra went back to work on the film. She cut more than one hundred hours of footage down to an hour of film. Then she turned to George Stoney, her former NYU professor, for advice. He told her to cut deeper. With the help of Erica Trautman, a film student, she cut another twenty-five minutes. Documentarian Deborah Hoffman, at the University of California, Berkeley, School of Journalism, took a look and encouraged Alidra to make Doris's biography even tighter.

But editing cost money, and Alidra's money was running out. She had used far too much of the $216,000 from the sale of her country house to support herself and to pay for the film. She hoped for a grant from the Independent Television Service (ITVS), which funds, presents, and promotes documentaries on public television, but she discovered it funds only experienced filmmakers. So Alidra sent veteran filmmaker and frequent PBS producer Janet Cole a rough cut of her movie and asked her to become her producer, so she could qualify for a grant.

Cole liked Alidra's project and thought it was right for PBS's audience. She also saw that Alidra needed relatively little money to complete it. Most important, "I was impressed by her drive and commitment. She had taken a tiger by the tail," Cole said. And she was honest about what she did not know. "A lot of first-timers don't know what they don't know. She had a degree of awareness, insight, and openness that made up for the lack of experience," Cole said. If Alidra would carry the ball, Cole would lend her name to the project.

Cole's influence was almost immediately evident. Alidra called PBS in Maine to request sponsorship, but was turned down. But on her next call, to New Hampshire's public station, NHPTV left the door open to a deal, and Cole quickly sealed it. NHPTV agreed to sponsor, promote, and hold an opening-night screening for the film if Alidra and Cole took responsibility for all postproduction work. They agreed and in November 2005, with the station as a sponsor, ITVS gave Alidra a $100,000 grant and one year to complete the documentary.

But with all Alidra would have to do on her own, that was not much time. Cole recommended an editor to shape the film quickly. Alidra hired him and began supplying notes and transcripts. But the editing went excruciatingly slowly and, Alidra thought, disappointingly. The film lacked emotion.

"You can't make feeling where there isn't any," the editor told her.

"There is feeling," Alidra insisted and sent off a barrage of notes indicating where the editor could find it in the footage.

With time ticking, Alidra readied herself to go to Joshua Tree National Park, California, in late January 2006 to shoot images she needed to illustrate Granny D's walk through the desert. But she was instead called to Florida where her mother was dying. For seven days, Alidra sat by her mother's side, playing her love songs sung by Ella Fitzgerald and Frank Sinatra. Alidra had time to reflect on how her mother—who had spent her life in busyness and shopping—had failed to develop her own life and unintentionally motivated Alidra to make something of hers. "She was a beautiful woman with talent, [but] she never fully engaged with life. I was determined not to live as she had." After her mother fell into a pattern of constant sleep, Alidra returned to California and her work. Her mother died two days later. "I didn't have time to grieve. I had said my good-bye. I had to keep moving. I was on deadline," Alidra said.

She drove fourteen hours south to Joshua Tree to film the sand and sky, and to re-create Granny D's point of view during the 1999 walk through the desert when she collapsed from dehydration. At Alidra's request, Doris sent the clothes and shoes she had worn. Alidra put them on, and a cameraman shot her feet on the pavement and sand and as she was placed in an ambulance. In the documentary, lights flash as the ambulance disappears in a dusty, sun-blanched haze.

Meanwhile, the freelance film editor continued to flounder. At $2,000 a week for his work and $800 a week for editing equipment, Alidra's budget was evaporating quickly. When, after three months, the editor announced that he was leaving to take on another project, Alidra was too panicked to feel relief.

Fortunately, Cole got Alidra another $20,000 in grant money and recommended that she hire Yasha Ajinsky, a veteran San

Francisco–based documentarian, film editor, and teacher, to help finish the film. His pedigree included Oscar nominations for two documentaries, *Forever Activists* and *Las Madres de la Plaza de Mayo*. But it was viewing *Outsider: The Life and Art of Judith Scott,* a documentary about a woman with Down syndrome who achieved worldwide recognition for her fiber sculptures, that convinced Alidra. "It was so sensitively and beautifully cut, I started to cry. I thought, *This is the editor I want*."

Alidra, the novice, and Ajinsky, the master editor, went to work reediting, adding narration, and streamlining her film. "From the start, we got along," Ajinsky said. "She was by no means a shooter, but she was passionate about the subject." She was also smart, tenacious, and courageous, and possessed a virtue too often lacking in filmmakers who come to him for help. "She was prepared to do her homework, to do whatever it took to keep up with the editing. Whatever I needed, she was there," he said. His admiration increased as he watched Alidra race almost single-handedly to pull together the various elements of production, jobs usually distributed among several people: writing narration, getting permissions, acquiring original videotape, dealing with the station, handling for postproduction, and pursuing publicity. "She was overextended, financially and physically. She was practically living out of her car," he said. "But she got it done."

When they finished editing the film, Cole submitted it to PBS Plus, which is responsible for supplying specials and series, from *This Old House* to *Charlie Rose,* to the nation's public broadcasting stations. PBS Plus liked it, too, and offered *Granny D Goes to Washington* to PBS stations around the country.

But there was no time to celebrate. Now, the pressure was ratcheted up even higher. Alidra had only three months to finish all the postproduction, including tracking down original archival footage.

With 40 percent of the documentary taken from archival footage, this was of major importance. Alidra had no idea how difficult and expensive getting ahold of the original clips would prove to be, or how stressful, with her money running out.

Then some angels appeared. Helen Appell, a former Zen priest at Green Gulch and a supporter of the arts, gave her $5,000. "As a fellow woman involved in the arts, I saw her sincerity of motivation, her dedication, and her fortitude. We all struggle with doubt, but she found a way to see herself through," she said. "She has integrity."

And when George Stoney viewed a completed version of the film, he was so impressed that, unsolicited, he secured a $2,000 grant from a family foundation to help Alidra pay for the film's publicity. "What she had done was amazing. What pleased me most is that she presented an extraordinary woman with economy and without condescension. The temptation is to make us older people look cute, and that demeans us as individuals. Alidra did not do that," said Stoney, who was ninety-two in 2009 and still teaching film at NYU.

Finally, on the evening of October 3, 2006, Alidra, dressed in a fitted black velour top and a skirt, drove to Saint Anselm College in Manchester, New Hampshire, for the PBS premiere of *Granny D Goes to Washington*. Before it began, the station staff had taken her to dinner and expressed curiosity and admiration. "They wanted to know how a neophyte had managed to bring a film like mine to completion," she said. "There was genuine interest, admiration, and acknowledgment. It felt nice." But the high point for Alidra came after the presentation. Doris's son, Jim, stood up spontaneously and encouraged members of the audience to support the film by buying the DVD. He said Alidra had put her "blood, sweat, and tears—and her own money"—into making the film and they ought to buy a copy.

Doris, who sat onstage with Alidra, was happy, too. The documentary had, after all, shown the power one person has to effect change against great odds. "I mean, a little old lady living in a backward state in a backward village suddenly at the age of ninety, walking across the country for campaign finance reform, was a pretty ridiculous thing. And now I am getting thank-you letters, inspiring letters, from all over the world, from Norway down to Australia," ninety-nine-year-old Doris told me.

The film ultimately aired on public broadcasting stations in forty-four states. The late Molly Ivins wrote of it: "You want to know where to get the strength, courage and optimism to keep fighting for change? Watch *Granny D Goes to Washington*. . . . The documentary of her work is inspiring." A *New York Times* review pronounced it "a stirring tribute, and an effective object lesson." It was named an official selection at ten film festivals and won several film awards, including the prestigious CINE Golden Eagle Award for Excellence, an award that once honored such first-time filmmakers as Ron Howard, Ken Burns, and Steven Spielberg. More important to Alidra, Democracy Matters, a nonpartisan student organization founded to counteract political apathy on college campuses, uses it to teach students about the importance of political engagement and campaign finance reform. "Granny D comes across exactly as she is—very down to earth, very serious, and an ordinary citizen who just said, *I've had it and I want to do something about it*. I can't tell you how many students have told me they were brought to tears by the film," said Joan Mandle, the group's executive director.

After a period of traveling to showings of the film, Alidra moved to Portland in late 2008. At age sixty-seven, with little money left but a film to her name, she began learning a promising new therapeutic treatment for one of the most difficult psychological diagnoses, and she began to kick around ideas for a new film. But she has promised herself she won't make another documentary alone.

While completing the work was sweet, perhaps no praise could be more satisfying than the one offered by Dennis Burke, who doubted Alidra so thoroughly when she began work on the documentary on Granny D. "Her film is *the* historical document on Doris. Alidra went to the kinds of lengths that a historian would to find the right clips. She could show it to any of Ken Burns's people and they would take her seriously as a filmmaker. It's a great film. I don't know what her compulsion was to do it, but I'm glad she did. I think everyone should have a compulsion that drives them almost to bankruptcy or suicide, and they should all come out of it happily. That's the story line of every great life."

Mission Impossible

*"I'm breaking loose from tradition
and laws of the tribe."*

Thomas Dwyer was finally embarking on a mission of his own when, after a long government career overseas in U.S. intelligence, he took up dance in his fifties. He gave himself the unexpected assignment one day when he saw his brother perform at a Washington, D.C., elementary school with an elder dance group known as the Dancers of the Third Age. "I had an awakening. I couldn't believe how amazed these kids were to see seniors running around and dancing these dances, many of them abstract, onstage. The seniors had ability and vitality. I told myself, *This is powerful stuff. It's important to show kids that their grandparents aren't just sitting in a rocking chair.* I already had grandchildren of my own and I found myself thinking, *I have to do this.* Destiny is given to you, and you have to make a choice to take it or leave it."

It is a matter for celebration as much as fascination and marvel that at seventy-six, almost a quarter of a century later, Thomas is still pursuing that destiny. Only now, he is encouraged by audiences who are moved by his performances as a principal member of the Liz Lerman Dance Exchange, an internationally recognized intergenerational dance company.

When he appears onstage audience attention often shifts palpably in his direction. Typically, his shoulders are pulled back, his spine oddly rigid, his silver-thatched head cocked as if he were sneaking a peek at the moon out of one eye. His face is sharply profiled, with its prominent nose, large flyaway ears, and squinting blue eyes. Where some see a resemblance to the Irish playwright Samuel Beckett, others think of Washington Irving's Ichabod Crane. Either way, there is no confusing Thomas's torso with that of a young Nureyev.

He extends lanky, marionette-like arms and moves his 127-pound frame on flamingo-thin legs. And it comes as something of a shock when he breaks from a pose of finger-to-lip concentration or of bemused distraction, and hurls himself to the floor, collides with another dancer, or bounds across the stage in rapturously self-absorbed reverie. A whispering curiosity spreads through the audience as the usual assumptions about what an elderly body can do clash with his sinewy defiance of them. Small wonder then that he draws steady notices as a company standout. The *New York Times*'s Jennifer Dunning has called him an "immense but understated presence," a presence Wendy Perron of *Dance* magazine wrote is by turns comic and poignant. It is a presence, too, that can be hauntingly sensuous or grave.

Thomas is still a bit incredulous that his work as a dancer receives notice at all. "If I watch myself on video, all I see is the gawky way I move and I see my skinny legs, and I just can't see what others see," he told me one night over drinks in a bar following a ten-hour day of rehearsals at the Dance Exchange studio in Takoma Park, Maryland.

"You know, if I lay on the floor on my back, I can't even put my hands on the floor. I've been missing that flexibility since childhood. But there's something in what I do as a dancer—Liz Lerman says it's the honesty in my movement—that satisfies her. She believes in me and she knows how to choreograph every move I make. And if it's good enough for her, it's good enough for me," he said. "Still, I can't believe I'm doing this."

His family could not quite believe it either. Doris, his wife of fifty years, and his three grown children were initially mystified, if not perplexed. When his children were young, he had a controlled, conservative demeanor, and never showed the slightest bit of athletic ability or artistic inclination. But there was something even more antithetical to his later life pursuit of dance. Thomas had only one quality of movement—rigid.

"When my father first announced that he was going to perform modern dance, it was a strange and almost unfathomable thing," recalled daughter Susan Frimmel, a forty-seven-year-old administrator for a robotics company. "It was like someone saying, 'I think I will take a Sunday drive to the moon.'"

It is no coincidence that Thomas relishes his ability to challenge assumptions—not just about his physical abilities as a dancer, but also about his most basic identity—often employing a sly sense of humor to do so. I learned as much the first time we spoke. As the phone call ended, Thomas wished me a Happy Hanukkah. I thanked him and said good-bye. But before I could hang up, he asked, "Aren't you going to wish me a Happy Hanukkah, too?" I was a little baffled. I said I would be happy to wish him a happy holiday, but I assumed that he was Irish Catholic. "I'm Jewish," he said, with a wink in his voice that made it difficult to tell if he was pulling my leg.

As it turned out, he was not putting me on in the least. Moreover, over time, it became clear that the story of Thomas's mixed parentage is critical to appreciating the search for expression and identity that brought him to dance. His father, Harry Francis Dwyer, was a Yellow Cab meter mechanic and a New York–reared Irish American Catholic. His mother, born Sonia Tsarkofski, was an Orthodox Jew. She was a child in Lutz, Poland, when the Germans invaded during World War I, and her survival was miraculous and terrifying. Her mother tried hiding Sonia and her nine-year-old sister from the Germans in a cellar. While in hiding, Thomas's grandmother died of natural causes, leaving her young daughters to await their fate. German soldiers eventually found the girls and beat them brutally, before they kidnapped Thomas's aunt, who was never to be seen or heard from again, and let Thomas's orphaned mother go. That is the story as Thomas knows it. "My mother never wanted to talk about her life in Poland. It was too painful," Thomas said.

A photograph of his mother visiting her father's grave in Poland and another of his aunt, his mother's abducted sister, hang on the wall of Thomas's study at his home in Taneytown, Maryland. The picture of his mother appeared as a photographic backdrop in one of Liz Lerman's most compelling works, *Shehekianu,* a dance in which members of the company share fragments of their family histories. Thomas appears early and moves gravely. He tells his mother's tragic story in a soft, raspy voice and evokes a wound to humanity that haunts the rest of the performance.

Thomas was born on July 31, 1934, in New York, a decade after his mother was widowed with a newborn—Thomas's brother Seymour—a few years after her arrival in America, when her first husband was run over by a taxi. She was on her way to stay with an aunt when Thomas's father helped her off a bus in Manhattan and a romance began. Defying the disapproval of Thomas's father's family, the two married. Not long after Thomas's birth, the family moved to Providence, Rhode Island. His childhood grew anxious after his father and brother Seymour enlisted in the navy and went off to fight at sea in

World War II. Eventually, his father returned home deaf, his brother with a sniper's bullet lodged in his groin.

The family's patriotism did nothing to protect Thomas from prejudice in Providence. His non-Jewish classmates assumed from his name and his looks that he was Irish Catholic, and they freely spat anti-Semitic slurs in his presence. Neighborhood kids pelted him and classmates with rocks and epithets of "Christ killers" when they played in the playground of the Hebrew school he attended in the afternoon. He was equally alienated at the synagogue where he was bar mitzvahed. The older men and the boys snickered and whispered at his looks. "I was treated differently because I was Irish. I found it foul. Eventually, I gave up on Judaism. I didn't fit in anywhere," he said.

His confidence was not boosted at home, where his mother, whom Thomas adored, profusely praised Seymour's intelligence and his father kept order with a heavy hand. Thomas retreated tight-mouthed to his room and grew up awkward and with little self-esteem. "I was the classic ninety-eight-pound weakling. I wasn't on any teams and I didn't go to any dances. I didn't even see any dances," he said.

When he graduated from high school in 1953, Thomas, in tribute to his father and brother, enlisted in the navy and served as a radioman for four years. On discharge, at age twenty-three, he followed the advice of Patricia, a nurse and one of two sisters, and trained to become an X-ray technician. He got a job at Peter Bent Brigham Hospital in Boston. He met Doris, another X-ray technician there, in an act of sublime clumsiness. He ran over her foot with an X-ray cart and then romanced her while insisting that she allow him to X-ray her foot. The film was negative for fracture, but his advances were positively received.

Married and with a child on the way, Thomas returned to school to get certified as an electronics technician so that he could pursue a more lucrative career. On the day of his graduation, the Department of Defense offered him a job. He and a pregnant Doris headed to

Taipei, Taiwan, for his first assignment and a life of service, sacrifice, and secrecy.

As a telecommunications officer—under the Department of State—he was stationed in far-flung and sometimes dangerous postings, including Kathmandu, Vietnam, Sarajevo, Leningrad, and Vienna. He would not say much about his work, and acknowledged only that he was technically responsible for sending and receiving back-channel intelligence communications from U.S. embassy message centers. Over the years, he would also do a stint at the Department of Defense's Warrenton Training Center in Virginia, which, according to unofficial documents found on the Internet, served as a high-frequency receiver facility and hosted a variety of satellite communications links to U.S. embassies in Asia from within its giant golf-ball-like structures.

While his fellow dancers enjoy conjecturing that Thomas worked as a spook, he is mum. He says his silence reflects only the habits acquired by a government employee who spent most of his career on assignments abroad. "I wasn't a diplomat. I didn't go to diplomatic cocktail parties. And it wasn't my job to talk with the political attaché, the cultural attaché, or the economic attaché. They had their counterparts. I was just a staff person. When you congregated after work you were always cautious about meeting strangers outside of that in the community, not knowing what their intentions really were, because you could easily become a target because of your work. You get to be pretty tough stuff," living through delicate moments in the Soviet Union, Yugoslavia, and Indonesia, among others, he said. "I've been around the block."

By the mid-1980s, Thomas was fed up with the way "politics" had intruded into the world of foreign intelligence and he wanted out.

He retired, at age fifty-two, and settled west of Washington, D.C. He had worked overseas and on special assignments for so many years that his pension assured him and Doris a comfortable retirement. But he had scant idea of how he would fill his time.

First, he contemplated boatbuilding. Then he flirted with becoming a painter, for during his career abroad, he had haunted the great museums wherever he was stationed and came to profoundly admire the works of the Great Masters. He especially loves Vermeer and Picasso. He passionately wanted to understand how they achieved the effects of their art. And in retirement, he began taking art history and painting classes at Warrenton Community College.

Thomas was also fascinated with the criminal mind. He loved watching television shows such as *The Forensic Files,* which he still tunes into when he rises at 3 A.M. He became so intrigued that he took a course in private investigation, passed a state licensing exam, and—hoping to look for missing children—was on the verge of opening an investigations business with a friend when his brother Seymour invited him to see him dance at the elementary school.

By then, Liz Lerman had been blending community building and storytelling for nearly a decade, and winning serious recognition for it. The recipient of such honors as the American Choreographer Award and, in 2002, a MacArthur Foundation "Genius Grant" Fellowship, she first worked with older dancers at the Roosevelt Hotel for Senior Citizens in Washington in the 1970s when she was choreographing a piece about her mother's death from cancer and needed to find older dancers. When she brought the older dancers she trained together with her college students, she discovered that both benefited in unanticipated ways.

Not only did the seniors become more flexible, they became

personal storytellers, and those who had been passive at the senior citizen facility became more active. The younger dancers performed better, grew as teachers, and developed a more profound understanding of the connection between life and dance. "I was driven to work with older people," Lerman said, "in part because of my personal story, but in part because of what I perceived to be the limits of the dance world. What some people would have described as professional, I would have described as a veneer. And I wanted to get down under that."

When Thomas first saw his older brother in the performance by the Dancers of the Third Age, the group was a mix of older nonprofessional dancers and dancers from Lerman's professional company, the Dance Exchange. Dancers of the Third Age performed almost exclusively at schools, senior centers, and nursing homes.

Seymour was then sixty-two and had been retired for three years from the State Department where he had served as an expert on education in the Soviet Union. He had stumbled into Lerman's company by accident after he signed up for a movement class taught by one of Lerman's professional dancers, who invited him to a rehearsal one day. Lerman, with her trademark topknot, encountered him there and invited him to join her company when it went to New York in 1985 to perform *Still Crossing,* her dance about the immigrant experience, at a centennial celebration for the Statue of Liberty at Battery Park in lower Manhattan. "I didn't do much. I was just moving in the background," Seymour said. But the overall effect of the dance was memorable.

The *New York Times* reported that more than one observer was moved to tears by the performance in which ordinary folks—old, young, several disabled—who had participated in a community workshop Lerman gave filled the stage along with dancers from Lerman's company to create a powerful metaphor for an ideal of a unified

American society. The performance was later hailed as one of the year's "ten best."

When, a year later, Thomas saw his brother perform at the elementary school with Dancers of the Third Age, and he committed himself to becoming a dancer, too, Thomas was already in reasonably good physical condition. A few years earlier, while stationed in Kathmandu, he had lost twenty-five of his then 185 pounds after he picked up an intestinal bug. Then, while posted in Vienna from 1983 until his retirement in 1986, Thomas quit smoking cigarettes and began a modest conditioning program, walking three hilly kilometers to work at the U.S. Embassy each morning and then home at night. That included climbing the 110 steps he counted every day on his way up to Peter Jordan Strasse, the street where he lived. His weight dropped to 142. Then, in 1987, he began taking dance classes at Lerman's studio, then housed in the Hall of Mirrors at an old amusement park in Glen Echo, Maryland.

Several months later, Thomas asked Lerman if he could dance in performances with the nonprofessional Dancers of the Third Age. She turned him down because he was still six years too young. But she encouraged him to continue taking classes and workshops at the studio. Thomas threw himself into learning dance with even more determined zeal and dedication. Occasionally, when the Dancers of the Third Age needed an extra dancer, the director of the troupe asked Thomas to fill in for a performance at a school or nursing home.

He had fun dancing with the elders, but he enjoyed even more being around the younger professional dancers. He was tickled by their creative and collaborative playfulness. "It looked like fun. I used to see how Beth Davis, one of the dancers, would cut up with the others. I was enthralled by her antics," Thomas said. "I remember one night, I went to a performance of the Dance Exchange at the

Kennedy Center for the Performing Arts. When it was over, I saw Beth leaving the stage.

" 'Don't worry, Thomas, you're going to be up here one day,' she called.

"I looked at her and I couldn't believe it," Thomas recalled. "At the time," dancing with the professional company "was the furthest thing from my mind."

A few months later, in June 1988, Thomas got his break. An older dancer in the Dance Exchange suffered an injury, and Lerman needed a replacement for performances in a dance festival in Zagreb and Belgrade, Yugoslavia. She also needed someone with a valid passport. Thomas jumped at the opportunity to dance—and to return to Belgrade, where he had served a decade earlier in the U.S. Embassy. His role, he says, didn't amount to much. "I played a Russian bureaucrat. He was supposed to be a silly person, as Liz asked me to portray him. I took off my stovepipe hat and bowed to a stool. And then I moved it around to various locations on the stage. It wasn't a big part, but I wanted to do a good job. That was uppermost in my mind," he said. He was simply pleased to be performing with the professionals.

Lerman was pleased to have him. So pleased that three months later, she asked Thomas to join the Dance Exchange. She had found what she was looking for. "With Thomas there was no veneer. Nothing. He is what he is. You see it all. I wanted to push that on my audiences. I also wanted it to rub off on my young dancers, who could do anything, but they came with a lot of physical baggage as a result of all their training. I'm interested in people dancing, not dancers dancing.

"From almost the second Thomas took the space, I knew we were in for something. After the first couple of performances, I had theater directors calling me and saying, 'I can't take my eyes off this guy. Can I borrow him?' " she said.

The response to Thomas's appearance as a dancer confirmed

Lerman's notion that dance technique should be a tool and not the master of the dance. "In dance, we have over-recognized technique, so that we've missed all the other critically amazing things. And Thomas, I think, helps audiences over the hump of that. You can almost see them as they adjust and start to think, *I'm going to stop looking for the high legs and jumps because I'm going to get something out of this other thing.* I'm so happy to see that."

The first morning I arrived to watch Thomas in rehearsal at the Dance Exchange studio—a converted post office—he had per usual arrived hours ahead of everyone else. Wearing baggy gray sweats and old, worn blue dance slippers ("They are like a badge of defiance; they mark that I came from poor beginnings"), he was already engaged in his demanding daily regime. He was holding himself in a rigid plank position a few inches off the ground. I was so entranced by the length of time he held his position that I forgot to check my watch to see how long he endured it. After that, he did an exercise in which, on his knees, he alternately stretched opposite arms and legs and held the position. Then, he stretched, balanced, did jumping jacks, and ran in place.

To strengthen his feet and ankles, he dragged a foot back as if pulling sand with his toes, slowly pushed his toes forward as if returning the sand in front of him, and then alternated feet. He gripped and squeezed rubber balls, juggled them high in the air, and then threw them against a wall and caught them to quicken his reaction time. He also did lung-strengthening exercises, breathing in deeply through his nostrils and expelling air by exerting pressure from the bottom of his diaphragm. "I go from the top of my head to my toes. I want everything to be exercised. So if I ever injure myself in rehearsal or performance, it won't be because I'm not prepared," he said.

He makes no concessions to the scoliosis, a curvature of the spine, he has suffered from since childhood. He is a stickler for doing his routine every day, a routine that often leaves his younger dancers awestruck. When the Dance Exchange does workshops at universities, college students watch Thomas warming up as if he were performing a circus act. "Which is part of what makes it so wonderful," Lerman said. "It changes what they think of old people, and it changes what we think of warming up, and it changes what we think of dance."

For Thomas it is pure practicality. "If I didn't maintain my regimen, I could really be hurt and not get out of bed," he said, adding, "No one here would ever challenge me in push-ups." Of that, there is little doubt. Every day, Thomas does at least 125, and that does not include the knuckle push-ups he throws in. In one of Lerman's most provocative works, *Ferocious Beauty: Genome,* a multimedia investigation into the history and ethical issues, such as endless aging, of genetic science, the choreographer uses Thomas's push-up prowess to great effect. He portrays an old man, genetically reengineered to live to an extensive old age, who tries to end his life by exhausting himself to death with push-ups. Thomas, wearing only his underwear, does sixty, with his feet elevated on a chair. The audience is usually gasping by the time he is done.

But conditioning was the least of Thomas's challenges when he began dancing. Never having taken music or dance classes in his youth, his spatial awareness, ability to memorize sequences of movements, and his rhythm were weak. He still works tirelessly to get the movements and timing right, and to duplicate important nuances such as when to shift his weight to begin a movement. He often seeks the help of younger male dancers, like Joffrey Ballet–trained Ben Wegman or Matt Mahaney. "I know if I can get near what they do, Liz will employ me in a dance. When I'm doing a movement, I want to make it as perfect as I can," Thomas said.

He has occasionally had difficulty finding his spots onstage during a performance or has lost track of the choreographed spacing between himself and other dancers. A strong sense of space and direction—always knowing where front, back, boths sides, and the diagonals are—is usually almost second nature to dancers trained from childhood. To compensate, when the Dance Exchange heads into an unfamiliar theater, the director puts Thomas on the diagonal and assigns another dancer to work with him repetitively. "As with the movements, once I have it in my body, I just go over and over it on my own, until I no longer have to think about it and can just do it," he said. "Choreography stimulates the brain. The body and mind are working to remember all these moves, and I'm firing all that gray matter," Thomas said.

Indeed, mounting evidence from brain imaging studies and other neurological research supports Thomas's sense that the work of learning to dance professionally has had cognitive and other benefits. In 2003, a twenty-one-year study of 469 senior citizens, seventy-five and older, that was led by the Albert Einstein College of Medicine in New York City and published in the *New England Journal of Medicine,* found that of the several activities it studied, frequent social dancing was the only physical activity associated with a significant decrease in the incidence of dementia, including Alzheimer's disease. "Dance is not purely physical. In many ways, it also requires a lot of mental effort," said the study's lead researcher Joseph Verghese. Among the participants of the study, those who danced three or four times a week, showed 76 percent less incidence of dementia than those who danced only once a week or not at all. Heightening interest in the neural benefits of dance, in 2005 McGill University researcher Patricia McKinley found that older adults who learned the Argentine tango, which combines the mental challenge of learning complicated dance steps with physical exercise and social interaction, performed better at multitasking—doing a complex cognitive task while walking or standing on one foot—than a group of older adults whose only exercise was walking. The tango dancers also improved in balance and motor coordination.

Investigators are continuing to search out the reasons the brain seems to benefit so distinctly from dance. Several neuroscientists with whom I spoke suggested to me that the level of physical activity and the "learning load," or demand, that Thomas has placed on his brain has, hypothetically, increased the blood flow to his brain and helped to stimulate the growth of blood vessels. Not only would such growth, known as angiogenesis, protect the brain against stroke, there is reason to suspect that his regular dancing and exercise have strengthened and stimulated the development of brain synapses (critical to learning and brain plasticity), neurogenesis (the growth of new brain cells), and the release of enzymes that help maintain the energy of brain cells that otherwise declines with age.

Bolstering that view are findings in 2007 by researchers at Columbia University who found for the first time that exercise targets a region of the brain within the hippocampus, the part of the brain that modulates memory and learning and which underlies normal age-related memory decline. The study was particularly significant because researchers, using functional magnetic resonance imaging (fMRI), identified neurogenesis within the region known as the dentate gyrus following exercise. "I, like many physicians, already encourage my patients to get active, and this adds yet another reason to the long list of reasons why exercise is good for overall health," said Dr. Scott A. Small, the study's lead author. Still other researchers have begun to find evidence that dance activates the pleasure centers of the brain, explaining in part why we like to dance, and that the sensory experience of watching other dancers move entrains movement areas of the brain in professional dancers, making it easier for them to replicate dance steps done by others.

Over time Thomas not only pushed himself to challenge his physical limitations, he learned to exploit them. His movements became even more authentic and arresting. "It's one thing to see someone move flowingly and energetically in their twenties, but a much different thing to see it in their seventies, to see someone pull it off in a container that is weathered," said Beth Davis, who is also a choreographer. "When an older person raises an arm, he raises it with a history of that person. There's a depth to the beauty to it."

Nowhere is that more evident than when Thomas dances a solo set to Willie Nelson's rendition of "Blue Skies." In the beginning of the piece, Thomas lopes around in a large circle, taking long, jaunty strides, his arms moving in opposition to his legs as the iconic country-western singer croons Irving Berlin's familiar verse, *"Blue skies/Smiling at me, Nothing but blue skies/Do I see."* The piece is one of a series of vignettes entitled *Nocturnes* performed by dancers of differing ages to a medley of Nelson's best songs. The set explores what Washington reviewer Lisa Traiger labeled "ever-green ideas of love, lust, loneliness and heartbreak." It premiered in 1996 and has remained one of Lerman's most popular and critically acclaimed works.

When she conceived it, Lerman did not have much confidence that "Blue Skies" would amount to much. She had been thinking a lot about men of Thomas's generation who served their country in the military, returned home, took jobs, and started families with a sense of vintage American optimism, expecting that everything would work out. "Then along comes the women's movement and the changes that occurred in the economy, and for many it all just fell away," Lerman explained before I watched Thomas rehearse the piece for an upcoming performance. Near the end of the song, Thomas falls hard to the ground and struggles to lift himself. In a gesture mixing frustration and determination, he smashes his fist into the floor and his wrist appears to break. Then he rises to his feet, the palms of his hands and his face lifted to the sky, as if resurrected by his last ounce of will and hope. Audiences are often shocked by the violence with which he pounds his fist into the floor. Even in rehearsal, other dancers—though they had seen Thomas perform the dance before—winced at the impact and the raw emotion he evoked.

"I'm breaking loose from tradition and laws of the tribe that have stymied me but are still very much a part of me," Thomas explained. If there is a more concrete personal history behind the dance piece, he is not revealing it. Half the meaning of a dance has to be hidden, even from the dancer, for it to come alive on the stage, he told me he had learned from Lerman. When I pressed him, he allowed only: "There was a lot I had to give up to be a dancer. I may look pretty simple, but I am a complicated man."

By striking out for dance in later life, Thomas broke with expectations of at least one person in the tribe of his family and stirred some mixed feelings. While she says she is proud of her father, daughter Diane Wimsatt has had misgivings about the amount of time that Thomas has devoted to dance at the expense of spending time with her aging mother. "I know what I would have liked," she said, "but my mother says she never asked him to spend more time with her, and I guess that's their business." Doris, at seventy-nine, suffers from hearing loss, and declined to be interviewed. She sent word through her daughters that she supported Thomas and was proud of what he has accomplished.

Aging and romance have proved fertile for Thomas and Lerman's troupe of intergenerational dancers. None of Lerman's works more richly challenges notions about age's limitations on romance and sensuality than the deceptively modest *Nocturnes,* and no part of that dance does so more touchingly or erotically than a duet Thomas performed in 2008 with Shula Strassfeld, a tall, graceful sixty-one-year-old career dancer who has performed with companies in Israel, Europe, and Canada as well as in Boston and New York.

No sooner had Willie Nelson's soulful singing of the ballad "Always on My Mind" begun during one of their first rehearsals for the piece than the other dancers in the Dance Exchange studio stopped what they were working on and focused on Thomas and Shula. At one point in the dance, Thomas touched her cheek with the back of his hand and then, kneeling with his head bowed, grasped her thigh in both hands and pulled his face close. Together, they conjured a relationship freighted with the complexities of remembered love, braided with hurt, loss, and desire.

As accustomed as we may have become to seeing physical intimacy between older adults portrayed in film, television, or in incessant advertisements for drugs that treat sexual dysfunction, the spectator still experiences an additional frisson watching intimacy enacted between two older adults so beautifully.

In rehearsal, however, the spell of the piece was broken after the first run-through. Something was nagging at Thomas. When he performed it last, ten years earlier, he was partnered with a dancer whose hair was straight and silky. His fingers easily ran through it. But they had snagged in Shula's lush, slightly kinky auburn mane. He was afraid that the gesture would not convey what it was supposed to. There were discussions and suggestions, and the dancers spent twenty minutes repeating the problematic part until Thomas was satisfied. "Thomas needs to know everything about what he is doing and why. His attention to detail is laser-like," Shula told me days later. Since joining the company in 2007, she has also come to trust Thomas as a partner. "I'm always confident that he's going to take care of me physically. He holds his own with the young guys."

His work ethic is impressive for a dancer of any age. During a daylong rehearsal, he seemed to go full out on every step. He rarely rested. Even when nothing was required of him, he could be seen practicing some small gesture or movement, including pliés, in a corner of the studio. "I always give one hundred and ten percent. I have to. I am working with professional dancers and I don't want to let them down," he said.

Since taking up dance, Thomas has evolved in emotional and social ways that can't be seen in a performance. Before he joined Lerman's company, he had lived his life embarrassed by his looks and doubtful that he had much to contribute socially. He made sure to stay in the background, unnoticed. "I hid myself within. But once I started dancing, I knew that I had to get over my neurotic stance if I was going to be successful with Liz Lerman. So now I'm not afraid to speak my mind or to ask questions I know are legitimate that no one else will ask. I'm not afraid of someone saying, 'You can't say that.' Now, I'm much more at ease speaking or moving. I take physical chances, too. Now, I'm a big ham."

Like many people of an earlier generation, Thomas also believed in the stereotypes about male dancers and owned his share of prejudices about homosexuals. He is disarmingly blunt about it. "I was bigoted. But once I started dancing in the company I came to see gay men as real people with real problems. I had to learn that they weren't going to come on to me just because I was a man, which like so many straight men, I thought would happen." He not only learned, he became close friends, confidant, and father figure to many of the gay dancers with whom he has worked.

By the time Vincent Thomas, a dance professor at Towson University and a 2006 recipient of a Maryland Individual Artist Award for Choreography, met him in 1996, Thomas had already long since overcome his bias. Vincent Thomas said he was the one who had to overcome prejudices working with Thomas Dwyer—working, that is, with an elderly dancer. When he was paired with the older dancer in his audition for the Dance Exchange, Vincent Thomas prepared himself to encounter a frail body that could not match his physicality and a dancer who would not be ready to take the risks of real improvisation. "When we made contact, his body wasn't frail and there was inventiveness to his movement. He didn't have a ballet vocabulary to draw on, so, instead, what he brought to the table was jarring, beautiful, and intriguing. You see Thomas dance, and your vision of what beauty is begins to expand," he said.

No moment stands in greater relief for him than when the two dancers were asked to improvise a duet for Lerman's *Hallelujah* project—a series of community-based performances that took place in fifteen cities over the span of three years. Vincent was standing behind Thomas, mulling what to do, when Thomas crouched down and sprang into the air and over Vincent's right shoulder. The high-voltage moment was immediately and permanently incorporated into *Hallelujah*. "It was as transforming a moment for audiences as it was for me," Vincent enthused.

Thomas's emotional and creative growth have been breathtaking, says his daughter Susan. "It's as if there was a small bud inside that lay closed for years but has burst forth and radiates a new being. I now see my father as someone who is artistic and creative. It is who he truly is. He is much happier than he used to be—happier with himself, happier with his life."

That is a good thing because Thomas's commitment to dance for the last twenty years has not made him richer. By 2008, he had worked his way up to a salary of $26,000 a year. But because of recession and the financial consequences it has had on the Dance Exchange, Thomas volunteered to cut his pay in half in mid-2009 to help the company. In addition to cutting his income, it means that he will not bed down as often in the monkish apartment he keeps near the Dance Exchange studio—with its bare walls, bed, bureau, and preacher's dais, which holds a bottle of Bombay Sapphire gin, his favorite drink.

No doubt, he will continue to rise early, read half a dozen newspapers, and send out a bevy of e-mails, with ribald jokes and conservative or contrarian opinion pieces to noodge his liberal friends and colleagues. He will continue to arrive before the other dancers at the Dance Exchange, tend to maintenance issues, change lightbulbs, and tighten screws. "Thomas loves in practical ways," Dance Exchange artistic director Elizabeth Johnson said.

Yes, he can be flirtatious. And he can be sardonic. And Thomas, who has been known to introduce himself to newcomers in the company as "Thomas the Great and Unforgiving," can be tough on fellow dancers who don't give maximum effort. When that happens, he can go stonily silent, looking down his nose in a frosty manner. But just like that, he can declare an end to a one-sided cold war, as he almost always does, with a handwritten greeting card or a gift of his own homemade biscotti.

A long way from his childhood in Providence and from his secretive work for the government, Thomas found his truest tribe in dance. It is a tribe filled with artists, young and old, he admires, for the qualities of their art as for the sacrifice they make to be dancers. "It's a very hard decision for their families to understand. What's the future in it? They take hundreds of hours of classes to perfect their techniques and movement. But it's a passion for them. It's not just about being up onstage and showing people how they dance. Ultimately, it's just that they want to dance. That's their passion," he said. "That they like dancing with me befuddles me."

As far as Liz Lerman is concerned, Thomas may continue dancing for her company as long as he is willing and able. And he is willing to, he says, as long as Lerman is happy with his work and remains the guiding force of the company she founded. He had no other timetable, unless the day comes when he has to care full-time for his wife.

Thomas has accomplished much of what he set out to do. A few years ago, he even got to dance with two of his granddaughters when the Dance Exchange performed at Appalachian State University in Boone, North Carolina, where twin sisters Joy and Anna Frimmel were in school. The piece referenced nearby Grandfather Mountain, the sharply profiled and tallest peak of the Blue Ridge range. "Grandpa's movements were sturdy like the mountain, legs spread wide as if nothing could move him," said Anna. "He stood tall above us as we leaned against his strong frame, a place of shelter and support. We held on to his arms and leaned away from him and knew he would never let us fall."

"I have succeeded in proving to seniors and to the children that there is something to look forward to other than resigning themselves to just being doddering, good-natured grandfathers," Thomas said. "The things I do might look silly. I don't care. I know who I am now. And I give that to the audience. I don't falsify anything. I'm satisfied with that, too. I was a messenger."

A Pie Maker's Place

"I could make a difference. . . . I could turn the diner into a place where people could stop, like they used to years ago for good food and good fellowship."

When a tall, blue-eyed dairyman's widow named Loretta Thayer rose from bed that September eleventh, it was still too dark to know how blue the sky would be. She put on her robe and went to the kitchen of her modest farmhouse on Route 11 in the village of DeKalb Junction, New York. Cars with their headlights on were already passing. Men and women were making their long commutes to somewhere else. The number of travelers that came through on the road had grown steadily over the years. But there just was not much to cause them to slow down anymore on this straightaway that cuts through dairy pastures upstate, close to the U.S.–Canada border.

Looking at the slender blue line of Route 11 on a map of the United States is a pleasant reminder of how this place is connected to a slew of small American towns and cities, strung north to south, for 1,646 miles, all the way from Rouses Point, on Lake Champlain, one hundred miles east of DeKalb Junction, down through such places as Shickshinny, Pennsylvania; Hagerstown, Maryland; Sweetwater, Tennessee; and Purvis, Mississippi before it ends at Bayou Sauvage in New Orleans. But here, at its northern end, Loretta looked across the two-lane blacktop toward the empty parking lot of the defunct diner. It was dark and still; the vacant truck stop next to it, the same.

Loretta was already sixty-nine then, and after the death of her husband two years earlier, her life had taken on a quiet rhythm. She had retired from a career of sporadic restaurant work with a well-deserved reputation for farm-style cooking and melt-in-your-mouth pies. Her main goal on this day was nothing more than to call her grandson Jason and wish him a happy twenty-ninth birthday. The two had always shared a close bond. It was one nurtured out of loss. Twenty-six years earlier, her son, Jason's father, was killed in an early morning motorcycle accident, not far from the house, on Route 11. He was twenty, and the boy only a toddler.

Loretta walked into the kitchen and put up her morning coffee. She did not notice what a visitor from elsewhere would: that hers was an iconic American kitchen. It was decorated with souvenirs of family history rather than granite countertops, zinc faucets, and other fashion accessories. When Loretta reached into the cupboard for a mug, she brushed against cabinets her father had built. A half-dozen porcelain teapots, including one given to Loretta as a wedding present sixty years earlier and another that had been her parents', sat on a shelf. Photographs of eleven grandchildren populated the refrigerator door. In the living room, separated from the kitchen by a wood-burning stove, were other tokens of her family: the colorful wool afghan a granddaughter had crocheted draped over an overstuffed sofa, the empty recliner where her husband used to sit and watch television.

Loretta kept a neat house but not a fussy one. During all the years she raised her five children and worked at area restaurants, she liked most helping Paul in the barn or working in the field. She particularly enjoyed driving the truck during haying. But she was in no rush to do chores or push through the papers piling up on the long kitchen table. She went into the dining room with its wall of windows looking out the back of the house onto a peaceful North Country pasture and sat down to read her devotional. She was lost in her prayers and thoughts when the phone rang. It was Jason. He was shaken. At first, she did not understand why. After a moment, he said, "Grandma, you don't know what's happening, do you? Turn on your TV."

She did and joined millions of Americans watching in horror as video images of the terrorist attacks on the World Trade Center and the Pentagon were played and replayed. The devastation in New York was still unfolding. As she watched the Twin Towers collapse, she felt anger. Then she felt bewildered and helpless. She had always been a pillar of strength for Jason, but when they spoke again she could not contain the anguish that had mounted throughout the day as she witnessed the desolation. "I tried to comfort her," Jason said. "She just kept asking, 'What can I do?'"

She kept asking the question of herself over and over in the days that followed as she watched the repeating footage of the hijacked jet-liners slicing across silent blue skies and plunging into the twin office towers, of the buildings collapsing into the world they once dwarfed, and of thousands of panicked people fleeing cascading debris and clouds of toxic smoke billowing through the streets of lower Manhattan. When she failed to answer her own question, a woman of strong Baptist faith, she turned her thoughts to God for an answer.

The attack punctuated Loretta's already growing sense of unease at what was happening to the once close-knit rural world she had known her whole life. So much had changed. So much was changing. It was not just Loretta's perception. The small towns between the St. Lawrence River and the Adirondacks were being hollowed out year after year by economic decline.

For nearly half a century, the area's dairy farmers—unable to survive on the puny prices paid for milk—had been selling out to the big dairies or just closing. It was true that more milk was being produced, but more barns and farm buildings were collapsing in disuse. More people had forfeited their work on the land. At the same time, St. Lawrence County's manufacturing industries and its former importance as a source of minerals were rapidly fading. The paper mill in Newton's Falls had shut down in 2000. A decade earlier the town's iron ore mill shut its doors. The zinc and talc mines in Gouverneur were laying off workers, too, and heading toward their various demises by the end of the decade. The crossroads communities, the pockets of communal life that once surrounded the small schoolhouses, such as in Richville where Loretta grew up, had been vanishing ever since the centralization of the schools. There just was no reason any longer for folks to congregate as neighbors as they once did, for a tree planting on Arbor Day or a Christmas recital before winter break.

So it was that there was a certain nostalgia that arose when the old daydream flashed through Loretta's mind. Once again, she imagined herself at work in the diner across Route 11 from her house, serving home-cooked food and talking to people who came there as to an old-fashioned haven.

It was hardly the first time she had daydreamed about it. From time to time, she had nursed this fantasy since the diner first opened in 1957. Loretta was then a pretty but shy strawberry-haired sixteen-year-old who worked as a waitress at the Silver Leaf. She served some of its first customers. Over the years, she had seen its name and owners change and watched as it went neglected and its popularity declined. She had hoped to restore the feeling it once had.

But she never had quite that much time, energy, or ambition. After all, she had a pretty full life, with much else to concern her.

Not long after the diner opened, she had gone on her first date with Paul, who picked her up in his father's Model T Ford. They went to see a movie at Grayland Movie Theater in Gouverneur and afterward went for a sundae at the Crystal Palace ice cream stand, where she also sometimes worked. After graduating from high school, she prepared to go to nursing school. But on Christmas Day 1950 Paul proposed, and they were married at her parents' house the following June. They borrowed a car, and, in one of the very few trips they ever took, they honeymooned in a cabin in Watkins Glen and visited Niagara Falls. But Paul, already a full-time dairyman, was worried about a couple of cows he expected to calf soon. So they returned home a week early. "Nobody could ever take care of his cows for him," she said. "We were country hicks, I want to tell you."

Loretta gave birth to her first child, Mike, in 1953 and her last, Randy, in 1966. In between there was Timothy, Linda Lou, and Ricky. To help pay the bills and to supplement the check that came from Kraft Foods once or twice a month for the milk the dairy giant bought from the Thayers, Loretta continued to work at the diner on and off, as waitress, short-order cook, chef, and baker.

She always had an accepting disposition. Of her children, only Timothy, who had a mischievous streak, tested her much—and, for the most part, even those moments were pretty lighthearted fare, things like putting a frog in a teacher's desk. Against her wishes, he bought his first motorcycle when he was in high school and promptly had an accident and broke a wrist. Then, much to Loretta's consternation, he traded up and bought a bigger bike. He got married at seventeen, separated two years after Jason was born, and moved home. During many late-night heart-to-hearts that followed, the two drew closer than ever. Then, in the early hours of May 2, 1974, the family's bucolic life was shattered when Timothy's motorcycle skidded off Route 11 into a culvert a short distance from the house. He and a friend were killed instantly.

Sitting in a booth in the diner, Loretta recalled how surprisingly composed she was at the church service. "You would think I'd be screaming. But I wasn't. I believe that was because I had and still have no doubt that I'll see him again." Loretta picked up a napkin, then put it down again, as she fought to keep her emotions in check. "That isn't to say there weren't times after I didn't scream with pain or feel like pulling my hair out from all that loss. Sometimes, I just had to talk about it with my friends all the time." If anyone tried to talk with her husband about it, "Paul would just turn his back and walk away."

Loretta's faith would be tested again in 1991 when a faulty electrical box sparked a fire one morning just as Paul was finishing up after milking the cows. The barn filled with smoke so quickly he barely had time to guess where the barn door was and dive out. He survived and spent a night in the hospital. But the Thayers' machinery, hay, and eleven cows were lost. The couple moved in with Loretta's father, Glenn Minnick, the same house where she still lives. Paul, who was nearly sixty then and also worked full-time running a control room at St. Joe Minerals, began negotiating to buy the farm next door. Loretta was not sure they should take on so much responsibility at their ages. One day, trying to decide what they should do, she took her bible out back and prayed. And, at that instant, "the sun broke through and I saw this beautiful rainbow come to the ground. It seemed to start near the last post on the property. The other end was in the farm's driveway. 'Okay,' I said, 'we'll buy the farm.'"

After the Thayers closed on the purchase, their children gave them a sign to post, naming the farm God's Promise. And eighteen months later, Paul Thayer was honored with the New York State Dairy of Distinction Award for what he had made of it. "It was the highest honor anyone could have given him," Loretta said.

It was not long, however, before he was diagnosed with colon cancer. Paul, who had an impeccable reputation but liked to call himself "a dumb old farmer," died in 1998. He was sixty-eight. Loretta's children were concerned about how she would recover from the latest blow, and to lend their support, two of her granddaughters moved into her house with her. "They made sure I was not alone much," she said.

Loretta's life became quieter and more composed but, one senses, was missing the kind of engagement with the community around her that had in the past defined her. When the diner, which was last run by an immigrant Sikh family, closed down she flirted with the notion of taking it over and then put it aside as the stuff of silly pipe dreams. Besides, why disrupt her placid routine? For what?

But when reopening the diner kept resurfacing in her thoughts as the answer to the question about what she could possibly do to help after 9/11, she felt compelled to heed it. "I couldn't go to Afghanistan and I couldn't drive down to New York City, but I could reopen the diner. I could make a difference to people. I could give people some enjoyment. I could turn the diner into a place where people could stop, like they used to, years ago, for good food and good fellowship," she said. "I had to reopen the diner."

Two months later, around Thanksgiving, Jason drove three hours north from his home in Cortland, New York, to visit his grandmother. One afternoon as they talked, she told him that she could not let go of her dream of reopening the diner. Jason, who had briefly owned a pizza restaurant before taking a job at a community college, started to get just as excited as Loretta. With his encouragement, Loretta phoned the property owner, Clyde Turner.

"I pretty much knew what to expect and what it would need: a fresh coat of paint, a new roof, and maybe an extra refrigeration unit," Loretta told me in her gently fluting voice as she toured me around the place, seven and half hours north of New York City, midway between Gouverneur and Canton.

She never had any interest in turning it into one of those kitschy re-creations of diners of the past. After all, the Silver Leaf had never been a sleek, chrome-studded, post–World War II, American beauty of a diner. It did not have intricately tiled floors. Its exterior was not sheathed in stainless steel. It was not built to make an architectural statement for the age of aerodynamic streamlining the way other diners were in the 1950s. It had always been an unpretentious restaurant, a beacon of comfort, familiarity, and good cheap food. For years, local dairymen had come there to meet, compare notes, and banter over coffee. Teens had come for hamburgers, fries, and Cokes after school. Parents brought their kids for a weekend treat. Night owls passed solitary hours. And long-haul truckers took sustenance and caffeine before heading onto dark upstate highways.

"No, I didn't really think about changing it much. I had my mind set on a little diner," Loretta said when I asked if she ever had any intention of replacing the worn gray Formica counter. Its original yellow chevron imprint had been all but scrubbed away by forty-four years of hands, elbows, plates, glasses, and bowls sliding across its surface. The old refrigerated Coke cabinet near the front door would do just fine as a pie keeper, she figured. And the twelve revolving counter stools could keep their original tan coverings, for the time being. "We saw what the place could be, rather than what it was. I really believed in it. I saw what I wanted to see," Loretta said, standing straight up behind the counter. When she speaks, she looks you in the eyes. And it was hard not to notice how blue her eyes were, or how closely their color matched the faded robin's-egg blue of her worn cotton blouse.

The day Clyde Turner let Loretta inspect the diner, with Jason in tow, Turner was not feeling so well. He waited outside, sitting in his van with the motor running. Loretta emerged from the diner forty-five minutes later and handed him the keys. She already knew he was asking $80,000 for the place. "What do you want to pay for it?" he asked.

"Sixty thousand," she said resolutely. ("It was just a number I threw out. I don't know why," she told me.)

"When you get ready to deal, Loretta, I live up the road," he said.

"When you get ready to deal, I live across the road," she said and nodded toward her house. That was the beginning and end of their negotiations.

The two had a long history. As a boy, Clyde—whom everyone called "Stan" for some reason unknown even to them—got into some trouble and was on the verge of being sent to reform school when Loretta's father intervened. He had a penchant for collecting strays. He persuaded the local justice of the peace to let him take Clyde home and set him on a better path than he was on. Later, Loretta watched carefully when her father came through the farm-house door with Clyde. "He was rough around the edges, with a mass of unkempt hair. Dad set him on a stool and took out the cow clippers and pretended that he was about to shave Stan," she said, with the same laugh that must have echoed through that farmhouse sixty-five years earlier. Her father saw something essentially good and smart in the fourteen-year-old boy. Her father was a fair, thoughtful farmer, and he laid down the law in his quiet manner. He did not believe in raising his voice if he did not have to, and never did so with his chil-dren or anyone else, as far as Loretta recalls.

Loretta was excited about having a new surrogate brother close to her age. She had a sister, Lois, but she was younger and too girl-ish. But instead of the camaraderie she hoped for, a sibling rivalry developed with Clyde. He, it seemed to her, was forever trying to get her in trouble with her father, and that did nothing to endear him to her over the next couple of years. Then, as soon as he could,

Clyde enlisted in the military and disappeared from Loretta's world for decades. "Until, that is, my father, who had kept in touch with him, talked Clyde into buying the diner and building a gas station next to it," she said. By then Clyde had a return-load trucking brokerage, which he ran for many years out of the gas station. Despite the family history, he was not now about to give the diner away to Loretta; she was not about to overpay.

Then one night a few weeks after her walk-through, Loretta went to dinner at the Circle Inn in Gouverneur. Clyde was eating at a table with his wife. Loretta had heard he still was not feeling well and went over to ask how he was doing. Before she could utter a word, he said, "If you still want the diner, you can have it for what you want to pay."

Loretta was dumbfounded. She did not know what to say. She eventually stammered that she would have to go home and think about it.

The next morning, she called her son Mike, who then ran an organic dairy with forty-eight Holstein cows on property just north of her house on Route 11. (The low price of milk—at ten dollars for one hundred pounds, about what it was twenty-five years ago—forced him to put the farm up for auction in March 2009.)

"What do you think?" she asked.

He considered her question. "It's a good idea."

"I figured that Dad had done what he wanted to do when he was alive, and my mother ought be able to do the same," he told me one morning, sitting with his family at a table at the Silver Leaf. Then he confessed. When he advised her to buy the diner, he was also thinking about how much he loved his mother's pies. With his sweet tooth, it would suit him just fine if she opened a restaurant across the street where her pies would always be readily available to him. So he encouraged her shamelessly. "Mom, we should have done this a long time ago. If you want to do it, do it."

She needed a mortgage and some start-up capital. The first banker she and Mike visited turned her down. He tried to discourage her from risking her time and money. Fast food was all anyone wanted, he warned. Undaunted, they drove over to the Savings and Loan of Gouverneur, where they met with bank vice-president Chuck Van Vleet. He had known Loretta for years and was glad to listen to her pitch. He considered what she said. Then he noted that the diner had been closed for a while and reviving it might be difficult. He paused and looked at Loretta. "But you're so enthusiastic about this, it might just work," he said.

Loretta closed on the diner in mid-April and started renovations. Her sons and daughter and their children all pitched in to help Loretta paint and spruce up the diner. She posted some hand-lettered food signs promoting specials such as chicken parmigiana and desserts such as strawberry shortcake. On the back wall, she mounted a two-handled saw on which she had painted a farm scene, à la Grandma Moses. Next to it, she hung the straw hat her husband used to wear in the fields when he was haying.

Forty-five years after she first waited tables at the diner, and a few weeks shy of her seventieth birthday, Loretta Thayer reopened the Silver Leaf Diner. Patrons lined up outside all day. Again, the family went to work: Mike, farmer and a former local police officer; Rick, a construction foreman at Fort Drum; Randy, a state police officer; their wives; Loretta's daughter, Linda Lou Green, and a flock of grandchildren. She also hired six full-time employees and a couple part-timers to keep the diner open from 5 A.M. to 10 P.M.

People have formed some bad pie habits since Loretta reopened the diner. On opening day, patrons devoured 156 slices from twenty-six apple, cherry, lemon meringue, berry, chocolate, coconut, and banana cream pies. Loretta did not bother to advertise. Still, it took no time for word to spread and for folks from the St. Lawrence River region and farther to start making pilgrimages to the diner for a slice of Loretta's homemade pies.

Wayne Fairbanks, a retired navy commander, is often waiting to eat breakfast and a slice of pie when the diner opens at 6 A.M. "It's always good because it's homemade. It's not made in a factory. There's a big difference. I guess it's the crusts that make it, but then, in season the fruit is always fresh, too," he said, after finishing off a piece of apple pie with vanilla ice cream. "Either I come by in the morning or around four o'clock and have a slice. Sometimes I'll have two. I don't often miss a day. I used to bring my mother here, and she'd eat two or three pieces of chocolate pie. I talked to the doctor, and he said, 'Let her, it's not hurting her.' I guess not. She lived to be a hundred and two."

There was an awful lot of chatter among the diner's pie customers who favored the banana cream pie. But I'm not a banana cream pie guy. I confess, it doesn't seem quite pie to me, though I was not about to argue the point with Loretta's fans. They, it seemed, had the right idea about how to talk about pie: simply. Pie, after all, does not bear much description. It is an existential product that prompts an either/or response. Either it's good or it's not.

I looked at the pies inside the pie keeper. My heart was with the apple pie, with its laced lid crust sprinkled with sugar crystals. It was not the most beautiful-looking pie. Neither were the other fruit pies. They were not pies perfected for a *Gourmet* magazine photo shoot. They had none of that plump puffiness. They also did not have that shellacked sheen of aged plaster that is found on pies mass manufactured for most roadside eateries. The pies themselves were the pie equivalent of the Silver Leaf: more reminiscent of the cozy imperfections of home than the efficiencies of business.

As soon as the pie plate landed on the counter in front of me, its cinnamon smell wafted upward. I had some misgivings about that.

This was filling made from fresh local apples. It would have been good to taste them pure, I thought. On the other hand, the filling immediately passed the eyeball test: neither too saucy, as when canned filling with corn syrup is used, nor too firm. In a journalistically careless way, I ate my pie without resting to take notes. I had a better idea why Wayne Fairbanks showed up at dawn, pie addict that he is.

Months later, when I could no longer remember the tastes of the pies, I asked Loretta to overnight me a few slices, for research purposes only. When I heard her reticence, I promised not to judge them on the basis of whether the crust held up in delivery. Sent on a Monday, they arrived Tuesday morning. In winter, the apple tasted even better than I remembered. The fruit had what others might call integrity. It tasted like what it was. It painted summer on the tongue. That was even truer of the blackberry and raspberry pies. Their fillings, with seeds visible, bore no resemblance to the gloppy berry fillings that are standard diner fare. And then there was the custard pie, which Loretta might think of renaming Comfort Pie. Even on 110th Street in Manhattan, where I live, a forkful of its honest dairy taste, of egg and milk, touched with nutmeg and cinnamon, was a momentary panacea for stress. These were not pretentious pies. Their mission, easily accomplished, was to soothe.

Customers may make a big deal about Loretta's pies, but she does not consider them special. "They're just pies. It's just that people don't bake like that anymore. They buy something pre-made out of a freezer. They don't roll their own crust as I do. My grandmother used to make pies like this and donuts this big," she added, shaping her hands into a circle the size of a large grapefruit. "She could be sick abed and she'd get up and say, 'I'm depressed, I'm going to make donuts.' That's kind of how I am." And so, Loretta, who almost always wears jeans and never much makeup, goes about her day humming to herself as she bakes for four or five hours on baking days. She makes pies, donuts, cinnamon rolls, and biscuits. She works and shapes the dough with effortless motion, with hands that know the way. "Hands that are always soft and smooth. But I suppose that has something to do with mixing pie all these years," says her look-alike granddaughter Tracy Kirker.

Meals with portions large enough to satisfy a hungry farmer's appetite are also part of the Silver Leaf's lure. Loretta understands the amount of food a farmer expects on his plate. "They don't want ten French fries on their plates," said Vicki Smith, a former short-order cook at the diner. Loretta does not worry about the portions cutting into her profit margins. She adjusts the portions to meet her patrons' appetites. "It all evens out," Loretta said.

She does not claim to be much of a chef. "I just know how to do home farm cooking. I don't know anything about spices. And I'd have a hard time telling you my recipes. People are always asking me for my donut recipe. But I never bothered to write it down and I don't really worry about making it the same every time. No one ever seems to complain," she said, laughing at the memory of how her father used to warn her that she would never amount to much of a professional chef because she never used the same recipe twice. "And I am guilty of what my father said. Just the other day, someone asked me for my recipe for strawberry shortcake biscuits. I started telling them, 'Well, you take a sprig of sugar . . .'" She stopped herself and laughed at the hopelessness of trying to provide the secrets of her magic.

"I don't know any fancy dishes. Besides, I couldn't charge the prices you'd need to get for something like prime ribs. We'll do them on Mother's Day, but that's it. If someone wants food like that, they go to a restaurant where they can have a glass of wine," Loretta said. Once, she recalled, one of the diner's earlier owners tried to turn it into a more elegant place. "She even put up lace curtains in the windows. It didn't last long. This is just a neighborhood diner, that's all. Good food and good fellowship is what it is. What more are we here for than to be good to one another? If you talk to people in this neck of the woods, that's the philosophy they have." Abiding by that philosophy herself, her cooking is truly done *for* others.

In the diner's small entryway, there's a saying: "Walk a little slower. Linger a little longer. Surround yourself with things and people you love." To the cosmopolitan, it might seem corny. But Loretta's customers seem to heed the saying. For them, Loretta is more than the diner's proprietor. "The food is fine, but that's not the reason I go there," says hook-and-line commercial fisherman John Miller, a retired navy cook. He regularly stops at the diner on Friday mornings en route to sell fish caught in Lake Ontario, fifty miles southwest, to restaurants in Massena, on the border. He joins a group of, at times, boisterous regulars, including car salesman Jim Hodgson and auctioneer Willis Shaddock, who commandeer the restaurant's round table. Loretta has been known to try to keep them in order, but she may have reached the point of accepting that doing so is hopeless.

Miller likes to order an omelet or a couple of blueberry pancakes for breakfast in the summer and oatmeal in winter. "The main reason I go there—in addition to the camaraderie—is I like the way I'm treated. The women who work there—Robin and Tracy and Loretta—actually care about you. If you don't show up after two or three days, they're on the phone asking if everything is all right. It's a family diner, and you feel as if you're part of the family, not just a number or a dollar bill or a tip." If a customer needs a sympathetic ear, Loretta becomes a trustworthy confidante who listens with care and true interest. "It's never just, 'Really?' or 'Okay.' She wants to know what's really going on. She has had a lot of hard knocks in her life, but no matter her age, she has come out with determination and she doesn't harp on what has happened in her life. This is her life now. And she puts her heart into it. She is the heartbeat of the Silver Leaf Diner."

Ken Taylor, a retired New York City high school English teacher and mystery writer, began eating at Loretta's diner to economize. The diner is an important part of his daily schedule. He usually wakes around 4 A.M. and later dresses and drives from Gouverneur to the Silver Leaf, where he often waits for it to open. "It feels like the whole area is dying," he lamented. "The lead mines and the zinc mines, the paper mills and the matchbook companies have all closed. But Loretta has carved out a pretty secure niche with her reasonably priced meals." It was more than thrift and more than her coconut cream pies that have made Ken a loyal customer. One morning when he arrived, he was surprised that the sign in front of the Silver Leaf listed more than specials. It also read, HAPPY BIRTHDAY, KEN! "That's not something that would happen in New York City," he said.

One day when Mark Macdougall, a middle-aged construction worker, was calling across the counter to a waitress, Loretta trained her eyes on him. "What are you asking for?" she said sharply from the table in the dining room where she was sitting.

"I asked for another roll," he said loudly.

"You can have another roll," she yelled back, relishing the verbal tennis match.

"Thanks, Grandma," Macdougall said.

Loretta took a breath, as if watching the word "grandma" form and dissipate in the air. "All of a sudden, I became Grandma. At first I resented it. But then I realized for a lot of people to say Grandma is a compliment. They mean it that way. So my only rule is this: you can tell me the pies or the food are *as good as* your mother's. But you may not ever tell me it's *almost as good as* your mother's."

As much as the diner has given to others, it also sustained Loretta during additional grief. In 2003, the year after it opened, Linda Lou died, after an eight-year battle with cancer. "She was more than a daughter, she was my best friend," Loretta said, adding that she drew on her daughter's example in fighting to turn the diner into a place that matched her dream.

In the spring of 2009, Loretta was still getting up at 6 A.M., having her coffee, reading her devotional, and heading across the road to cook, bake, and greet her loyal customers. Though the diner has, for the most part, been a happy distraction, at seventy-six Loretta had begun to wonder how much more time she wants to spend filing paperwork to meet state regulations and worrying over the day-to-day operations. After eight years, the diner's novelty had worn off a bit. But when she was made an offer, the year before, she decided to give herself an extra day off instead of sell. It has worked out well, even as the current recession has brought plant closings to General Motors and Alcoa in Massena, to Corning glass in Canton, to a cheese factory in Heuvelton, to the zinc and talc mines in Fowler and Gouverneur. "It can be very depressing to listen to the news. But then I go to the diner, and we have a great day. I'm amazed by how well we're doing. We're doing even better than last year," Loretta said. The reason, she believes, is that people see in the diner something dependable. "I think, too, people want to be spoiled a little, they want to feel like someone cares."

Of course, Loretta never got into the restaurant business to make a killing. "My father used to say, you reap what you sow. I think of that each week when I go to the bank to make a deposit. I take out twenty dollars to give to someone who really needs it. At my age, what difference does it make, as long as I have enough money to eat? I don't want to travel. I don't need to shop. I'm very content with what I'm doing every day. I enjoy people saying to me, 'It was a good meal.' I have people who travel twenty miles each way several times a week. They come because they feel comfortable here, for the fellowship. I guess that's what I'm here for. And I'm going to keep coming in here until I don't have the strength to make pies anymore."

Few ever thought otherwise. "She's someone who doesn't feel good about herself unless she's working," said Tracy, who has an undergraduate degree in professional writing but waitresses at the diner and cares for her two-year-old daughter. Customers often point out that the pretty, expressive redhead is a young clone of the grandmother she idolizes. "Grandma has touched a lot of people through her strength and her faith. This isn't just a place where people only get good food. People feed off the feeling of the place and her good advice. She's everyone's grandma. But she's not that grandma who sits in the corner. I tease her all the time," she said, glancing at Loretta talking to a couple of middle-aged men at the counter. "She gets hit on in this restaurant more than I do."

Erotic Woman

"Until I began collecting, I had lived . . .
in a narrow and suffocating world.
I became my own pioneer."

Naomi Wilzig was in midlife when she took an imaginative approach to declaring her independence from her husband, a powerful New Jersey banker. To protect her husband's sense of decorum, she had not yet told friends or her rabbi up north that she was living in a clothing optional community. She had, however, confided to her playboy son, who had taken to calling himself "Sir Ivan." He was already aware that, to make up for the absence of her children and grandchildren, she was spending a great deal of time antiquing to fill her days. It was not, therefore, that bizarre when he phoned one day and asked, "Ma, do me a favor, find me a piece of erotic art for my apartment." He figured she was now worldly enough and that she could easily find what he wanted while shopping for antiques. The problem was that despite her new nudist environs, Naomi, who grew up in an Orthodox Jewish home, did not have a clue about erotic art. "What is it?" she asked.

Ivan was as dumbfounded by the paradox of her not knowing

as she was by his request. "Really, you don't know what erotic art is?"

"No," she said.

Ivan tried to explain. He was not interested in pornography. "I want something unique, provocative, creative, mysterious, and sexy," he said.

If still unsure about precisely what erotic art was, Naomi was certain about one thing—why her son wanted it. "He wanted something to turn the girls on. He didn't say that, but I understood the inference, bachelor that he was and still is," Naomi said, with a throaty laugh one day in her office in the World Erotic Art Museum in Miami's South Beach, which she opened in 2005, when she was seventy and after a fifteen-year journey that began with her son's request.

Newspaper headlines trumpeted the museum's opening with variations on a salacious and misleading one that ran in the *National Examiner*: GRANNY PROVES YOU'RE NEVER TOO OLD FOR *PORNO*! The museum, as widely reported in news reports around the world, housed much of Naomi's extensive personal collection of four thousand objects of erotic art, valued at $10 million.

Naomi, a zaftig, five-foot-three woman with deeply tanned olive skin, began her quest timidly. She may have declared her independence from her husband, Siggi Wilzig, CEO of the Trust Company of New Jersey and a founding member of the governing council of the U.S. Holocaust Memorial, but she had done so very discreetly. She was, after all, hardly a child of the sexual revolution. The closest she had come was reading about it in newspapers and women's magazines.

Over the years, Siggi, a slim, vain man, had regularly criticized Naomi for her fluctuations in size and her tendency to put on a few pounds. He believed his wife should be slim and attractive. "I never had a model's figure. And it became a problem in our lives," she said. "I spent a lot of time in spas trying to lose the weight."

Indeed, in 1982, at age forty-seven, she was at a spa in Strouds-burg, Pennsylvania, trying once again to lose weight to please Siggi, when she picked up a local magazine and came across an article about a nudist colony in nearby Haddonfield, New Jersey. She was tired and dispirited by the monotonous daily spa routine of exercise classes, group walks, and spa diet. "Being bored, I was curious," she said and, on a whim, she decided to call and see if anyone would be admitted into the colony. She was given directions and instructed to bring a beach towel and a folding chair.

The nudist colony was off Route 80 and, "as they always are," at the end of a road. After Naomi signed in and paid her entrance fee, she was directed to park and then walk up a hill to "the sun field." "I felt a little timid, so I wrapped myself in the big beach towel I had brought and then I walked up to the crest of the hill carrying my chair. And all of a sudden, the land falls away. And I see several hundred naked people laying there, young, old, men, women, and children. So I think, *This looks pretty interesting.* And I walked down and opened my beach chair, keeping my towel around me at first." After a while, she summoned the courage to open her towel. Soon thereafter, she heard someone say, "You're new here, aren't you?" Much to her embarrassment, there was a naked, elderly man loom-ing over her chair. "I nearly went cross-eyed trying not to look at him," she laughed. When he soon asked her if she wanted to go to see the nature walk, she excused herself, saying she was quite allergic to bug bites. "I figured if I survived that moment, I could survive anything."

As funny as her initiation into nudism was, becoming a nudist proved a serious revelation.

"It was a discovery to see that people were looked at because of who they were and not because of their bodies. Curiously enough, there are very few perfect bodies in the nudist world," Naomi said. "People were overweight and they were skinny. They had mastectomies. They had bulges. They had amputations. They had people who were grossly overweight. Nobody cared. Either they liked you because you were a nice, pleasant person and interesting to talk to or meet, or they didn't care to meet you, whether you had clothes on or not."

A couple of years later, while vacationing in Florida, she visited a clothing optional resort near Tampa and decided to check it out. "I had no idea how I would feel. I saw this community of children and parents and grandparents who were nude, complete families sitting around, and it seemed very natural. So I went as a visitor the first time and kept going back. People have a total misconception about it. They imagine people fornicating under every bush. They don't understand that it's a liberating, honest experience. It removes all those social barriers, whether you're wearing designer clothes, designer pocketbooks or jewelry. It's a leveler of society. You become more interested in people rather than the manifestations of wealth or accomplishment."

Most important for Naomi, she felt fully accepted. "These people didn't give a damn that I was overweight. They liked me and they spoke to me. I was no longer in my husband's shadow. I didn't have to worry about his criticism, and I blossomed as a person. I literally became more assertive in my thinking, in my talking, and in my behavior. I realized that just because my husband had fancy ideas about what I should look like, that didn't mean that's what life really is. Becoming a nudist enhanced my image and gave me comfort and allowed me to accept my own body. If Siggi wanted to make it a problem, it was his problem, not mine. I was still a decent person.

I did good things. I was charitable. I was loving. I was kind. I did community work. And just because I wasn't a perfect size number, whatever that was at the time, it shouldn't have reflected on our relationship or my life."

Naomi told Siggi about her venture. While curious, he feared it would ruin his reputation to be seen among nudists and he never joined her.

It was against that backdrop that Ivan had asked Naomi if she would pick out a piece of erotic art for him while she was antiquing. But Naomi had not completely outgrown her ingrained modesty. She came by it naturally. Her Orthodox Jewish mother was so strictly observant that she did not permit graven images in their home. Naomi was still too embarrassed to ask antiques and art dealers about erotic art directly. Instead, for months she silently marched up and down the aisles of stores and shows in New York, New Jersey, and near her home in Florida. She hoped that she would know what she was looking for when she saw it as she shopped for conventional antiques: Art Deco jewelry, Royal Worcester porcelain, English card cases, and giftware for friends.

She was browsing in an art store in the Willowbrook Mall in New Jersey, of all unlikely places, when she came across a dreamy pastel-colored oil painting of a nude Euroasian woman ascending from a giant rose. She thought it was beautiful and readily paid $500 for it. She confidently brought it to Ivan. He rejected it on sight. "She still didn't get it at all," he said. "She thought because it had a nude, it was erotic."

Naomi returned to the trenches and bought more of what she thought was erotic, mostly nudes. Her son continued to reject her offerings. As far as he was concerned, they lacked eroticism. Finally,

Naomi became frustrated enough that she summoned the nerve to ask an antiques dealer directly if he had any erotic art. "It's everywhere and it's nowhere," he said. Mystified, she asked what he meant. "We all have it, but none of us display it," he continued. "It's under the table, and only if someone specifically says, 'Show me the erotic art that you have,' do we take it out. We don't want to offend religious people or parents with children. So we just don't leave it out."

Naomi was more than a year into her quest when the proprietor of a store in St. Petersburg, Florida, approached her and asked what she was after. Still self-conscious about being "Mrs. Wilzig, the banker's wife," she answered by listing her respectable quarry. Just before she stopped speaking, she spit out, "And erotic art."

The owner shrank back. He glowered at his young assistant. "Did you tell her that we have it?"

"No," the young man responded, "you must have told her."

"I didn't tell her, you . . ."

Offended accusations shot back and forth between the two men until Naomi interrupted the squabbling. "Gentleman," she said, "stop arguing and tell me what it is that you have!"

"Go get it," the owner ordered his assistant. The young man walked to the back of the store and emerged with a seven-foot ladder. He leaned it against a tall breakfront. After climbing as high up as he could, he reached behind the molding and descended clutching something to his chest. The owner of the store took it and carefully presented a Japanese *shunga,* or pillow book, to Naomi. "It was amazingly beautiful. I had never seen anything like it. I knew it was old and rare, and I felt a rush. *Don't let this get away from you,* I told myself," Naomi said.

The book, a gift to newlyweds in the late 1800s, contained twenty-five hand-painted pictures illustrating the ways a man and a woman might give each other sexual pleasure. At $2,500, the *shunga* book was more than Naomi had guessed she would have to pay for erotic art, but she did not flinch at the price.

The pillow book wowed Ivan, too. "What was phenomenal about this book, apart from the fact that it was done on parchment, was that if you open it from right to left, you see a dozen illustrations of a wealthy, upper-class couple in ornate robes, making love in plush surroundings. Turn it around and upside down, and it showed a poor couple in simple robes, without jewels, having sex in forests and streams. This was the coolest book I had ever seen. The rich and the poor, alike, still had to have sex in different positions."

The *shunga* book ignited Naomi's curiosity and interest as nothing else. That day she also bought her son a pair of Chinese engravings and a bronze sculpture of a threesome, with two men balancing a woman between them, held by her ankles. Now armed with the secret that dealers hide their erotic treasures, out of fear that they may offend some buyers or run into trouble with the authorities, and need to be coaxed to show them, Naomi began to hunt in earnest.

Born December 5, 1934, Naomi grew up in an affluent universe, the daughter of New Jersey cemetery owner Jerome Sisselman and his wife, Lorraine. "I wasn't exposed to the world at all," she said. "A kosher hotel in the Catskills and a kosher hotel in Miami. Those were my boundaries."

That world began to expand when she was eighteen and babysitting an older sister's children in Clifton. The fruit and vegetable vendor stopped by in his truck. Naomi went out to buy some things on a list her sister Harriet had left for her. When the transaction was complete, the peddler asked, "Who are you? Where's Mrs. Cohen?"

Naomi had thinned out from her chunkier childhood, and the peddler had not recognized her. She explained who she was.

"That's you. You look like a *kalleh moid,*" the grocer exclaimed, using the Yiddish expression for a girl of marriageable age. He asked if she had a boyfriend or was engaged. When she answered no to both questions, the peddler asked if a friend's nephew might call her. "Sure," she said. But as the peddler walked back to his truck, he turned. He had forgotten to mention one thing. "My friend's nephew is a refugee," he said.

Naomi was a little confused about why that might be an issue. "He's Jewish, I presume," she said, believing that as long as she dated a Jew her parents would have no immediate objections, a notion that proved mistaken.

When Siegbert "Siggi" Wilzig called, she agreed to go on a date. As they talked that first night, she learned that he was ten years older than she was and, more important, that he was a survivor of the concentration camps at Auschwitz and Mauthausen. Naomi assumed that her parents would be even more likely to embrace him for having suffered through the worst of the Nazi nightmare. Moreover, Siggi was ambitious. He had arrived in the United States penniless in the midst of a blizzard in 1947. His first job was shoveling snow in the Bronx. Five years later, he was already moving up in the world. He had started a business with another entrepreneurial refugee, buying stacks of fabric that matched the material used by manufacturers for their current handbags. The two men sewed and sold matching change purses, then the fashion. But it was too early in Siggi's career for Naomi's parents to see beyond their prejudices.

Not only was Siggi an uneducated refugee, but as a concentration camp survivor, he was suspect in their eyes. "They thought he was damaged goods. They worried that he was sick or weak or psychologically injured. *He survived. How? Maybe he was a collaborator?*" Naomi said, rehearsing her parents' questions. "One night, six months after our first date, we went to the movies in Passaic with my parents to see *From Here to Eternity*. When we got home, Siggi asked them if he could marry me." They responded with an unambiguous "No."

So, on New Year's Eve 1954, Naomi and Siggi eloped. They tracked down the only area justice working that night—the police court judge at the Passaic County, New Jersey, jail. After they were married, Naomi snuck home with the marriage unconsummated. She pleaded again for her parents' consent and was denied. A few weeks later, Naomi summoned her courage and left her parents' fifteen-room house in Newark. She moved in with Siggi, and his aunt and uncle, in a furnished apartment behind a kosher butcher shop in downtown Passaic. She went to work as a bookkeeper for a butcher supply company. After three months, Naomi's parents relented and threw a wedding at the "Little Hungary" catering hall on the Lower East Side in Manhattan. It was a tense affair. Naomi's family shunned Siggi's immigrant relations, with their heavy accents and broken English and impoverished looks.

But Siggi Wilzig, sent to Auschwitz at sixteen along with his entire family and tattooed number *104732,* didn't survive twenty selections for the gas chambers or a death march to Mauthausen in the final days of the war to fail or be sneered at in America. He worked steadily to better himself. He pursued one trade and business after another. He went from being a presser of bow ties in a Brooklyn sweatshop to a traveling salesman, first of school notebooks, then furniture. "I was the original *Death of a Salesman*. My fingers got arthritis from holding cases," he told Roger D. Friedman of the *New York Observer* in a 1999 feature article. By the 1960s, he was managing a furniture store in Hillside, New Jersey, while Naomi was busy raising Ivan and his siblings, Alan and Sherry.

Then Jessica Mitford's book *The American Way of Death* exposed the monopolistic practices cemeteries used to market and sell funeral services, caskets, and equipage. It prompted the federal government to step in. As a result, Naomi's father was forced to separate his business into two. He would continue to sell the plots; Siggi would take over the headstones. "If you can sell men's goods and furniture, you can sell monuments," he told his son-in-law. And Siggi did. He built a million-dollar headstone company and began investing everything he could into undervalued gas and oil stocks.

One night he came home and told Naomi about a big investment he had made in Wilshire Oil Co. of Texas. " 'You bought more stock,' " she scolded. "There was never money to pay the bills, because he was always buying stock." By 1965, he had orchestrated a proxy fight and, despite objections to him because he was a Jew, Siggi was awarded four seats on the board. Six months later, he became the oil company's chief executive. Next, he took over the Trust Company of New Jersey, a consumer-oriented bank, to offset the risks in oil exploration. "Picture Tevye as J. R. Ewing," Friedman wrote.

Naomi played a traditional and subordinate role as Siggi's wife. In addition to doing the child-rearing, she was active in Jewish affairs and charities for synagogues and local Jewish women's groups. She also served as chief event coordinator for the Trust Company's elaborate annual dinners, a sought-after gala invitation in New Jersey.

A great deal of Naomi's time was consumed by a fifteen-year landmark dispute that followed the death, in 1980, of her father, who was known as "the czar of the Meadowlands." He had been buying up land there since the end of World War II and had developed plans to build a billion-dollar mini-city, with a regional shopping mall, hotel, offices, parks, and museums, not far from the current Giants Stadium. A family feud pitted Naomi's brother, Selig, and her mother against her and her four sisters. The battle ended with a court-directed sale of the land to the state. "It all went down the drain. It was a monumental loss for the family and—with stupid judges pulling us into court every day all those years—it just wiped out the rest of my family financially," Naomi said.

As one after another of her children graduated from Ivy League colleges and began working for their father, Naomi and Siggi began to live increasingly separate lives. She spent more and more time in Florida, appearing at home as Siggi's wife for Jewish holidays and important ceremonial or business events as Siggi continued to work fourteen-hour days. Naomi needed something meaningful in her life. "I was always a homebody. I wasn't working. And I couldn't play tennis anymore because if I had it would have killed my knees," she said. "How many days can you sit by a pool like a dummy?"

After finding the shunga book, Naomi was hooked on erotic art. If she found something she thought was beautiful or interesting, she'd buy it and keep it for herself. In 1992, at fifty-eight, the floodgates opened after she moved from a one-bedroom apartment to a 3,500-square-foot condo. She began buying paintings, drawings, sculpture, ivory carvings, boxes, mechanical objects, and virtually anything that might be described as erotic. "There was no quality control going on at all," said British novelist Geoff Nicholson, the author of *Sex Collectors: The Secret World of Consumers, Curators, Creators, Dealers, Bibliographers, and Accumulators of "Erotica."* "Anything that had a nude woman, she wanted. Anything that had a penis, she wanted. At the flea markets and antique shows, she became known as the old lady who collected erotic art."

Despite her obsessive enterprise, Naomi did not notice that she was amassing a collection. "I never anticipated becoming a major collector of erotic art, certainly not an authority, and I surely never dreamed that I would write books or open a museum. It just snowballed," she said. She did not, she says, collect the art because she was a nudist. But living in a clothing optional community made it easier for her to display the art and it had a social advantage. If she had gone to an antiques show, her neighbors would come by at night to see what she found. Without the presence of her family she had limited social contacts. "Collecting the art became an integral part of my life. People would tell each other, you have to go see Miss Naomi's collection. It became the center point of my existence and my community."

Naomi remained concerned about how Siggi would react when he learned the extent of her collection. When she first told him what she was collecting, he recoiled. He didn't think it was appropriate for her, Noami recalled with evident sadness. Once, bringing a portfolio of photographs from Florida, she broached the idea of publishing a book of her collection with Siggi. As they sat together in their three-story Georgian house in Clifton, he rifled through the pictures. When he was done, he ridiculed Naomi for her foolishness. A publisher would surely rip her off and Asian factories would make knockoffs of her prize possessions without paying her a dime, Siggi lectured.

On another occasion, Naomi brought an inoffensive piece of Deco sculpture to New Jersey. "It had three nude ballet dancers lined up symmetrically. But there was no sexual activity. I took down a flower vase from a pedestal in our dining room, put it there, and went out for the day. When I came home later that night, the piece was gone and the vase of flowers was back on the pedestal. He resented my even bringing a piece like that into the family house."

Naomi retreated. From then on, she hid her activities from Siggi and his conservative, European sensibilities. "I decided not to inflict it on him anymore. Collecting erotic art became something I just did privately, on my own."

She never had to worry about Siggi visiting her home. When he ventured to Florida, Siggi preferred to hobnob with powerful, wealthy cronies and schmooze poolside with the card players at the Fountainbleau Hotel in Miami Beach. As genial as Siggi may have been with bank customers, he was dictatorial at home, where he monopolized the conversation and the limelight. "He knew better than everyone else. He was brilliant, but he never gave anyone else an opening," Naomi said, as she struggled for words that would honor Siggi's intelligence as well as the truth of what drove her to seek her own identity and authority in something as unconventional as erotic art.

To the end, Siggi failed to comprehend Naomi's motivation. He died, at seventy-six, in 2003, without ever seeing Naomi's collection. He may have viewed it as indirect commentary on their sex life together, Naomi speculated. "He thought it cast a shadow over our relationship. It suggested that maybe something had been wrong or missing. Maybe it was his sense of guilt," she said. "The way people act outside the bedroom is often the way they act in it, too. And that's not always such a good thing. He once asked his doctor, a personal friend, 'Why is she doing this?' I suppose if they got me on a couch somewhere, I'd say it was a statement of independence, that I could choose what I wanted to do with my life and not have someone dictate it to me."

Naomi received validation from some unexpected sources, including her longtime rabbi Shmuel Katz, then the rabbi emeritus of Congregation Adas Israel in Passaic, which he led for forty years. After he was retired, she often visited him at his home when she returned to New Jersey. Unfailingly, he asked why she was spending so much time in Florida. To protect the rabbi, she says, she concealed her marital problems and her passion for erotica. She told him she went to Florida because she needed to buy antiques. One day, in 1999, when she was sixty-five, she was again sitting in the rabbi's study when he asked, "What's the matter, there aren't antiques in New Jersey?" Naomi asked Rabbi Katz if he really wanted to know the answer. "Of course, what are you doing in Florida?" he said.

"Rabbi, sit down. I'm doing something a woman doesn't ordinarily do."

He looked up, startled.

"I'm doing something an Orthodox woman doesn't ordinarily do."

"What are you talking about?" the exasperated rabbi said.

"Rabbi, I have become the country's authority on erotic art. I've written two books. I lecture in colleges. And I've got a major collection that people come from all over to see."

The rabbi looked up and said, "Naomi, you're a smart woman. I always knew you were going to do something important."

"That gave me the absolution," she said, bursting into laughter. "There was no stopping me after that."

Before long, erotic art began to take over almost every available inch of Naomi's apartment. "At first, it was just a very exotic way of decorating. I put a statue out here, a painting there. My friends and neighbors couldn't get over the stuff. Soon people were calling me day and night to ask to bring a friend or a relative over and show them something. After a while, it became a pain in the neck."

It also sparked an epiphany. The collection had become more than a curiosity. "I suddenly said to myself, *This art is really important. It's unusual, it's unique, and it's a genre that's been passed by and hidden away. Why?* I kept asking myself. It's life as it is. People who were guests in my house would say, 'How can you sleep here? We were up all night looking at the artwork. Aren't you turned on by the art?' And I answered, 'No. I'm turned on by finding it!' It was such a challenge to find it hidden away, and so pointless to hide it away from society as if it didn't exist. People have been doing these things for centuries in every country, in every culture, in every generation, in every lifestyle, and we're acting like sex didn't exist. How do you think we all got here? So, I put it simply and realistically, 'Why have people been stupid for so long?'"

Naomi's collecting may, of course, have resulted from multiple motivations, conscious and otherwise. There has been ample psychoanalytical, behavioral, and cultural speculation about why people collect, from Sigmund Freud's view of collecting as sublimation of anal eroticism to New York psychoanalyst Werner Muensterberger's assertion in his book *Collecting: An Unruly Passion* that collectors use objects to soothe emotional pain experienced in childhood. "Collecting can become an all-consuming passion, not unlike the dedication of a compulsive gambler to the gaming tables—to the point where it can affect a person's life and become the paramount concern in his or her pursuit, overshadowing all else: work, family, social obligations and responsibilities," he wrote.

Collecting, however, turns out to be a routine human behavior. Studies by Russell W. Belk, the author of *Collecting in a Consumer Society,* and the Kraft Foods Canada Chair in Marketing at York University in Toronto, has found that about one in three people in North America collect. Most don't start out intending to collect something, but instead realize only once they have a few of something that there is a bounded category in which they have begun to have objects. "This can lead to feelings of mastery, competence, and success, all of which can be gratifying. Collecting enlarges our sense of self and this can make us feel unique," Belk said in an e-mail. "The collection can also provide the numinous benefit of contact with something perceived as transcendent, almost sacred."

Finding important or beautiful pieces of erotic art had a liberating effect on Naomi and she began to experience a metamorphosis that is anything but novel among collectors. She began to feel a higher purpose than just the accumulation of a rampantly heterodox collection. She divined a calling in liberating erotic art from those who were afraid to display it. And as she collected it, the art educated Naomi. "I'm a realist in life, and I'm a realist in what I like in art," she said.

"But I learned about surrealism, expressionism, and folk art. I made myself into an art historian." She has since self-published and had published a total of five books, reproducing parts of her collection with scant explications.

Naomi traveled extensively to shows, exhibits, and museums. She met with dealers and sellers wherever she could, often accompanied by J. C. Harris, a striking-looking, six-foot-two African-American private detective she met in Tampa. Now in his early fifties and the general manager of the museum, Harris's imposing stature, no doubt, dissuaded anyone from greeting Naomi's curiosity with any disrespect. In turn, she shared the process of buying, judging, and authenticating the art with him. Collecting, he said, "rejuvenated her. It gave her an agenda, it perked her up. The woman is phenomenally intelligent and tenacious. It makes me happy to see her fulfill her dreams."

Finding erotic art in Europe was, at first, as difficult as it has been at home. Naomi's first buying trip to Paris was a complete flop. Belatedly, she realized that many of the antiques dealers in the flea markets came from rural France, and that she had failed to unearth a single piece of erotic art because most of those dealers spoke little English and she spoke no French. When she returned a decade later, she had a stroke of genius. She wore a cardboard sign around her neck, proclaiming: *Je cherche de l'art erotique.* Soon, antique dealers were virtually running out of their booths and pulling her into their shops to show their hidden erotica. The method worked so well, she had signs made up in languages for every foreign country she visited. Even in flea markets at home she began wearing a black plastic placard emblazoned with "Buying Erotica."

One afternoon during her second trip to Paris, Naomi decided to visit the Musée de l'érotisme on the Boulevard de Clichy. The museum, which opened in 1998, included about 1,500 exhibits displayed on seven floors of a nineteenth-century town house. To show off, Naomi says she brought along one of her books about her collection. A year later, the museum's owners contacted her through their investment adviser in Miami. They wanted to know if she was interested in joining her collection with theirs to open an erotic art museum in London. When she turned them down, fearful that prudish British customs officials would seize pieces of her collection, the Frenchmen offered to lease Naomi's collection to open a museum anywhere in the United States she chose.

She considered Las Vegas, New Orleans, San Francisco, St. Petersburg, and Miami. But finding the right location for a sex museum was more challenging than she expected. Each time Naomi found a suitable city and location, opposition arose. The search took nearly five years.

Then there were issues with her prospective French partners. Initially, the Parisians agreed to pay a fair return on the collection's value, set at $5 million. Naomi hoped to manage the museum and share in the gift shop profits. When it became apparent to her that the Frenchmen intended to create a spacious museum, Naomi began buying significantly larger pieces of art. Her purchases eventually doubled the value of the collection. Everything was going smoothly until the day before a scheduled Miami Beach zoning board meeting, to seek a change of use permit for the site leased for the museum. Her partners' lawyer e-mailed her that they would pay a rent based only on the earlier $5 million value. "Very good, we have to go one step further," a seething Naomi said. "I'm not going to have anything to do with you. Go back to Paris. You're not going to treat me like I'm an idiot."

Great, except Naomi now owned $10 million worth of erotic art and had no museum to hold it and no permit for one. She quickly reviewed the papers that had been submitted to the city. She was startled to discover that her former partners were seeking a permit to open an adult business, which would have restricted the museum from being near other adult sites, schools, churches, and residences. The museum's future looked doomed. "So the business is down the drain and I have more art than I can live with. I can't even entertain in my house anymore because I'm afraid people will fall over the art and get hurt." Naomi made a tactical decision. "I say, 'Baloney with this. I'm not an adult business. I'm not going to sell dildos, porn, and vibrators. I'm an art museum.'"

At the zoning board meeting, she waited for five hours to be called as her dread mounted. The board was rejecting one application after another. When her turn came, Naomi requested permission to open her art museum in a building she had found in South Beach that had, coincidentally, formerly been used as a recording studio by one of hip-hop's original bad boys, Luke Campbell, aka "Uncle Luke," a former front man of 2 Live Crew and a pioneer in popularizing explicit sex as a musical theme. The board deliberated for five minutes and then unanimously approved a permit for the World Erotic Art Museum.

Still, Naomi had no idea how she would promote her unique business, so she called "Mr. Miami Beach," as Michael Aller, the director of tourism and conventions and chief of protocol for the City of Miami Beach, is known in South Florida. Given the theme of her museum, Aller didn't know quite what to expect as he waited for Naomi to arrive for an appointment. He was surprised and tickled when an attractive, older Jewish woman was ushered into his office and began to tell him the story of her collection. "Then she started to pull out of her bag the coffee table books of her collection. I was flabbergasted. I said, these are magnificent," he said. "Eventually, we started to talk about food and she told me she was a good cook. I said that I adored sweet and sour cabbage. And she said, 'You stay right here. I'll be right back.' And off she went to her apartment, and before I knew it she came back carrying a container with two pieces of sweet and sour stuffed cabbage. I was overwhelmed by her attitude. It reminded me of the Yiddish phrase: *Esa ga zinta hate* [Eat in good health]. I thanked her profusely. She said, 'Wait until you taste my kugel.'"

Aller put Naomi in touch with Charlie Cinnamon, the "dean" of Miami Beach publicists, and he helped her mount a promotional campaign that has garnered her museum international attention. Among those who took interest in Naomi was Geoff Nicholson, the novelist who was himself collecting collectors for his book *Sex Collectors*. In it, he profiled people who collect and catalog sex objects, porn, illustrations, art and artifacts, from casts of rock stars' genitals to Chinese lotus shoes.

Nicholson visited Naomi in her home before her collection was moved to the museum. Jet-lagged, he spent a sleepless night trying to catalog the art in the guest room alone. "The majority [of the art] would probably be more at home in the Kinsey Institute than in any regular art museum, and a certain number look like thrift-shop paintings, which I suppose is to say they're probably best considered as examples of erotic folk art, which is fine by me," he wrote. After taking notes on some seventy pieces of sexually diverse art, from tasteful pre-Raphaelite nudes gamboling down a hillside and a painting of Bettie Page in primary colors to more explicit, raunchy, and occasionally ridiculous pieces of art such as a Minotaur with a monstrous, mythical erection, he abandoned his effort to inventory the 3,500-square-foot home.

Frequently, collectors seem happiest in detailing the pursuit of objects of desire. That is not true of Naomi. Her relationship to the works appears purer. "One meets collectors who are interested in showing off their expertise or for whom the story of how they got a certain piece is what occupies them, but she's not an academic and she's not a theorist," Nicholson told me. "She's also not interested in showing off what she knows. She doesn't seem to care very much about how she got things. She's just a very joyous collector who gets a lot of pleasure out of it. She's not interested in objects for connoisseurship or as souvenirs of experience. She just says, 'Here's some cool stuff.'"

When the museum opened, in October 2005, Naomi was three months shy of her seventy-first birthday and had spent fifteen years hunting, acquiring, and researching erotic art of every period, genre, and origin. She had succeeded in establishing one of the most comprehensive collections of sexual art in the world, and had transformed herself into an authority on sexual art. She had also acquired a library of more than 250 books on erotic art, artists, and collections of erotic art of the East, the West, Japan, China, and France. (The library is available only by appointment: "You can't have people with sun tan oil touching them every day.")

"I was totally free to absorb it. The human mind is like a sponge. It absorbs information at any age, if you challenge it," she said. "Collecting erotic art has been important to my outlook on life, people, and sex. Until I began collecting I lived in a narrow and suffocating world. I became my own pioneer." She added, "Sometimes you have fantasies and you wonder if they are normal or are they good or bad. Then, when you see the artist portraying things that have been in your mind or experience, it gives you comfort to know there are others out there with the same thoughts, fantasies, and experiences. So it validated and enhanced my own sexuality."

The World Erotic Art Museum sits almost unnoticed in the heart of South Beach's Deco district. Despite the area's reputation for ostentatious sexuality, at midday it looks like nothing so much as an upscale shopping district set in vibrant period concrete color-banded buildings, many of which were funded by organized crime in the 1920s. A small neon sign announces the museum over its innocuous, recessed entrance. The downstairs lobby might just as easily serve as a vestibule for a dentist's office. By design, there is nothing to offend passing pedestrians, only an unclothed mannequin, decorated with a potpourri of language associated with the erotic, to signal the art upstairs. A visitor can therefore be unprepared, as I was, for the museum's eclectic excess, which ranges from the sublime to the hopelessly kitsch. Glass display cases lined the walls of three large alcoves and were crammed to capacity with phalluses, amulets, ancient oil lamps, carved boxes, representations of human genitalia, and a panoply of symbols of power, protection, and fertility, the oldest dating to 300 BCE.

A tour led by Naomi is a brisk, dizzying, Alice-in-Erotic-Wonderland feeling. It evoked, for me, the wonder-cabinets that proliferated all over Europe in the sixteenth century, filled pell-mell with marvelous curiosities from global expeditions, which Lawrence Weschler wrote about in *Mr. Wilson's Cabinet of Wonder.* But unlike the disorienting hodgepodge of the Wunderkammern, Naomi has tried to impose some order on the World Erotic Art Museum.

"We start with Adam and Eve and a little Garden of Eden art—the original erotic art," Naomi explained, in a flat, I-have-seen-it-all intonation. We moved swiftly from a glazed clay sculpture of God admiring the resting figures of Adam and Eve, to a Spanish colonial altarpiece, circa 1850, to Naomi's favorite Adam and Eve piece, perhaps her favorite piece in the entire collection, a one-of-a-kind white plaster statue of Adam being created out of the dust of the earth. The young Cuban artist who made it had intended to cast it in bronze but ran out of money. "I love the simplicity of it, the way the arm is coming out of the swirl of dust and the hands are resting on the space of eternity and the perfection of the man's body, as if God got it right the first time," Naomi said.

But Naomi does not dwell. She practically race-walked—despite her bad tennis knees—into a large room grouping about one hundred paintings and sculptures based on the myth of Leda and the swan. In the ancient tale, the Greek god Zeus took the form of a swan and seduced the beautiful, mortal daughter of the Aetolian king Thestius after she resisted his advances. Naomi believes her collection of Leda art is the world's most extensive on the theme that has fascinated artists for centuries. From there, we moved through the centaur and satyr art, stopping momentarily in a narrow gallery to consider an oil painting, by contemporary American satirist Charles Bragg, of an obese satyr embracing an overweight woman. "There are no Twiggies in erotic art; the women tend to be Rubenesque. It's the voluptuousness of the female body that captures our attention," Naomi said. We pass a painting of an elderly religious Jew who can't seem to get a close enough eyeful of a naked woman and an Inuit soapstone carving from Alaska of a tumescent native hunter. "The spark of eroticism is within us all, regardless of age or background," she notes.

Erotic art often has a hidden aspect. And it was that element of surprise and subterfuge that came to most fascinate Naomi. And so we made a quick stop in a room filled with erotic music boxes, double-lidded boxes, boxes that unscrew or have a painted erotic lid hidden beneath a false lid, painted with a commonplace subject. "A lot of it is meant to show a sense of humor," she said. "See this one. You wind it, the curtain opens, and you see a couple going at it. Other things were erotic for their time, even though there's no sex act going on, like the paintings in which women lift their skirts and show their undies and garters and belts." We practically careen from Art Nouveau and saloon pinups ("Their purpose was to entice men and keep them in the saloon, drooling and drinking") to one of the museum's showstoppers: a hand-carved, gilded replica of the throne of Catherine the Great, the supremely powerful nineteenth-century empress of Russia, whose legendary sexual appetite is hinted at in the carvings (though, truth be known, she died of natural causes, not in nexus with a horse). We stop, too, at a room-filling eight-piece bed created by German carpenter Dieter Sporleder. All 138 sex positions described in the *Kama Sutra* are carved on its giant phallus-shaped bedposts, foot rails, and headboard. Naomi bought the bed set from Sporleder off eBay for an undisclosed price.

My head was spinning by the time we passed one of WEAM's most noticed works, a polished white fiberglass dildo-sculpture prominent in Stanley Kubrick's film classic *A Clockwork Orange*. Slapping it lightly, as did the movie's protagonist, played by Malcolm McDowell, Naomi laughed. She swore her glee was unrelated to the object's five-fold increase in value from the $3,000 she paid at auction for it.

Lori Mitchell, a professor of human sexuality and a certified sex surrogate, is among Naomi's biggest fans. She requires students who take her course at Barry University in Miami to visit the museum. Mitchell's goal is to help students step outside the narrow views of sexuality inherited from their parents and community. The museum helps to teach her students the distinction between the erotic and the pornographic, and to appreciate that throughout human history, men and women have been experimenting with sex and sexuality and representations of it, she said. Students are often reluctant to make the visit. "Most of them end up saying that they love it, that it broadens their outlook," Mitchell said. "But they're taken aback when they meet Naomi. They just don't expect to see this grandmother talking to them about these things or to be so knowledgeable and fascinating, as she tells them the history of every single object."

Naomi is proud of having achieved the stature of an expert, a role in which she is often asked the difference between the erotic and the pornographic. "I explain that porn has only one message: Get it on! Erotic art is art, and should be addressed as any fine piece of art. You consider the talent of the artist, the meaning of the art, the connection between viewer and the work, the psychological or sociological reaction to it. In a simple sense, the erotic is sexual. But it can also be sensual, romantic, beautiful, suggestive. And one usually has an intimate reaction to erotic art."

"What did I understand before about what people do sexually and why? Now, I have much more understanding of what motivates and drives people. That they're different sexually doesn't make them wrong. Give me my soapbox and I'll tell you. The public only thinks of the erotic as pornographic. They go to see movies of chain saw killings and people being massacred and Halloween horror movies, but show a naked body and they go berserk. Let the government and the church mind their own businesses. If it's consenting adults—Hear! Hear! Do what you want, just don't do it by force and don't do it with children," Naomi said.

About 2,500 people a month visit the World Erotic Art Museum, and Naomi spends much of her day working to build attendance and planning a monthly thematic series. In 2009, they included a show of black artists' work about Josephine Baker, the expatriate African-American dancer and entertainer, and exhibitions of objects illustrating the *Kama Sutra,* and erotic art on surfboards. She spends hours every day continuing to search for erotic art, reviewing offers of objects made to her online, and trying to upgrade the collection. She was pleased recently to have snagged a handsome and witty wood sculpture, by Connecticut artist Andrew Giarnella, titled *G String,* of a nude female torso. Using resin and wood filler, the artist built breasts and buttocks over a violin, and then ran a single string from the neck to the base of the pelvis.

Naomi is often kept busy, too, attending benefits, sometimes several a week. In the space of two weeks, for example, she attended benefits for the Buoniconti Fund to Cure Paralysis, the Israeli Defense Forces, the Greater Miami Jewish Federation, the Rabbinical College of America, and one honoring her publicist as a "Champion of the Arts" in Miami. At the benefits, she frequently meets people who, learning what she does, say, "You're the face of erotic art in Miami?"

" 'Sure am, and I'm proud of it!' I say. Several times a week people stop by my office, not to say how beautiful the art is, but to thank me for showing it. I feel proud of what I have ended up doing with my life."

THEODORE LUDWICZAK

Rock Star

*"You never know what you'll find
on the side of the road."*

It was low tide when Theodore Ludwiczak put down his trowel and stepped back from the sixty-six-foot bulwark he had spent more than two years building. A series of powerful storms in the early 1980s had taken a considerable bite out of his property along the Hudson River in Haverstraw, New York, just north of the Tappan Zee Bridge, and Ludwiczak, a retired contact-lens grinder, hoped the seawall would protect it from further erosion. As he assessed his handiwork, he felt a flash of disappointment. Aesthetic concerns replaced practical ones. "The wall looked bare and primitive," he said, with a Polish accent. "It needed something."

He looked around without knowing precisely what he was looking for. Buried at his feet in the river sand he saw a large, clay-colored rock. "It spoke to me," he said. "I looked at it and I saw a face. I saw eyes and a mouth. I grabbed the broken lawn mower blade I used working on the wall. I ran up to the garage and got a hammer and a screwdriver, and I started carving a head. I kept chiseling all day."

Twenty-one years later, the eighty-two-year-old Ludwiczak hasn't stopped. Since carving his first head, he has chiseled about twelve hundred others, using stone found on his walks along the river, on roads, and in nearby forests. Some smile with twisted lips, others are inscrutably serene and mysterious. Some have long, thin noses and jutting chins. They do not have eyes yet they seem to see nonetheless. Dozens of his sculptures are embedded in the seawall along the riverfront an hour north of New York City. Hundreds more populate a small yard, one hundred feet above the river, making it a remarkable folk-art environment and garnering gazes from curious sailors who pass Ludwiczak's place. "They call it Easter Island. I know what they mean. I've seen pictures of the statues in the South Pacific. I guess I made my own Easter Island—an Easter Island of the Hudson."

In recent years, the late-blooming sculptor's reputation as one of America's most accomplished living folk artists has grown well beyond those who ply the river on boats. Although he is a reluctant seller of his work, several pieces now reside in the American Folk Art Museum in New York and the American Visionary Art Museum in Baltimore, which recently purchased ten pieces to create a fountain that will serve as the centerpiece of its lobby. His works are also on display in numerous private collections, including that of the Oscar-winning actress Ellen Burstyn in Nyack. Ludwiczak has been interviewed by National Public Radio, filmed for HGTV, and featured in popular roadside travel books. Before he was first represented by art dealer Aarne Anton at his American Primitive Gallery in New York City, Ludwiczak often sold his heads to admirers for sixty or seventy dollars. Now, the larger heads fetch thousands of dollars. Anthony Petrullo, a collector of self-taught and outsider art, explains why: "His pieces are pure and simple. And if you remember the primitive tools that he used to make them, you begin to see the intuition they embody."

When I phoned the artist to make an appointment to visit, a man with a thin, energetic voice answered. He sounded sweet, buoyant, and grateful that I was interested in his work, but not eager for a visitor. We were in the middle of a heat wave, and he wanted to wait until it cooled before submitting to an interview. When, after several days, the heat showed no sign of abating, I phoned again. This time, he resigned himself good-humoredly to my request.

Ten minutes north of the Tappan Zee Bridge, the road to Ludwiczak's house angles down a hillside off Route 9W and toward the working-class village of Haverstraw, with its odd mix of elegant Victorian houses and tightly packed, shabby, low-income housing for an increasingly Dominican population. I missed the correct turn and quickly got lost in this village that Henry Hudson first visited in the seventeenth century on his ship the *Half Moon,* and which the Dutch settled in 1666, calling it *Haverstroo,* meaning "oat straw."

For a century and a half, from the mid-1770s, Haverstraw supplied a significant portion of the bricks used to construct New York City's buildings. At the height of their productivity, its brickyards sent as many as a million bricks a day downriver to build the metropolis. To do so, brick makers dredged deeper and deeper into a spectacular deposit of powdery blue clay left in the Hudson River by melting glaciers of the Ice Age. In 1906, despite signs that the riverbanks were becoming unstable, the dredging continued, and clay supporting the embankment in Haverstraw slipped away. A hole opened and swallowed three blocks of houses, claiming nineteen lives. Soon, lighter European bricks and other building materials gained favor, and the Rockland County brickyards began to close, leaving Haverstraw in economic freefall for decades.

After passing a new waterfront condominium complex being marketed to an upscale population and promising to revitalize the area, I found my way onto a street gray with dust from the surrounding

Tilcon gravel company and noisy with its mixing trucks and conveyors. Just as I was about to turn back, I entered a dead-end suburban street in the small, secluded area once known as Dutch Town.

Toward the end of the street, a congested colony of enigmatic stone heads appeared on the low-slung front porch of a green two-story frame house. I pulled to the other side of the street and sat for a few minutes gawking at the sculptures. Moon-shaped heads hung from the porch roof and were nailed to its posts. Square, oval, and oblong heads were stacked on shelves, perched around the mailbox, piled atop one another, and corralled in a side yard.

Before I had a chance to gather my thoughts, a tan, unexpectedly youthful-looking Theodore Ludwiczak appeared at the side of the house. He flashed a warm, self-effacing smile that quickly settled into a tighter, more impassive mien. His face was handsomely grooved. A thin tuft of sun-bleached hair topped his high forehead. He was dressed in a thin, well-worn grayish T-shirt, smudged unbelted khaki shorts, and sandals—his work uniform for the summer. His left hand was bandaged in a dull white piece of cloth. Instead of reaching out to shake, he held it in front of him apologetically and explained, "A bee stung me yesterday when I was working. So I won't be able to work today. It's too hot anyway."

With the sun blazing and the temperature in the high nineties, Ted quickly ushered me into his unair-conditioned house. I barely had time to catch a glimpse of the dense throng of stone heads and statues—some weighing several hundred pounds and standing four feet tall. But I was already mystified: How did a person who spent much of his life grinding contact lenses in a one-room "factory" transform himself into the sculptor of these statues? What inspired him in the first place? Where had he acquired the skill, strength, and compulsive will to carve so much striking and original art so late in life?

ROCK STAR

Ted showed me into his spartan living room. There were two kitty-corner couches in disrepair with cotton throws over them. A small wood coffee table was cluttered with magazines, newspaper clippings, and a grandchild's plastic army tank. A dark desk in one corner of the room held a hodgepodge of papers, pens, tools, and a large stone head. Rows of small carved heads sat on a couple of tables next to a vintage television set. The walls were hung with a copy of *Les Saltimbanques* by Picasso ("I like him because he worked right up till the end"), a few framed newspaper articles about Ted's sculpture, and four faces—suggestive of Old Testament prophets—Ted had carved in relief on two large flat jagged clay-colored rocks.

Flushed with modesty, the sculptor began to recount how carving his first head led to making another: "When I got finished, I cemented it right in the middle of the seawall, so *he* could see the sunrise on the other side of the river," he said, speaking of his first carving as an animate being. "I was pleased. But the next morning when I came down to the wall to admire my work, I was disappointed. The day before, he looked so happy and I was so proud, but now he looked sad and lonely. Maybe he needed a companion. Maybe he needed a friend. I found another rock and went and got my tools and began chiseling another stone into another head. At the end of the day, I cemented it into the wall, too. The next day, I began another."

That summer of 1988, Ted chiseled a dozen primitive heads and cemented them to the breakwater. It wasn't long before sailboats and powerboats slowed and stopped and their occupants called ashore to ask if Ted had made the heads, how and why. "They were curious. There were a lot of photographers who came and took thousands of pictures," he noted. Their curiosity and praise encouraged him to continue working at his newfound art, which he did, working even through the winter months in his garage.

Over the next four years, he carved four hundred heads of varying

191

sizes, shapes, and expressions. As his skill increased, so did the size of the stones he used and the sophistication of his designs. After originally concentrating on the softer red sandstones he found on the beach along the Hudson, he began experimenting with a wider range of rocks—granite, quartz, limestone, basalt, marble, and glacial stone. "I discovered a method. I pick up rocks and turn them round and round until I find a face. Once I do, I peel away what's there. I take pleasure in it. It's just fun. I can't stop. I wake up at night and can't wait to go out and get to work. But sometimes, it's too early to start, especially now that I use a compressor. I don't want to wake the neighbors with the noise. So I have to wait. I make myself some oatmeal—for lunch I make a large salad, for dinner fish. I listen to classical music on the radio and I wait. Every day, I chisel. It's my life."

The only child of Tadeusz Ludwiczak and Jadwiga Szelong was born in Otwock, Poland, on January 2, 1926, and named after his father. He remembers little more of his mother than her sitting in a chair. She died of tuberculosis during an epidemic when he was four. "I probably missed my mother at first, but you get used to these things when you're so young," he said.

If he speaks of the event matter-of-factly, it is not difficult to understand. Even when there was no epidemic, tuberculosis was a constant in Otwock, a picturesque resort town on the Swider River fifteen miles south of Warsaw. With its mild climate, pine tree woods, unique alpine Russian architecture, and proximity to the city, it was the ideal location for the first tuberculosis sanatorium in lowlands Poland, founded there in 1893.

By 1933 Otwock had become the first town connected to Warsaw by electric train, and during Ted's childhood it developed into a cosmopolitan resort. As the home of a Hasidic dynasty of revered rabbis and yeshivas, it attracted a large number of Jews. Its full-time population swelled to thirty thousand residents, half of whom were Jewish.

Ted's father had a good job as the secretary of the Otwock court, and the family had a comfortable existence. For Ted, there was school in the morning and handball and soccer in the afternoon. The Catholic family lived in a villa with four private houses—three of the families were Jewish, and Ted counted Abraham Orbach, Nathan Hirschberg, and Anthony Hoffman among his best friends. "When they had matzoh and gefilte fish for Passover, we did, too. We lived together from the day we were born."

September 1, 1939, should have been a happy day for young Ted. It was the day he learned that he had been accepted into the local gymnasium to begin his secondary education. Just before dawn, however, more than a million German troops, in five armies, stormed Polish borders on several fronts. They marched through towns, throwing grenades, making arrests, and plastering buildings with swastikas. By 9 A.M. German planes had bombarded Warsaw, and German soldiers had entered Otwock. The Nazi nightmare had begun.

The beautiful Goldberg synagogue on Warszawska Street in Otwock quickly went up in flames. Within weeks, the Wajnberg synagogue was demolished so its bricks could be used to build a Nazi administrative building. Jews were randomly attacked, shorn of their beards, and arbitrarily arrested. The cruelties mounted. Jewish women were forced to strip and wipe the floors of the Nazi barracks with their own undergarments. Still, the Jews of Otwock, like those elsewhere, held out hope for a rapid end to the war and a return to the way things were. With that in mind and to protect their belongings, they signed over their property to non-Jewish Poles for safekeeping.

In December 1940, shortly before Ted turned fifteen, the Nazis established a Jewish ghetto in Otwock, as they had in Warsaw and other Polish cities. To create the ghetto, non-Jewish Poles were forced to vacate their apartments and to "swap" with Jewish residents. The Ludwiczaks were forced out of their home and into a three-room house that had belonged to a Jewish optician. "It was small, but we weren't looking for comfort. Life was so strenuous. People were disappearing overnight. You never knew who would be next. The small stores had all been in Jewish hands. And suddenly the Jewish merchants disappeared, and there was no food—no fruit, no vegetables, no medicine. We were only looking to survive."

On August 19, 1942, the hope of survival for the majority of the Jews of Otwock vanished. At 7 A.M. a truckload of Ukrainian soldiers drove through the main gate of Otwock's ghetto firing their rifles. A limousine carrying S.S. officers followed. A Jewish woman—a dentist and the mother of two young children—rushed forward to show the Ukrainians her official certificates. Without a word, they shot her in the head—the day's first victim but hardly its last. "We heard them as they began rounding up the Jewish population. It took a whole day. The Germans herded them into columns and then into cattle cars, one hundred people in each one, and sent them to Treblinka. It was terrible. It's hard to imagine," Ted whispered.

Under the Nazi master plan, educating Poles, whom the Germans planned to use only in forced labor, was pointless. They ordered gymnasiums to eliminate all academic subjects for Poles and offer only a trade-school curriculum. "But secretly, the teachers taught us the forbidden subjects—history, literature, math. It was very risky. When someone found out what we were being taught, teachers disappeared to the concentration camps. Everyone was quiet."

Ted once came frighteningly close to losing his life. Ironically, the German he had learned to speak in the trade-school classes most likely saved him. One morning, as he was putting on his coat and leaving his house, he looked up to find two German soldiers pointing rifles at him. Behind them, a Nazi van sat idling. Poles arrested off the streets huddled inside it. " 'What's your name? What are you doing?' the soldier asked me. I answered him in German. I said I was a student. And he let me go."

After the war, Ted began a three-year program in accounting at the University of Warsaw thanks to a certificate stipulating that he had completed standard high-school studies in secret. But in 1948, the Stalinist era introduced Poland to mass intimidation, arrests, deportations, and murders. And while Ted was working at a summer job as a dockmaster at the ancient port city of Stettin, now known as Szcezin, he was befriended by an officer on a Greek-owned merchant ship, who helped him stow away on the S.S. *Epiros*. "Poland had changed only from an occupation by the Nazis to an occupation by the Soviets," Ted recalled. "The country was ruined, and I didn't see any future in it."

He believes his artistic impulse was born during the several months the ship was dry-docked in Bombay and when it stopped in Alexandria, where he got the chance to explore, respectively, the Buddhist temples, caves, and ruins of India, and the pyramids of ancient Egypt. In Ancona, Italy, he ran into a group of demobilized World War II soldiers from the Polish II Corps, who warned Ted not to return to their homeland or risk being sent to a Soviet labor camp or, more likely, to his death. He went to Rome to get aid from a Polish refugee organization. While waiting for a visa to the United States, sponsored by an aunt in Flushing, Queens, he survived by giving tours of the ancient city to some of the hundreds of thousands of German-speaking tourists making pilgrimages for the Holy Year of 1950. He assumes that that experience added to the feeling for art that he would later draw upon. "I went to the Colosseum every day. I knew every stone in the place—the obelisks, the columns, the statues," he said. "I must have stored up what I saw and forgot about it until I started carving my own work," he said.

Instead of a visa from the U.S. consulate, he received an invitation to work as a civilian for the United States in Germany (because of the linguistic ability noted on his visa application). In anticipation of the Cold War, the United States was expanding its bases and needed non-Germans fluent in the language. Ted was actually in no rush to get to America and took up the offer. He was sent to Frankfurt, where he became a quartermaster, providing soldiers with food, clothing, equipment, and living quarters at a nearby army base. As American officers began to get transferred to the conflict in Korea, Ted gained seniority at the base. "I had my own jeep and driver, my own staff, and girlfriends. I was like a boss."

He might never have left Germany if his aunt in Flushing hadn't grown impatient (because there were other family members who wanted to be sponsored for visas) and given him an ultimatum. Either come to New York now or forget about it. "I won't sponsor you anymore," she wrote. So on February 3, 1956, Ted Ludwiczak sailed for the United States from Bremerhaven, Germany, aboard a government transport, the USNS *General W. C. Langfitt,* and arrived in New York harbor on Valentine's Day. After briefly working at a Bohack Supermarket in Bayside, stocking shelves, slicing cheese, and cleaning machinery, he took a job at a contact lens factory on Forty-second Street in Manhattan that he had heard about from a landsman from Otwock. Contact lens manufacturers needed employees who were exacting and mathematical. The cutting tools were mostly made in Europe, and prescriptions had to be converted to metrics, and Ted had a facility for math. He wasn't excited about the job, but it was a living. Besides, it had its benefits. "It was close to the library and to Tad's Steakhouse. You could get a good T-bone steak, a baked potato, and a salad for a dollar nineteen. That was great!"

In the late 1950s one of the lab's customers, an ophthalmologist from Westchester County, asked Ted if he would help him open his own contact lens business in Mount Vernon, thirty minutes north of Manhattan. Ted wasn't ready to risk giving up a steady job, so he convinced a friend, Dusan Milkowicz, to go instead. He promised Milkowicz, a foreign national whom he'd met in Germany, where Milkowicz was working as a translator for American intelligence, that he would take the train to Mount Vernon every night after work and on weekends to help. Within a year, the doctor lost his entrepreneurial zeal and offered the business to the two immigrants. By then Ted had saved enough money to cosign a loan, and they bought Optimum Contact Lens for $1,000.

The popularity of contacts grew quickly, and Optimum burgeoned, along with the skill and reputation of its new owners. "He was a very gifted young man," Ted said of his partner as a sad dreaminess entered his face. "We were the only contact lab in Westchester County or even New Jersey. We were going to be millionaires."

Ted's personal life advanced, too. One night, he met Anna Spang, a pretty seventeen-year-old, at a dance in Manhattan. They were soon married, and a daughter, Renee, was born in November 1961.

With the Berlin crisis coming to a boil, world events would once again have a powerful impact on Ted's life. Soviet Premier Nikita Khrushchev was making threats about the future of democratic West Berlin, then surrounded by Soviet-controlled East Germany. President John F. Kennedy responded, first by reminding Americans of the sacrifices that had won Germany's freedom from fascism and then by calling up 117,000 army reservists. Milkowicz was among them. Ted and his partner were convinced the call-up would be only a temporary inconvenience. The following spring, the twenty-nine-year-old Milkowicz, stationed in Georgia, was granted a leave and headed home, with another soldier, to see his fiancée. "They were driving through North Carolina and a big rig ran them over," Ted said. "I was left all alone with the business, and without my friend."

Ted poured himself into the company, but the dream of what might have been receded. "I couldn't expand. I hired someone to help, but it just wasn't the same," he said. He worked longer and harder, while his young wife grew unhappy and restless. She wanted to go out dancing, to spend weekends in the Catskills, to celebrate the Fourth of July. "She wanted to have fun. She couldn't understand why I wouldn't take time off," he said. And it was not long before she left him with his infant daughter (a judge awarded Ted full custody).

It wasn't long after the dust settled that he went looking for a new wife to help him raise Renee. He pulled out his dancing shoes, and in 1963, he met Margaret Riley at a dance at the Roosevelt Hotel in Manhattan. Peggy, as she was known, was thirty, widowed, and the mother of a five-year-old. Her husband, a New York City police officer, had committed suicide a year earlier. Ted asked her to dance, and she says he danced well: "I'm a Catholic from the Bronx. Usually, if you went to a dance, you'd ask someone what parish they were from. If they were from another parish, you never heard from them again. But we just clicked."

A few months later, Ludwiczak and his one-year-old daughter, Renee, moved into Peggy Riley's three-bedroom ranch house on a cul-de-sac in Garnerville, New York. Most of the neighbors were, like Peggy, Catholic natives of the Bronx who began moving to Rockland County when the Tappan Zee Bridge opened the way over the Hudson River in 1955. Ted and Peggy's son, Christopher, was born in 1964, and their daughter, Susan, three years later. With Peggy at home with the children and Ted devoting himself to his business, the family attained a semblance of suburban happiness.

Ted expressed his creativity mostly through his frugality. If he had a mantra, it was: *Don't buy what you can make or fix.* And, according to those who knew him best, he bought little that was new. His children got bicycles, but they were castaways that he repaired and sometimes souped up. But no bike was ever delivered in a factory box. "We were never happy about it. My friends would always say, 'Gee, I wish my dad could do something like that,'" said Christopher, now a FedEx driver. Their friends were less envious of other ways Ted expressed his Old World parsimony. "The worst day of the year came the night before school pictures had to be taken. There'd be a lot of crying, but my father would insist that we go to the basement, where he gave us a haircut. If you look at the pictures now, you'll see a lot of scowls. We were definitely different. You might even see a resemblance between our heads and the ones he carves now," Ted's son joked.

Over the years, Ted transferred his love of the sea into a passion for the Hudson River, and found another outlet for his creative energy when he joined the Seaweed Yacht Club at Stony Point, New York. Founded in the mid-1950s, it was a working-class club, limited to fifty families who paid an annual membership fee of ten dollars. The members, including skilled electricians, plumbers, carpenters, and other construction tradesmen, worked collaboratively to turn a mothballed barge, bought for a dollar, into a family oasis. Ted worked diligently alongside his new compatriots—so diligently that he was eventually given a plaque of gratitude for his dedication. He absorbed skills that, along with those he developed as a lens grinder, were apparently later applied to stone carving. Every day on his way home from work, he stopped off at the club for a couple of beers and, in good weather, to work. His family spent its weekends at the club and on the boats he came to own, including a thirty-seven-foot Chris-Craft. "We had a lot of good parties," Ludwiczak said, delighted at the memory. "It was real America!"

By the late 1970s the good times waned, and Ted's business and domestic life foundered. Communications between husband and wife had never surpassed the obligatory, and the pressures of blending their families eventually overwhelmed them. A painful period of feuding led to separation in 1979 and, eventually, divorce. Taking seventeen-year-old Renee with him, the fifty-three-year-old Ted moved to the house in Haverstraw, which he bought from a financially distressed owner for $13,600—a fraction of what the property alone is worth today. He went to work fixing it up. He cleared the woods at the back of the property, terraced the land, and, over a couple of years, built a winding stairway down to the river. He was, as in all else, regimented.

"Every day, he'd carry down a couple of pails of cement and do a little work," recalled his daughter Renee Sabini, an archivist. "My father has always been good with his hands. For years, my father rented a room to a man who lived upstairs. He had an old Volvo. Once, when it needed a new shock absorber, my father fabricated one for him out of a can. For a long time, it worked. He could fix anything."

By the start of the 1980s, Ted's profession faced extinction. Two decades earlier, a Czech scientist named Otto Wictherle, who discovered the nylon used to make stockings during World War II as well as the material used to make soft lenses, invented the spin-casting machine to produce soft contacts. In the 1970s, Bausch & Lomb introduced the first commercially available soft contact lenses. Within a decade they had become so popular that if Ted hoped to stay in business he would need to learn a new technology. He had neither the desire nor the interest. "I was too old. I didn't want to be bothered with learning all that at that age." In 1986, at the age of sixty, he sold out and retired.

When, two years later, he carved his first heads, his family was astonished. "Yes, I was surprised," exclaimed daughter Susan Santic, a full-time mother. "I think even he was surprised." It was the urge to create art, not the manual skills, that surprised everyone. Ted had, after all, perfected the craft of cutting a 10-millimeter lens blank from a plastic rod. And he could maneuver a diamond tool to cut the lens while it spun at high speeds. "I had that touch," he said, rubbing the roughed ends of his fingertips together and assuming, probably correctly, that all the years of repetitive work with his hands had trained his brain and given his fine motor skills additional finesse. "Even if what you're doing is primitive, you've got to get the details of eyes, the lips, the mouth. You need to create expressions."

Stone, particularly the kinds of stone he uses, can be as unforgiving as glass. Chisel too hard or too deep or choose the wrong place to strike, and all may be lost, he explained.

Ted's work first gained public attention after one of his tenants called a friend and insisted that she had to see Ted's sculpture. Kathy Gardner, a photographer who works for the *Journal News,* a Gannett-owned newspaper, showed up—with her camera—and was amazed by the work. "It was wonderful. The faces had humor and intelligence. I felt privileged to meet Ted." In September 1990 the newspaper published a full-page feature article, accompanied by Gardner's photos. Larger media outlets picked up the story, and Ted was soon fending off unannounced visitors wanting to see and buy his work.

The enthusiastic responses stoked the artist's ambition. The publicity also led art dealer Aarne Anton, a resident of Rockland County, to Ludwiczak's doorstep. "I was astonished. Here's his house, this folk-art environment, in this untouched pocket, almost a forgotten place from the *Twilight Zone.* I got very excited about his work. There aren't many stone carvers out there. At first, I liked the heads in the seawall best. They were really weathered. Some of the noses were broken or smoothed down. Lichens were growing on them. Ropes were hanging down around others. Some heads are battered by logs and objects floating on the river. They continue to change and evolve. That's part of what I like about the work," Anton said.

He also likes that Ted is not a slave to realism. His heads achieve their power organically, their expressions seemingly dictated by the stone. While many of the faces wear bemused expressions, the emotional impulse behind them remains elusive and devoid of obvious sentiment. They possess the electric authenticity of the work of the self-taught, but they are neither precisely primitive nor derivative. Ted isn't interested in trying to appeal to academic, formal, or even folk-art styles. The work, like the artist, is self-reliant and self-contained. "Ted's work is almost antimodern," art dealer Anton said during a conversation in his New York gallery. "He's not making any attempt at arriving at abstraction, though the work has abstract qualities. Some of the faces are like [Alberto] Giacometti's." Anton lifted one of the artist's small heads from a shelf. A band of milky quartz accentuated the roundness of a cheek. "There's a subtlety of expression in his pieces that he gets by using the features native to the stone. In a way, they're closest to Native American sculpture in that what he's trying to do is bring out the spirit in the stone." For others, they evoke ancient Eastern or Buddhist works of stone.

For all the interest in buying pieces, Ted has held his work closely. He doesn't want to haggle over prices and has gladly given over the worry of sales to Anton, who said, "He's financially free of the need to sell for money, but he's still carving. That's a really pure place to be."

In the weeks that followed my introduction to Ted and his work, I found myself trying to sleuth out what had tapped the psychological spring from which his work had suddenly poured after he turned sixty. The first time we talked, he made almost no mention of World War II, and he said almost nothing about his experiences as an adolescent in Otwock. He made only one reference that gave any clue, but it continued to reverberate. When asked about his religion, he had said, "There are so many gods. Besides, after the Holocaust, how could I believe in God?" At the time, he did not care to expand on the comment.

Could the experience of World War II, of seeing his friends and half a town disappear, be at the root of his late blossoming and his compulsive carving of heads? Was he trying unconsciously to reclaim those taken from Otwock? Was he trying to repopulate the world? In the years since World War II, he had scarcely shared his experience under the Nazis, even with his children. His ex-wife Peggy did not recall him ever mentioning it. His friends—including several women artists—say that Ted's sculpture has the joyful and antic qualities of the artist's personality and are best seen as an affirmation of life rather than as memorials for those who were lost. Ted himself declined to probe.

"Everyone wants to know what my motivation was. Who knows? There was what happened during the war, but then I traveled. I married. I had to work and I had to take care of a family. I forgot. Maybe it's coming out now." Then, speaking of his reluctance to part with his work, he said, "I don't like to sell them because they are my family."

While Ted claims to be slowing down, anyone who trails behind him as he climbs the steep riverbank or tries to lift one of the heavy carved stones has good reason to doubt him. Every morning he takes a two-hour walk with his neighbor Norman Alpert, a sixty-three-year-old retired New York City social-studies teacher. They hike through the woods along the river to Rockland Landing and back, three and a half miles each way. Alpert, at six feet, three inches, towers over Ted. They share a love of the way the river is forever changing and an almost transcendental point of view. "Even though I'm Jewish and he's Catholic, we think alike. Sometimes we joke that when we die, we'll come before God and He'll say, 'You were those guys who thought the trees and the river were so beautiful. Come on in!'"

Ted Ludwiczak doesn't get bogged down thinking about his mortality. "My hearing and eyesight and balance are perfect. I don't feel my age. Maybe it's my good genes or maybe it's the spirit of creation. Maybe it's what I eat. Maybe it's that I continue to look for things. After all, you never know what you'll find along the side of the road."

NANCY GAGLIANO

A Time to Teach

"I have a knack with kids."

Nancy Gagliano's second-graders were squirming around, knocking their desks into each other and playing demolition derby between lessons when their teacher flashed her stoplight eyes. They got still quickly.

"You know, you are so lucky that you weren't born when I was born," the youthful sixty-eight-year-old told her pupils at Banyan Elementary School in Sunrise, Florida. Her students were on notice—and delighted. They could tell she was about to begin one of her far-fetched tales. "Because," she picked up, "when I went to school our seats were bolted to the desks, and the desks were bolted to the floor!"

"Oh, no they weren't!" the children shot back serially, certain that "Mrs. G" was making it up. After all, she always seemed to have another apocryphal story to tell them, such as the one about the time she raced her hot-pink stock car at Raceway Park in Chicago or the one in which she was a fashion model.

One day Nancy decided to put an end to doubt and dug up her old photographs. The children were amazed by her feminized Monte Carlo stock car and wowed at the sight of her modeling a cranberry evening gown at a fashion show in Chicago, where she lived before moving to Florida. Then, too, there was the framed black-and-white school photograph of her seated in a sixth-grade classroom in 1950. And yes, the desks were bolted to the floor. Nancy's second graders could even recognize the pretty, erect eleven-year-old girl at the center of the picture as a younger version of their effervescent teacher, though her hands were folded tightly and placed firmly on her desktop instead of flying around like wild birds as the students were used to seeing them do. What the children could not see in the picture was that as she sat in that Southside Chicago classroom fifty-seven years earlier, she knew she would become a teacher. What she did not know, however, was how long it would take for her to realize that ambition.

She was born Nancy Andjelic. It would matter little that she had excelled in every possible way to ensure that her dream of teaching would come true. When she graduated from Bowen High School in 1957, Nancy was class vice president and salutatorian. She also had a reputation as one of the school's best athletes, in particular as a power-hitting member of the girls' softball team (in an age when girl athletes were not as common as today). In senior class voting she won seven of nine superlative titles. School officials had to intervene and divvy up her stockpile among other graduating seniors, crowning Nancy simply "Most Popular." In addition, she worked after school at Ernie's, the local soda fountain, for $10 a weekend, and at the Chicago Public Library for four hours every day after school and on Saturdays.

At the end of her junior year of high school, she went to her mother, Agnes, a beautician who had recently added a gift shop to her hair salon, and her father, Joseph, who worked as a painter at the General Mills plant for forty years. As girls did at the time, she asked her parents, both native-born Americans of Croatian parents, for their permission to apply to college. "They looked at me as if I was nuts," she recalled.

"You don't need to go to college," her mother said. "You're going to marry Jimmy and he's already in college."

"In those days, that was it. The book was closed. You didn't question. You didn't say, Huh? Why? How come? Nothing. I was destroyed, just destroyed. The door was just shut," Nancy told me. Disappointment flared anew in her voice, and her face froze with hurt as the inequity of the scene replayed itself in her mind. "The Monday after I graduated from high school, I went to work at the public library, as assistant librarian, and I worked there until just before my first baby was born."

Nearly fifty years after graduating from high school, at five feet, eight inches tall, Nancy Gagliano was still a striking presence as she circled her seventeen students in their low-slung seats. She conveyed a veteran teacher's energetic authority as she hurried them to open their reading books. Dressed in sharply creased navy blue pants, a red blouse with a robust floral design, and open shoes that showed off nails with bright red polish, she seemed a supercharged and larger-than-life figure as she strode about the twenty-five-by-thirty-eight-foot portable classroom.

Portable classrooms are a fact of life in South Florida's schools. School construction in Broward County has had great difficulty keeping up with decades of booming population growth and immigration. Portable classrooms have been the only solution to its Sisyphean battle with overcrowding. For Nancy, whose classroom is just steps from the main school building, there are benefits to being apart from the hubbub inside the building. And, after all those Chicago winters, she enjoys the advantage of keeping the door open to the Florida light and air as much as the thrill for her students of the occasional sparrow that joins the class.

Her classroom walls were covered with samples of student writing, bright paper butterflies, a chart of the constellations, night-blue illustrations of outer space (including a chart Nancy favors, showing how minuscule our solar system is within the known universe), vocabulary words in English and Spanish, a math board showing place values, a calendar, and the traditional class jobs list. Soil and materials for a Delta Science earthworm project were mounded in the center of the room. "I'm so glad we're done with the maggots," she said when she showed me around the classroom. She was, admittedly, more comfortable in the reading nook with its lively book-tree rug. She noted the sign with her one unbreakable rule: NO SHOES. ("This rug cost too much," she said.)

"Mrs. G, you forgot to collect lunch money," one of the boys called before reading began.

"Okay, if you've got lunch money, bring it up to me," she said. Then, when the students were resettled, she checked to be sure they were all on the correct page before she turned on a tape recorder. A narrator began to read *Chinatown,* a children's book by William Low, in which a child visits New York's Chinatown with his grandmother. Nancy hiked herself onto a desktop at the side of the room and marked the students' planners, as the children read along with the narration. In the story, a boy and his grandmother encounter Chinatown's small-town life in a big city where they watch tai chi practitioners, greet a street cobbler, and visit the fish market, an herbalist, and a kung fu class. The story culminates with a parade celebrating Chinese New Year. *Chinatown* ends with the salutation, *"Gung Hay Fat Choi!"*

The students mumbled the phrase.

"Come on, say it again, like you'd say, 'Happy New Year!'" Nancy said.

"*Gung . . . Hay . . . Fat . . . Choi!*" they yelled in unison and convulsed in laughter. Nancy laughed, too.

Next, she asked students to read aloud, individually. For someone who has not sat in a second-grade classroom in recent years, it was a reminder of how little should be taken for granted—and of how patient and questioning a teacher needs to be to be sure that young children understand what they are reading. When one of the children stumbled while reading the word "composition," the mistake became an opportunity for Nancy to lead her students in an exploration of the ending sound and then of the word's meaning. "We don't use that word, 'composition,' much in elementary school anymore. We use the word 'writing,' but you need to know it," Nancy said.

With playful, unchallenged control, she turned the students' attention from reading to a discussion about the difference between main ideas and supporting ones in the construction of a paragraph. After schoolwide writing scores flatlined three years earlier, her principal, Bruce Voelkel, had made improving student writing a priority at Banyan. And Nancy was determined to not let him down.

"So, what do we call that sentence besides a main idea?" Nancy asked. Her students raised their hands and called out their answers. Most were pretty far off the mark. She repeated her question in a different way, and then another, and then another, until finally a look of comprehension spread across the faces of the children. Then she recapitulated: "A main idea is the most important idea in a piece of writing. So isn't that appropriately named? The main idea? 'Main' means the central, doesn't it? Main Street, isn't that the most important street in town? It has all the important stores and restaurants. The main idea is like that," Nancy said.

Even in this prosaic terrain she remained a study of constant animation. Her red-nail-polished fingers—one with a ring set with a chunk of coral—danced in the air, as she searched this way and that to recast the lesson until certain her students had hold of it.

"I have so much fun with the kids," she said. "I'll put something forty ways until they get it."

Admittedly, her methods can be unorthodox and much of her success depends on her students—and their parents—"getting her." At Banyan, these days, that can mean bridging numerous cultural and language barriers. At the start of the school year, for instance, she watched for two weeks as a short, neatly dressed Bangladeshi woman who spoke little English followed her son, Nasra, into the classroom each morning. "Momma was happy, happy, happy," Nancy trilled. "Every day, she'd come into the classroom and hang up Nasra's jacket and book bag. Then, Momma would put his homework paper and pencils on his desk for him. She was sweet. She meant well, but I realized I had to step in. I said, 'Momma, Nasra must do it himself.' She looked at me, puzzled. I said to her, "If you do it, in third grade, children will laugh, Ha ha ha, at Nasra!" I hated to say it, but I had to. The next day, Momma started to walk into the classroom and stopped at the door. She looked at me, and I knew it was hard for her. I put my arm around her and said, 'Good, Momma, good.' Now, I knew we had only dealt with part of the problem. Nasra is a big boy, but still he sat at his desk, hunched over and cowering.

"Then one day, when one of the other kids answered something easy incorrectly, I did one of my dumb brick things, something that will probably get me in trouble one day. I said, 'I'm going to throw a brick at you for that,' and I hurled an imaginary brick. And all of a sudden, this big belly laugh came out of Nasra, 'Ho, ho, ho.' I didn't even know he was capable of laughing like that. But the brick thing did it. It opened him up. One day, he said, 'Mrs. G, maybe two bricks.' I said, 'You're right, Nasra, maybe two.' I made him my cohort. 'Bam! Bam!' Lots of laughter."

A little while passed, and then one day, Nasra pulled his teacher aside when he came into class: "Mrs. G, I made something for you."

"Oh, yeah, what'd you make me?"

"It shoots three bricks!" he said, offering only his imagination as evidence.

"How does it work?" Nancy asked.

"Put a brick and a brick and a brick, like this, pull back the lever, and let go," he said, conjuring his contraption in the air and flashing a collusive smile at his teacher.

"When the kids said something really dumb that day, I turned to Nasra and I said, 'Now?' He nodded. 'One, two, three,' I said. No one else knew what I was doing, but he was dying with laughter. And from then on, he just opened up. When his parents dropped him off today, they told me how much Nasra loves me and how happy he is and how much he has changed. You know, those are the things. You do nine things wrong and then you do one good and right. These things don't show up in the curriculum, but they're often what matters most."

The first day I visited, Nancy was not about to let the opportunity of having a writer in her class go unused. With a persuasiveness that was impossible to resist, she asked me to tell her class how I became a writer. I first became interested in writing, I told them, when I was eight, in third grade, and lived just thirty minutes away from Tamarac, in Hollywood. In 1958, my older brother Geoff and his best friend Buddy Nevins started a newspaper and enlisted me as their reporter. I wrote one story that got a lot of attention. It was about a boy who leaped from a dresser onto his parents' bed while playing Zorro. The boy's teeth, still attached to his mouth, sank into the headboard and stuck. His frantic babysitter called the police.

The police called the closest dentist, who, as luck would have it, was the boy's father. I explained, too, how, in a world before computers and cell phones, which all of the students in the classroom had, we printed our one-page newspaper on something called a mimeograph machine and sold it on store counters for a nickel. The *Miami Herald* picked up my story and boxed it on its front page along with an article about *The Item*, our newspaper. The students were pleased with my tale, but, a bit unsettling for me, they wanted to know just who Zorro was and what a mimeograph machine and the *Miami Herald* were.

At recess, Nancy marched her class double-file to the playground. Some of the children went off to play kickball on the grass while Nancy watched the children who began climbing the jungle gym, hanging from rings, and playing on the swing set. Even though it was time for them to run freely, several children, some from other classes, gravitated to Nancy and seemed compelled to touch base with her regularly. A few children began to talk giddily to me about "Mrs. G." Shenaya, a heavyset girl, bubbled, "I like Mrs. G because she's funny and because she tells great stories and because she's nice." Then she ran off to swing from the rings. When she leaped for them, she fell onto the black rubber mat and began to cry.

Nancy carefully comforted her. She did so with the practice of a woman who has been drying tears for five decades, and instinctively knows the difference between physical injury and humiliation. But she showed no sign of doubting the girl's complaint. She hugged Shenaya and soothed her with maternal intelligence. Then she called over two other girls and asked them to escort their classmate to the nurse. Sniffling, the girl hobbled off. "They don't want you to touch the children anymore, these days, but sometimes you just have to," Nancy said.

Since she was hired to teach full-time four years ago, Nancy Gagliano has not only won the affection of her students, she has won the admiration of the administration, fellow faculty members, and parents. Elisha Carr's son, Nathan, entered Nancy's class in 2006. He was undersized, fearful, and withdrawn, the result, his mother said, of a bad experience in first grade. But it was forgotten and his behavior changed in Nancy's class.

"She brought my son out of his shell. By the end of the year, he was a different child. She's very loving, caring, and nurturing. Not every teacher provides that. Her teaching style made him comfortable. It's true, she does expect a lot, but when her students go into third grade, it's easier for them to make the transition. Nathan has been on the honor roll every semester since he had Nancy in second grade. She's an amazing teacher," Carr said. In fact, she was so impressed by Nancy that, at thirty-one, she adopted her as a mentor and returned to college to become a teacher, too.

Until she moved to Florida in 1998, Nancy Gagliano lived her entire life in Chicago and, once married, in Hegewisch, a small, tightly knit neighborhood on Chicago's far South Side, founded in 1883 by industrialist Achilles Hegewisch. Hegewisch became a working-class enclave for Polish-Americans and the families of Chicago's police, firefighters, teachers, and steelworkers, a distinction it retains.

Nancy Andjelic and Jim Gagliano grew up a couple of blocks apart, just west of Calumet Park and Lake Michigan. They met one summer when they were fourteen and sixteen, respectively. She had gone on an outing to Wicker Park pool with a teen group from St. George's Catholic Church. "I was standing with my friend Sandy and I see this handsome *dago,* with this beautiful build, climb up to the board. More often than not, kids would turn around and go back down the ladder, or just jump, it was so high. But this guy does a perfect swan dive into the pool. After that, he climbs out of the pool and goes back up the ladder and does a perfect jackknife. So I asked Sandy, 'Who is that?'"

It was James Salvatore Gagliano Jr., otherwise known as Jim, who, it turned out, was Sandy's boyfriend's good friend. Nancy and Jim were introduced and, riding home on the bus that night, exchanged their first kiss. Jim likes to tell a different tall-tale version of their meeting. "One day I was walking home and passed her house. I saw her swinging a giant sledgehammer, and with just a few blows, she demolished a garage shed. That's when I knew that she was the girl for me."

Nancy credits her mother's voracious reading habits with her early passion for the library. Every two weeks her mother sent Nancy to the local branch of the Chicago Public Library with a red leather shopping bag to pick up a new batch of books, principally mysteries, that the librarian, Miss LaPrez, selected for her. What most interested Nancy, though, were not the books themselves. It was the graceful way the assistant librarian checked them out. "She was a tall girl named Janice Smith, and she had the most beautiful hands and fingers you can imagine. I would stand there and watch her take each card out of its book and then stamp it, perfectly on the line, with those beautiful hands and nails, with the tip of a pencil-like marker. It was like heaven. It was an art. And I thought, *I want to do that*." When she was fourteen, she told Miss LaPrez as much. "Come here when you're sixteen," Miss LaPrez said. The morning of her sixteenth birthday, Nancy was at the library when it opened. Miss LaPrez sent her downtown to fill out the necessary papers so she could hire her. After graduating from high school, she became the assistant librarian, only taking time off in 1960 to go on her honeymoon with Jim at the Castaways Motel in Miami Beach. She quit a month before her first son, Jimmy, was born the following year. In quick succession, she gave birth to two more sons, Joey and John, and relished her role as a mother.

But the joy of motherhood vanished for a while after Monday night, April 18, 1966. Instead of watching Elizabeth Taylor receive an Oscar at the Academy Awards on television, Nancy found herself waiting for the pediatrician to make a house call to treat her husband and sons Jimmy and John, then five and two years old respectively, for the flu. Citing the close quarters that they were living in, Dr. Harvey DeBofsky, then the junior member of the pediatric practice, gave shots to the entire family, even Nancy and Joey, age four, who had no apparent symptoms. Jim spent the next day on the couch, watching the three boys work in coloring books on the living room floor.

On Wednesday morning, everyone was awake by 9 A.M. except for Joey. "I called in, 'C'mon, Joey, get up, Lazy Bones, time to get up!' I went into the boys' room. Joey was lying there in his crib, completely discolored and lifeless. I knew immediately that he was gone." Nancy ran out of the room, screaming to Jim to call the fire department and then out of the house and into a neighbor's house, crying, "Joey's dead! Joey's dead!"

As she recounted the tragedy on the screened patio of her house in Tamarac, Nancy's eyes filled with tears. She stopped and gazed out at a placid lagoon. An ibis stood still at its edge.

"There wasn't any trauma. There wasn't any suffering. It was an easy death for him. God just took him. I went nuts. Just went nuts. It was really awful. There was no warning and nothing anyone could do. It was just supposed to happen. And still I near died."

A clerk in the coroner's office told the Gaglianos that night that the cause of Joey's death was lower lumbar pneumonia. It seemed implausible to them because he had shown no signs of illness, but the couple was so grief-stricken they never questioned what they were told.

Life recovered in the house with the births of daughters Lisa and

Denise in successive years. Of course, quarters in the 1,108-square-foot house in Hegewisch were always tight—as tight as a family budget that depended on Jim's modest salary as cost accountant for Interlake Steel. But as long as there were children around, Nancy says she was happy in her life. "As a mother, she was always a natural teacher," said her oldest son Jim. "She was always on top of things. All of my friends respected her. She treated us as kids, but she treated us as adults, too. If we toed the line with her, we were the best. If we crossed her, she let us know it." She was an active participant in the schools' PTAs, a leader of the Babe Ruth baseball league, and a softball coach.

But when her daughter Denise entered third grade, or, as Nancy would say, "When the dirty rats left me alone with no one to play with," she became restless. She needed something to keep her occupied and made her first foray into business, as a Mary Kay Cosmetics representative. Knowing just about every family in the four hundred homes of Hegewisch and possessing good looks and a cheerfully persuasive personality, Nancy did well. She could almost always count on making $200 at each Mary Kay party.

Soon, however, the occasional night work was not enough to satisfy her. She applied for a teacher's aide job at a local elementary school. As she was waiting to be interviewed for the job, she heard someone in the principal's office say, "Hey, looks like we got our new school secretary." She had no idea that the speaker was referring to her, and remained incredulous even when the principal greeted her and asked her to step outside. He informed her that he wanted to hire her as the school secretary. "No," she protested, "I'm the school aide."

"I'm sorry, we've already hired a school aide," the principal said.

"No, there's some mistake," Nancy said, fearing that her chances of working in a classroom were slipping away again.

The principal ushered her back into the office and, typing the air with his fingers, asked Nancy if she could type. When she said she could not, the principal said, "That's okay, you'll do fine. I'll teach you." The next day was the first day of school. One after another, teachers paraded before her demanding supplies, book orders, and schedules, and headed off to classrooms where Nancy craved to be. After a couple of years, because of cutbacks, Nancy got bumped from her job to one as a part-time clerk in two of Chicago's toughest elementary schools, Atgeld and Kershaw. Shootings outside the schools were frighteningly routine in those days. On more than one occasion Nancy considered herself lucky that she had been working at one school when a shooting occurred outside the other.

Perhaps it was the pressures of the time or that the trauma of Joey's death just caught up with Jim and Nancy's marriage, but after months of trying fruitlessly to induce Jim to talk about the state of their marriage, Nancy went to a lawyer and filed for divorce. Jim wouldn't discuss it. He wouldn't answer legal papers. And he wouldn't go to court. In 1981, after twenty-one years of marriage, the couple was divorced. It is an event that both of the Gaglianos gloss over when describing their lives, and not without reason. On the day that Jim moved out of the family house, he asked Nancy for a Saturday night date to the movies. "Right there, he had me all over again," Nancy recalled. They continued to see each other exclusively for the next seven years.

Then Jim proposed marriage for a second time. Nancy said that before they could marry again, they needed to live together. Three years after Jim moved back home, ten years after their separation, they re-wed on what would have been their thirtieth anniversary. "I know, we're nutty," she said.

Meanwhile, before the divorce, in the spring of 1980, life on Chicago's Southeast Side, once a leading center for steel production in the United States, had also changed. The area suffered a major blow when Wisconsin Steel Works closed its gates and tossed out three thousand workers. Symbolically, it marked the beginning of the end of Chicago's industrial might. Other plants followed. The South Chicago Development Corporation was established to retrain the droves of unemployed steelworkers. The then-powerful South Side political boss Ed Vrydoliak hired Nancy as the program's office manager. She was a quick study and was soon promoted to assistant director, for $18,000 a year. It proved an important step. She leveraged that work, first into a job as a loan officer for a Hartford, Connecticut–based insurance company. She went from there to Montgomery Ward, the Chicago catalog and department store chain, once the nation's largest retailer, and worked as an executive secretary to one of the company's vice presidents.

Nancy's prospects brightened still more when she came across an advertisement for a then-novel program at St. Joseph's College in suburban Indiana. By documenting their life experiences, perspective students could receive college credits and reduce the total number of credits needed to receive a degree. Nancy, then forty-five, spent months tracking down information and gathering testimonials for her various work experiences. When Jim delivered five bound notebooks she had compiled, the college's dean was astonished. He granted her more than sixty credits. At once, Nancy Gagliano was college bound and nearly half finished.

Her corporate ascent ended abruptly four years later. She came down with the flu and for the first time since starting work at Montgomery Ward she had to call in sick. She returned to work a few days later. But by 10 A.M. her first day back, she slumped over her desk and could barely move. Eventually, she pushed herself up, walked to her car, and drove the 175 blocks to the nearest clinic. She collapsed as she entered its doors and was rushed to the hospital. Doctors performed a battery of tests, but were stumped. Nancy was sent home, but got no better. Day after day, she lay in bed, increasingly filled with despair.

"Everyone thought I was dying. To get out of bed, I had to hang on to the walls," she said. Finally, on a hunch, one of her doctors tested her for lupus, Epstein Barr, and rheumatoid arthritis. She tested positive for all three, a hallmark of chronic fatigue syndrome.

"She was flat on her back for months. We were lucky I worked close by then and could come home and feed her lunch," her husband, Jim, said. When she didn't return to work by Labor Day, Montgomery Ward terminated her without benefits, though she was literally days from being vested with long-term benefits. "They didn't want to get stuck. I could have managed to come in for a day or two. When I found out that they were pushing me out, I said, 'You know what you're doing is crooked.' But I didn't have the strength to fight." (Two years later, Montgomery Ward went under.)

Despite bouts of debilitating exhaustion, after five years of night school, Nancy finished her studies at St. Joseph's and was awarded a bachelor's degree in business administration in 1990. At age fifty, with the last of her children in college and the others establishing lives of their own, Nancy finally had the credential she needed to substitute teach in Chicago, at least on the days she felt strong enough. She had little expectation that she would ever be well enough to do more.

Fate is formidable. In August 1992, Hurricane Andrew, the second-most-destructive hurricane in United States history, slammed into southeast Florida at Homestead, causing $26.5 billion of damage. Some eighty thousand housing units were destroyed or badly damaged. One hundred sixty thousand people were left homeless, and forty-three were killed. Nancy's daughter Denise had recently started work for Prudential Insurance and volunteered to go to Florida for the company for a year to help with the massive number of insurance claims. When her year was up, she decided to stay in Florida permanently and found an apartment to buy. She asked Nancy to drive down from Chicago to take a look. Nancy had just walked into her daughter's place and dropped her bags when Denise said, "Mom, let's go."

"Where are we going?"

"I found you and Dad a house."

The "What?" was barely out of Nancy's mouth before mother and daughter were on their way. "As soon as the saleswoman opened the front door and I saw the water out there [through the sliding glass doors at the back of the house], I did everything a buyer's not supposed to do. I dug my nails into my daughter's arm and I screamed, 'Oh, my God! Oh, my God!' She said, 'What's wrong with you?' I said, 'I don't know, Denise, I just want this house.'"

Nancy phoned Jim at his office. Hearing her voice, he, too, asked what was wrong. "Nothing," she said.

"Then why are you calling me?" he asked.

"You've got to drive down here on Monday," Nancy said.

"What's wrong?" he repeated.

"I think we're buying a house," she said. Then she heard the phone drop.

As it turned out, the Gaglianos' son John, a professional golf instructor in Illinois, was about to drive down to Florida, and gave his dad a lift. Within a week, the Gaglianos' offer was accepted and financing approved to buy Nancy's dream house. That was 1994. "It took another four years for Yakshemash to finally retire," Nancy said, referring to Jim. In preparation, Nancy began subbing more in Chicago and planned to continue to substitute in Florida when she and Jim retired there. She would at least realize a bit of her girlhood ambition.

A lifetime of cigarette smoking, however, had already caught up with Jim. A stellar athlete once known around Chicago's baseball diamonds for his silky play and sure glove at second base as well as a former all-city basketball star, Jim had been diagnosed with emphysema. X-rays showed the right lung black halfway up. "It's sad; when he was young, he was so athletic he could have been a decathlon champ! No kidding, he played every sport there was, and played them well. God gave him an exceptional body, and he just destroyed it." As he approached sixty, the disease made it hard for him to endure the Chicago winter. He agreed to retire at the end of May 1998.

With a date for retirement in hand, Nancy took charge. She fixed a firm price of $110,000 on the little house the Gaglianos had inhabited for thirty-seven years—and soon had buyers. Nancy filled out the paperwork for substitute teaching in Florida and mailed it to the state Department of Education along with a check for $56. On April 28, she finished packing the family Hi-Lo camper with everything that was precious to her, including her bedroom set and two heirloom sewing machines, hooked the camper to her prized 1988 black Lincoln Town Car, and pulled out of the driveway in Hegewisch, with her son, Jim, his wife, and three kids on the curb to wave her off.

By the time schools opened in August, Nancy had plotted out routes to the seven elementary schools nearest her new home on a Broward County School Board map. She began subbing at each of the schools and weeding out some. There were those where she felt poorly treated, dismissed as a "lowly sub," and she eliminated them. She was most happy at Banyan. She liked the pleasant, upbeat, and efficient school secretary, Nancy Farndell, and principal Voelkel. They made Nancy feel welcome and wanted. She became a regular substitute at the school over the next three and a half years. Then, during the 2001–2002 school year, Voelkel told her that a second-grade teacher was taking maternity leave in January and offered her the interim position. "I jumped at it. And I just loved it. I had found my home. I had a class of thirty second-graders! It was wonderful," she recalled, her face lighting up and her voice as animated as if she had just received the news.

The offer proved critical in unexpected ways. Shortly after Nancy accepted the job, Jim Gagliano noticed that health insurance deductions hadn't been taken out of his retirement check. When he called Chicago to inquire, he discovered that Interlake Steel had gone out of business, and his and Nancy's medical insurance had been discontinued. "Trick or treat!" Nancy said.

While most of the symptoms of her chronic fatigue syndrome had vanished, the effects of Jim's emphysema were worsening. With the costs of oxygen and medications escalating, they faced certain financial ruin. After much discussion, their insurer agreed to let them pick up insurance in Florida. But they could not possibly sustain the premium of $1,370 a month. Luckily, Nancy's new paycheck allowed them to hold their ground until Jim's Medicare kicked in a few months later.

Nancy delighted in the experience of having her own class, and one day near the end of the year, she approached the principal's secretary. She wanted to ask Voelkel a question. "He's such a good guy, I'm afraid he'll lie," she sputtered. "So I figured if I asked you to ask him, he would tell you the truth." Farndell was puzzled. It wasn't like Nancy Gagliano to be indirect or fearful. "My God, Nancy, what is the question?" she said.

"I would like to become a full-time teacher, but is there a principal in his right mind who would hire a sixty-six-year-old woman as a new teacher?" she asked.

Nancy had already computed that it would take her three years to complete the twelve basic elementary education courses, five ESOL (English as a second language) courses, and three state exams required for certification by the State of Florida. Farndell laughed and headed down the hall to the principal's office. The would-be teacher didn't know what to do with herself while she waited. She went into the faculty mailroom and pretended to look for her mail. Then she heard the principal's secretary yell, "Nancy, Mr. Voelkel says that no principal in his right mind would hire an old bag like you to be a teacher!"

Knowing with certainty that Mr. Voelkel was too sincere to ever say anything of the kind, she just imagined him raising his eyes and thinking, *God deliver me from such women!* Realizing that she was about to step across the threshold to the dream of her lifetime, Nancy Gagliano doubled over in laughing disbelief.

She began her course work that summer and, though it did take her three years to complete, as soon as a regular full-time second-grade teaching position opened for the start of the 2002–2003 school year, Voelkel hired Nancy.

"I don't look at age. I look at the person. Life experience brings a lot to the teacher and the classroom. I know this may get me in trouble with some, but a college degree doesn't necessarily make you a teacher. It's your understanding of children and your compassion for them. It's your ability to relate to children and get across concepts that is most important," said Voelkel, a big, pale, gentle man. A career educator, he had been the principal at Banyan for twelve years. During that time, he frequently had to struggle with changing teaching requirements to meet augmented state standards and new statewide student testing. Finding qualified teachers for an expanding student population was not easy, he said. He was already anticipating the difficulties that would arise when his school population was divided in 2009, for the fourth time in his tenure. By the spring of 2008, the school's population of 995 had surpassed its designed capacity by more than two hundred students. (In 2007–2008, 10 percent of the students were Asian, 35 percent black, 20 percent Hispanic, and 35 percent white.)

As an educator, Voelkel was tickled by Nancy's vivacity and motivation. Her complete dedication to her students has been even more impressive, he said.

"She has the kids' best interest at heart, and that's what's important. She will go out of her way to make accommodations for a child. She wants kids to succeed. We're a school that has a lot of after-school events, and Nancy is always there. She doesn't have to be, but she is. If it's McDonald's Night or Dairy Queen Night, Nancy is there, and she'll probably bring a camera to take pictures of the kids." In a school with so much transition, Nancy's energetic, engaged, and nurturing presence is critical.

Typically, she arrives at school at 7:30 A.M. She is often still in her portable classroom, grading papers or preparing her lessons for the next day, long after dismissal. Her colleagues love to tell the story of the night she became so distracted by her work, she lost track of time. It was already 7 P.M. when she realized she needed to get home to make dinner for Jim. She hurried from her portable classroom and across the walkway to school's rear entrance. But the door was locked, and the only way to exit the fenced-in school was through the main building's front door. She banged on the back door and called out, but no one answered. Everyone else, it seemed, had left for the night. Afraid of the embarrassment she would suffer, but believing she had no choice, she called the police. "I'm a teacher and I'm locked in at Banyan. You've got to get me out of here. I'm too old for this," she said.

While the officer was recovering from his laughter, a janitor appeared at Nancy's door. "It's Tony! It's Tony! I'm saved!" she shouted.

Her co-teacher, Jody Stapleton, who has three decades of teaching experience, says the first time he saw Nancy marching her second-graders along a sidewalk at the school, he assumed—watching the children's cooperative behavior—that she was a veteran teacher. It was only later, when he discovered a minor gaffe—she was sending home the next marking period's empty report cards with the graded report cards—that he learned she was a rookie. He had the students hand over the ungraded report cards before they left the classroom. "I knew I would like Nance after that because she came to me and said, 'Thank you, Jo, thank you for saving me.' She wasn't at all defensive," he said.

His appreciation of her grew steadily afterward. "She loves her students and will do anything for them. Her mothering skills kick in a lot, and though a lot of us have had that trained out of us, she knows how to use it. She's organized, high energy, and full of life. As all good teachers, she questions everything she does. I look forward to coming to school every day because of her." Stapleton, at fifty-two, had hoped to retire in a couple of years, but his investments in rental properties have suffered badly and his retirement will probably be postponed for a decade. "I sometimes wonder how I'm going to do it, then I look at Nancy and I laugh. If she can do it, I can. She's a role model to me."

As I watched Nancy Gagliano teach her second-grade class, I found my mind drifting a bit. What could be more of a challenge or more worthy of the word "success"? What could be of greater significance than becoming a master teacher of second-graders and helping them build a foundation for their own successful lives?

It's doubtful that her students will even consider Nancy's age when, years hence, they look back at their own class photo to remember who they were and see her standing there. More likely, they will remember her stories, her sense of humor, her warmth, and her ferocious determination to teach them.

"I'll continue to teach for a few more years, until after Jim is gone," Nancy told me in her quietest voice. "Then, who knows?"

She was modest and cheerful about what she had accomplished. Maybe if she had started earlier, she said, or had more seasoning, she might have been better at analyzing her students' learning issues or at formulating teaching practices. "But as a teacher, I think I'm very good at making them understand what they need to know. Where I shine is being someone they know they can trust. Someone they can come to with their problems, in the classroom and outside. I have a knack with kids."

Reflecting Success

"What keeps me going . . . ?
The universal 'oohs' and 'aahs.'"

In October 1989, single mom Myrna Hoffman faced a minor dilemma. Her daughter, Nell, was turning seven in Montclair, New Jersey, an affluent and competitively child-centered suburb where it had become de rigueur for parents to stage elaborate theme parties for their children's birthdays. Nell petitioned innocently for something special of her own. Myrna was then forty-seven years old and struggling, financially and emotionally, with the protracted aftermath of an ugly divorce. She did not have the wherewithal to indulge her dark-haired second-grader with a bash. But an artist, illustrator, animator, and educator, Myrna was nothing if not resourceful.

When parents arrived to pick up their children after Nell's party, they opened the burgundy-colored door of Hoffman's large, century-old clapboard house on Montclair Avenue and were baffled by the quiet that greeted them. "Where are the kids?" they asked one after another.

Each time, Myrna directed the parents to gaze into the dining room. There the seven rapt young guests and Nell were huddled over mirrored paper cups on the cherrywood dining table. The cups were sitting on sheets of paper on which Myrna had made mysterious line drawings. The children were coloring intently between the lines with crayons and giggling. It quickly became apparent that commonplace coloring book pictures alone were not generating their intense concentration or their laughter. Every time they looked up from coloring the distorted shapes on the pages before them and at the mirrored cups, they saw something magical. Their drawings were somehow being transformed into their own vivid versions of Mickey Mouse and Minnie Mouse. Parents joined their children, exhaling delighted "oohs" and "aahs."

"It was just an entertainment for me and for Nelly," Myrna said. But the parents saw more than just amusement in Myrna's creative birthday party activity. "They kept saying, 'You've got a business there. You've got to do something with it!'"

So began Myrna Hoffman's twenty-year, multi-chaptered, sometimes treacherous entrepreneurial epic. The enthusiastic parents promised to find investors and stoked Myrna's belief in what she had made, her ambition, and her daring. She soon formed her own educational art activities and toy company, which she named Ooz & Oz to echo the beguiled responses. She was possessed by a novice's naïveté as she launched her quest to make her art toy as familiar to American households as such iconic toys as Etch-a-Sketch and Slinky. That has not happened yet, as close as she has come during two decades. Instead of a fairy-tale ending of a fat fortune made, she has a cache of nineteen national toy awards and a going business that seems poised for a commercial breakthrough. But even without crossing the tipping point, to use Malcolm Gladwell's phrase, hers is no small accomplishment. Her story is an example of gutsiness, of iconoclastic achievement that comes from personal resilience, creative resourcefulness, and faithful devotion to an idea.

The seeds of her toy were sown one day, a decade before Nell's birthday party, when Myrna happened into an exhibit in a pocket museum at Harvard University in Cambridge, Massachusetts. She was then still single, childless, in her thirties, and working as a free-lance technical illustrator and an animator at MIT and Harvard. She was drawn to the little exhibit by its display of ancient optical astrolabes, sextants, and other esoteric brass optical instruments and devices for measuring distances and movements of planetary objects and stars.

"I loved that stuff. I had always been fascinated by mirrors and reflections. Among the optical instruments, one caught my eye. It was a skinny, shiny cigar tube standing on a little, unrecognizable drawing. When I saw Puss and Boots reflected on the tube, I asked myself, *How do they do that? How?*"

That was Myrna's first encounter with an anamorphoscope, a curved reflective cylinder on which a deformed image appears in its true shape. "I fell in love with it and wanted to figure out how it was done. It stuck with me," Myrna said, nodding toward the living room of the house in West Seattle, Washington, where she now lives. Mirrored cones and pyramids of various sizes sparkled on a glass coffee table, a desk, and a mantelpiece. Her shelves held books about mirror art and optical illusions. File drawers were filled with historical information about anamorphosis. A buoyant, five-foot-three-inch woman with styled white hair, Hoffman, at sixty-seven, proclaimed, "Everything of mine is mirrors."

After her introduction to anamorphosis at the Harvard exhibit, Myrna began obsessively researching its history and techniques in her spare time. (At the time, there were few books readily available on the subject and, of course, no Internet from which to instantly fetch information.) In response to written inquiries, curators at the Science Museum in London sent Myrna images of anamorphosis and photostatic copies of pages on the subject from the 1830 edition of the *Edinburgh Encyclopedia*. It reproduced grids and the mathematics of plotting used by artists to distort the design on a page in a way that a rounded mirror would reconstitute into art.

She also learned about the long and fascinating history of anamorphosis as an art form. It is well known that Leonardo da Vinci was intensely interested in using mirrors for his art. Among other things, he used mirrors to critique his paintings, according to Mark Pendergrast in his absorbing book *Mirror Mirror: A History of the Human Love Affair with Reflection*. "Why does a painting seem better inside a mirror than outside it?" da Vinci puzzled in his notebook, a question he posed using a mirror-writing technique in which characters can only be deciphered with the aid of a mirror.

Such esoteric aesthetics were far removed from the world that Myrna was born into in 1942. Growing up in Union, New Jersey, the first of two daughters of Victor Goldblatt, a successful accountant, and his wife, Lillian, a homemaker, she considered herself the black sheep of the family. Her childhood was "ninety-eight percent miserable," a condition she attributes to her father's persistently critical nature. "Nothing was ever good enough. 'Are you sure you've looked at this?'" she recalled being asked regularly, as if everything one did could be computed like a column of figures. Her greatest accomplishment as a child was winning a citywide poster contest on the unfortunately worded theme of "Help the Helpless. Give to Sister Kenny." Myrna turned the language around and created a poster that read: "Help the Helpful. Give to Sister Kenny." Her victory validated a vague sense that she possessed creative talent.

Still, she had little idea what she wanted to pursue when she left home for Syracuse University. She graduated with a degree in fine arts in 1965 and then moved to Cambridge, Massachusetts, where she began work on a master in art education degree at Lesley University.

She moved to Montclair, New Jersey, in 1978 and taught art at a school for the developmentally disabled. The next year, she married a lawyer six months after meeting him at a party. Nell was born in October 1982, the day before Myrna turned forty. Myrna was divorced three years later, after six years of marriage.

Since she first stumbled on mirror art, she has doggedly experimented with anamorphosis. She began by manipulating illustrations on the page over and over again until she nailed the right amount of distortion of an image and, reflected upward, it reassembled itself into a recognizable image on a reflective cylinder, usually placed near the top of the drawing. It is an admittedly difficult concept to grasp in the abstract. But seen and experienced, it beguiles and captivates. "I just did it for the fun of it. It was trial and error. I kept looking in the mirror and adjusting as I went, to get my drawing right," she said. "After a while, your brain starts to lay down new neural pathways, and you know how to distort the images to make them work."

A few months later, she hired a mathematician and a computer programmer, who used the grids she had gotten from the *Edinburgh Encyclopedia* to create a proprietary computer program that would allow her to morph any image, including photographs. She also commissioned illustrators to make drawings she could morph with the help of the computer program. She included them, along with a Mylar-wrapped cup, in a children's coloring activity kit, which she patented. Now she had a product to sell, and investors "wanted in on it from the beginning. But they usually wanted a big chunk. Or they wanted to put their nephews in charge. But at that time, I didn't really need the money. I knew who I wanted to work with and what I wanted to keep. I didn't want to give up creative rights and control. And I still don't."

However, keeping tight control of her idea and spending her own money meant sacrifice and financial struggle, especially after alimony and child support were reduced and she was forced to sell the house in Montclair. She and Nell moved into a vacant apartment Myrna's mother owned in nearby West Orange. "I recall the shock of realizing my financial situation. *How can I make money and still be there for my daughter? What do I have that I can turn into an advantage?*"

To help pay the bills, Myrna went to work as a wallpaper hanger. "I was a mommy and I had to make ends meet. I'd renovated three houses, I'd torn down walls, I'd done tiling and Sheetrocking, and I was really good at hanging wallpaper. My girlfriends' husbands always used to call me for advice on laying floors and other things. So I registered myself at a paint store in West Orange" and started getting jobs, she said.

Meanwhile, she pushed forward with her product. By 1991, she began to self-manufacture three "Party Fun & Favors" kits that contained an assortment of morphed images and a reflective cup on which drawings took shape as they were colored in. The following year, a friend asked Myrna to make an activity kit to keep her kids entertained during a plane ride to Europe. Myrna whipped up what she dubbed the Awesome Art Activities Kit "Circus," an anamorphic coloring kit designed to fit on an airplane tray table. Her friend was so ecstatic about how well it worked, Myrna brought it to the 1993 Toy Fair for its debut. And Ooz & Oz won its first recognition: a gold "Doing and Learning" award from Parents' Choice, the nation's oldest nonprofit guide to children's media and toys. "To get the award right out of the box was incredible," Myrna said.

Over the next year, Myrna found herself awash in more than $750,000 in purchase orders, pro forma invoices, and earnest inquiries from buyers in twenty-eight countries. But as a one-woman company without a lot of capital, she could not possibly manufacture the merchandise to fulfill those orders. So when representatives of stationery giant Pentech International, which manufactured and sold art and school supplies, offered to license and distribute the Ooz & Oz line of products, Myrna signed a two-year contract and sold all her existing stock of kits to the stationery company. Pentech was then reporting nearly $60 million in annual sales. The New Jersey company had licensing agreements with Walt Disney, Coca-Cola, the NFL, the NHL, and the NBA, and sold its products through Wal-Mart, Kmart, and Target, among other stores. Myrna figured she was on the cusp of the big payoff.

But, in what seemed like the next breath, Pentech's sales plummeted in its newly formed teen cosmetics line, it lost a costly patent infringement case, and it became mired in internal disputes. The company never made or sold a single one of Myrna's toys. Worse, Myrna was prohibited by contract from contacting potential customers. And despite her pleas—evidenced in ample correspondence between Myrna and the company's president—Pentech never informed her potential customers that it had taken over her toy line or when it might deliver on orders. "Customers, like Radio Shack, reserve money and shelf space for purchase orders. When items do not materialize or when there's no communication from the manufacturer," the buyer loses trust, she said. "Pentech tied me up for two years, and for two years I could not do anything. They wouldn't manufacture and they wouldn't contact my customers. I kept begging them, 'Let them know where things stand.' But they wouldn't. They had lawyers and deep pockets, and all I had was me. It was excruciating. They had taken this wonderful idea and this wonderful company of mine and basically killed it. It hurt so much I couldn't go into toy stores for almost ten years."

She was so devastated that the details of that period remain a blur to her. "You're trying to make ends meet, you're trying to raise a child, you're fighting in court, your heart is broken because your little pot of gold at the end of the rainbow has been buried or trashed or something. It's hard to go back to all of that."

After two troubling local events—the mother of one of Nell's friends was carjacked from her home in Nutley, New Jersey, and killed, and a former postal worker killed four people at a small post office in Montclair—and after her mother put the condo in West Orange up for sale, Myrna decided to move to Falls Church, Virginia, where she had friends. Serendipitously, the move proved an unexpected boon for mother and daughter, then fifty-three and thirteen, respectively.

Myrna got jobs teaching art in the Fairfax and Alexandria schools. And after completing eighth grade and taking competitive entrance exams, Nell, a precocious learner, was admitted to the Thomas Jefferson High School for Science and Technology, considered one of the nation's best high schools. Nell did extremely well there—particularly in playwriting and Shakespearean studies—and made a slew of new friends. With her daughter happy and achieving, Myrna returned to experimenting with anamorphosis, using it to whet the appetites of her students for art and drawing. Her toy was moribund, but her obsession was intact.

Six years later, when she was fifty-eight and Nell was heading off to Carnegie Mellon University (where she majored in computer sciences and Japanese and minored in robotics), Myrna spotted a small article in the local newspaper. It reported the opening of the Women's Business Center of Northern Virginia, with the support of the federal Small Business Administration. The center then amounted to a small classroom with five computers and two telephones. After her crushing experience with Pentech, she was almost phobic about business. But in the spring of 2001, she got up the nerve to visit the women's business center. "When I strolled in, they put an arm around me and they gave me chocolates and cookies and they asked me, they really asked me, how they could help," she said. "It was a very welcoming environment. The whole intimidation factor disappeared." "I said to myself, *You have no more excuses, your daughter is safely ensconced, you have time to yourself. Use it!* I wanted to confront myself because I had been avoiding finding out what had gone wrong and how to fix it. I didn't have a specific question because there was so much I didn't know and so much I needed to know."

When Myrna first appeared at the center, "she was in bad straits and very discouraged," recalled Barbara Wrigley, the center's founding and executive director. "Myrna is not an uneducated woman, but she had been taken advantage of because she had a small, woman-owned company, and she was older." In her assessment, Myrna had fallen prey to one of the most common mistakes made by first-time women entrepreneurs. She had gone into business without spending enough time planning, doing due diligence, and lining up trusted accountants and lawyers able to put strategic business elements in place. She badly needed to rewrite her business plan.

Myrna began anew, gradually this time. She started hanging out at the center, networking, and attending classes and conferences. She read books on business. And she drilled herself with flash cards: What is a spreadsheet? What is profit? What is loss? "The whole numbers side of business had been a barrier to me. I said to myself, *You've got to deal with this. You've got to know this side of things if you want to succeed. You can't just tra-la off into the sunset anymore.*"

Later that year, one of the center's administrators showed her a flyer from Oprah's Oxygen Channel announcing the second annual "Build Your Own Business" contest. Entries were due in days. Though she did not yet have all the answers she needed for her new business plan, the contest only required an executive summary. Myrna figured she could write that well enough. She went to Long Beach Island, New Jersey, and spent a long weekend interviewing kids on the beach and writing. She got her entry in by the September 10 deadline.

The next day, as she waited in a school cafeteria for her students to arrive, she learned of the attacks on the Twin Towers in New York and on the Pentagon. Suddenly, the results of Oprah's contest seemed trivial. Like teachers and parents all over the country, she forgot about personal concerns and was absorbed in dealing with the aftershock of 9/11.

A few weeks later, Oprah's Oxygen Network notified Myrna that she had been selected as one of three winners, from more than five thousand contestants. Her mentors and friends at the Women's Business Center were jubilant. "Oh, my God! It was huge!" Wrigley said. Not only would Myrna, then fifty-nine, receive a computer and other equipment, business workshops, and a $10,000 award, she would also be flown to New York to be interviewed on television by Gayle King, television talk show host and Oprah Winfrey's best friend. Almost overnight, the hits on her Ooz & Oz website skyrocketed by the thousands. "Oh, honey, every time you trot out Oprah's name, people perk up. To have won that was a very big deal," Myrna said.

There was only one problem. She still had no product to sell. Filled with urgency, she cut back on her teaching schedule and set to work developing a new packaging design. But a personal crisis thwarted her again. Myrna's mother was on a cruise in the Caribbean when she was injured in a car accident on the island of St. Thomas. Her traveling companion had reboarded the ship and sailed, leaving Myrna's mother alone at the hospital in need of emergency surgery. Myrna turned in the final grades for her students and flew down to be with her mother. Frustratingly, her Oprah moment slipped away.

It was not until later, in 2003, that Myrna, having turned sixty, remanufactured, repackaged, and renamed her product Mirror-aculous Art Activities "Circus" Kit, complete with thirty-two distorted drawings, crayons, and mirror decoders. By year's end, her unusual, interactive toy and drawing activity kit had racked up a string of the nation's most prestigious toy awards, including being named one of Dr. Toy's "10 Best Creative Products 2003" and "100 Best Children's Products 2003," and received the National Parenting Center Seal of Approval and the Canadian Toy Testing Council's highest ranking, and won *Creative Child* magazine's Seal of Excellence.

The "Circus" kit is a unique way to teach children to draw that is intellectually stimulating and fun, according to Stevanne Auerbach, Ph.D., the educator otherwise known as Dr. Toy, whose imprimatur has been sought after in the toy business for nearly a quarter of a century. "It was easy, creative, and inexpensive. It took a lot of courage to take on a project like this and take it to the marketplace. To do that, you have to be a forward-looking person with stamina. Myrna invented something and has been able to sustain it by reinventing it several times. It has a classic quality, like yo-yos and Hula Hoops, that will allow Myrna's product to be constantly rediscovered."

Of course, her long entrepreneurial journey has occasionally been so challenging that she considered giving up. But each time, her passion for mirror art and her faith in her toy have pulled her back on track. In 2004, her vision was rewarded when the federal Small Business Administration for the Washington, D.C., district named Myrna the Entrepreneurial Success of the Year. "She has been indomitable," said Maggie Constan, a friend. "She has been determined and flexible, trying angle after angle. She is organized just the way her desk is organized."

Her desk, in fact, has no junk drawer. Paper clips are sorted by color. Multicolored Post-its, reminding her of tasks and timetables, are plastered around the two walls of the L-shaped desk that dominates her living room. Each night, she reads through all of her note cards—some of which have been written out numerous times, a habit she attributes to her accountant father's relentless questioning. No matter what time she goes to sleep (she often works late into the night when she is struggling with a creative problem), by 5 A.M. she is usually back at work fulfilling orders, corresponding with customers, writing copy, and working out new designs.

In 2005, Microsoft hired Nell and moved her and Myrna to Seattle. Since arriving there, Myrna has been steadily building her business. Restless to improve her toy, she designed a reflective cylinder that eliminated the paper cup. And goaded by a new friend from a business networking group in Seattle, Myrna began a six-month struggle to find a new, more felicitous and memorable name for her product. She was stymied until one night she went to an outdoor showing of her favorite movie, *Who Framed Roger Rabbit?* (Myrna's car keys even dangle from a Roger Rabbit key chain.) "That night, I dreamed about the Acme Suck-O-Lux vacuum cleaner scene [in which Roger Rabbit's face gets sucked into a vacuum cleaner]. When I woke up, I had the new name: Morph-O-Scope!" she said. She also added a new tagline, "Brain-powered play. No batteries needed."

Myrna's rejuvenated toy received fresh acclaim. Bernie DeKoven, the games-loving maven, gave her products a Major Fun Award and waxed ecstatic about Myrna's kits and anamorphic products. In addition to being affordable, they made an esoteric, mathematically based Renaissance art form accessible to children. "It's a unique contribution to the game world. It's a wonderful play experience that challenges a child's brain. It goes way beyond a coloring book."

And when Myrna asked the Toy Man Product Guide to update her product image in its online review, she was informed that while she already had the Toy Man Seal of Approval, the guide's policy required her to submit her latest version for an entirely new review. As a result of the evaluators' report, the Toy Man awarded her Morph-O-Scope kit its highest honor, an Award of Excellence—her nineteenth national toy award since turning sixty. At the start of 2009, The Toy Man Product Guide gave Myrna's Sports of All

Sorts kit, containing 32 pages of sports images to color, both an E-Choice Award, for its high potential for causing cognitive and critical skill growth, and the Award of Excellence. The Reverend G. W. Fisher, who founded the product guide to publish credible and unbiased reports on toys' safety, educational value, and capacity to engage children, said the kit is "a unique, innovative toy, with long-term effects. It's something that engages, from children to adults." He was fascinated, too, to see that when his evaluators tested the product in New York City, Yonkers, and Las Vegas, even reclusive children were stimulated to interact with others as they played with Myrna's kit. "People in this industry are so blind. They say, 'It's not a name I recognize,' so they don't pay attention. But the potential value is astounding. Stores could sell this in a heartbeat. It's one hundred percent child-safe, even eco-conscious. Once it hits the tipping point, this thing will scream, and companies will wonder why they didn't buy it. The potential is unlimited."

Amazon.com began carrying Ooz & Oz products on its website in 2006. Over a one-year period, ending in the spring of 2008, sales increased eightfold. The company's actual sales figures remain a closely held secret. Myrna shared only that she has sold thousands of kits. But by August 2008, she had sold out of all product. And, in the midst of the deepening national recession, she faced a critical decision. Should she, at last, pull the plug on her dream or manufacture again?

She weighed the financial risks against the vision to which she has clung for twenty years. While there is always guesswork in economics, Myrna felt confident enough to plow forward. She developed yet another new product, prepared for discussions with Wal-Mart and toysrus.com, and, in 2009, placed an order with a Texas factory to begin manufacturing ten thousand Morph-O-Scope kits.

Still, I've wondered more than once why, after all this time, she is still willing to risk her time and money, including her retirement fund, betting on her mirror toys.

"Becoming educated in business and applying that knowledge to my passion may well prove to have been a sounder investment of time, money, and effort than my contemporaries made," she answers without hesitation. "Millions of other seniors have lost their portfolios, their pensions, and their jobs. I, on the other hand, have an independent, established business." Besides, she added, "I'm honoring my brain and children's brains rather than just worrying about the marketplace. But I'm not in this just to diddle my brain. I'd love to be free of money worries. I confess I covet nice clothes. And perhaps by some measures, I am not *successful* Y-E-T. But I am succeeding in the process. It is all a journey, sometimes a lifelong journey! While I am learning and refining the line, and increasing sales, I am succeeding. I am getting closer and closer to making the kind of income that allows me to grow my company, build financial security, and be of help to others beginning businesses. I'm paying it forward. What keeps me going, in addition to more sales? The universal 'oohs' and 'aahs' from kids, the praise from all quarters for the products, and offers of licensing deals." Sooner or later, she is certain, the right one will come along.

Recycling Lives

"These have been the best years of my life."

Ira Smith was fielding questions in the middle of the warehouse filled with rows of secondhand sofas, chairs, dressers, and other household goods. "Where are the beds?" "Where are the linens?" "Where are the microwaves?" He is a genial man and answered each query warmly and efficiently, mixing a host's welcome and a ringmaster's élan.

Ira's wife, Barbara, was standing at a counter just inside the warehouse's steel double doors. She was busy logging the increasingly steady flow of things people were carrying out to their waiting cars, vans, and rental trucks: beds, bedding, cribs, car seats, clocks, china, sofas, settees, stemware, and flatware, as well as desks, tables, rugs, vacuums, sewing machines, televisions, stereos, toaster ovens, coffee-makers, vases, artwork, and assorted knickknacks. There was even the occasional bagel toaster. "I guess our price is right," Barbara said.

That is because there are no prices. Everything at the Household Goods Recycling Ministry, as it was then still called, was free. It is, therefore, hardly surprising that business was up by 30 percent in the midst of the nation's worst economic downturn in decades. Or that, year after year, business has increased at that pace at the unlikely all-volunteer operation that Barbara and Ira started 1990 when they were sixty. (It has changed its name, replacing "Ministry" with "of Massachusetts" to avoid unwarranted conjectures about its religious nature.)

More than two hundred agencies, from the American Red Cross to the Veterans Administration, operating out of some five hundred offices, have grown dependent on the charitable enterprise over the last nineteen years. After quite literally carrying HGRM on their own backs for the first decade, the Smiths are only too happy to boast about the 220 active volunteers who have helped to build and expand HGRM over the last decade. Annually, it now serves about three thousand individuals and families from Acton and sixty surrounding communities, including Boston, Boxboro, Lowell, Lawrence, and Worcester. By and large, the clients are recovering from domestic violence, drug addiction, mental illness, financial failures, and homelessness. They are making transitions from shelters, rehabilitation programs, and halfway houses back to lives in their own homes. Political refugees, from El Salvador to Iraq, have also received assistance from HGRM. The acronym is often pronounced as Hug Room to reflect the contagion of warm embraces between its beneficiaries and the volunteers who staff the organization, including the Smiths. And why not? The nonprofit furnishes the equivalent of about fifty apartments a month. In 2008, it distributed more than twenty-seven thousand pieces of furniture and about ten thousand boxes of small household goods, worth an estimated $1,178,000.

Not bad, considering that when Barbara and Ira began giving away furniture and household goods, they did it out of their house in Acton. For ten years, the couple picked up and hauled almost everything by themselves in a vintage orange Datsun truck.

"There would be stoves and refrigerators and half a dozen sofas covered with plastic sitting out here," Barbara said one day as we walked up the long driveway to the modest, brown-shingled, five-bedroom house in which they have lived for nearly fifty years. "Furniture filled the garage. And all the household goods were crammed into every inch of the basement."

When Barbara and Ira began recycling furniture to needy families, Barbara had finished raising their six children. Ira had spent thirty-five unfulfilling years as an electrical engineer, helping develop surface-to-air (SAM) missiles for the United States Air Force and then working on various projects for Raytheon.

"My work was mainly filling slots and doing work that was not a heck of a lot of value. I spent my time caught in a lot of red tape and writing reports on this or that that never amounted to anything," he said. Admittedly, there had been some exciting periods, such as helping develop Patriot missiles, which would become the U.S. Army's main medium-range tactical air defense and the army's anti-ballistic missile platform. "It was a fantastic thing for our defense, as were some of the other projects I worked on, like helping us to figure out how to send the second wave of ICBMs over to Russia or how to keep the Command Post alive so that we could send another wave over after a preliminary attack. But after a while, those things really got to me. I had work-related depression for years and was never really happy in my work.

"If someone had told me, 'Well, Ira, now, at age sixty, you're going to enter into another career, and for twenty years, you're going to work six days a week, and you're going to go out and carry refrigerators in sub-zero weather, and you're not going to get paid anything,' I would have said, 'Oh, God, don't let me live.' I would have taken a gun and shot myself in the head," he said. But no one warned him. And instead of all he might have dreaded, Ira—a trim, handsome white-haired man with a slim mustache hugging his upper lip—says, "These have been the best years of my life."

It began with a phone call to Barbara in 1989 from a fellow parishioner at Saint Elizabeth of Hungary Catholic Church in Acton. Barbara was writing the church bulletin in those days. The church member asked her if she would include a notice in the next bulletin requesting donations of furniture and household items for a fellow church member's sister who was arriving from war-torn El Salvador. The twenty-six-year-old woman, Cecilia Palma, had fled her country with her two small children. She had lived next to the church building where six prominent Jesuit priests, their housekeeper, and the housekeeper's teenage daughter were slain by twenty armed and uniformed men while they slept. In fighting that had followed, government forces destroyed Palma's house. With her sister's help, she scraped together enough money for plane tickets to the United States and for rent and security on an apartment in Acton. But neither she nor her sister had any money left to buy beds, linens, or any other furnishings.

The slaying of the Jesuit priests was big news and a stinging reminder in the United States of the four American nuns murdered with Archbishop Oscar Romero in El Salvador nine years earlier. It galvanized concern in the United States about the systematic violence and human rights abuses carried out by the Salvadoran death squads and the military against suspected leftists. It also heightened questions about President Ronald Reagan's vocal support of the Salvadoran government and the billions of dollars in military aid that had been sent to Latin American nations in the 1980s. That support came under even sharper focus in Massachusetts after the late

Representative Joseph Moakley, an old-school Boston politician, initiated a congressional investigation.

Acton residents responded to the plea to help Palma by dropping off so many goods at the Smiths' house that a week later the Salvadoran woman wanted for nothing. "It was a blessing for my sister, and for me, and for a lot of people. It was something wonderful. They had beds and didn't have to sleep on the floor. In my family, whenever we talk about that time, we say, 'Thank God,' because when we needed it, Barbara was there," Palma's sister, Reina Hernandez, said.

The Smiths were left with a pile of leftover items. To get rid of them, Barbara called the Acton Housing Authority to see if it knew of any tenants who could use household goods. There was, in fact, plenty of need. And the local housing authority soon began to think of Barbara as a resource for residents in need. Someone from the housing authority would call, and she would place a notice in the Sunday bulletin.

It was not long before the residents of Acton, an affluent suburban community, got into the habit of dropping off donations in the Smiths' driveway and basement, whether there was a notice or not. "At the time, we weren't connected with any agencies. But word about us spread like wildfire through the Brazilian community. For many Brazilians, we were literally the first stop after they arrived at Logan [International Airport]. They were honest, hardworking tradespeople who just couldn't make it in Brazil. We would just leave the door to our basement open for them, even on Thanksgiving Day, and they would take away what they needed. It was a blessing, because if they hadn't taken the stuff away, we would have drowned in it," Ira said.

For the next five years, Ira Smith continued to work full-time as an engineer, most interestingly on a futuristic urban people mover called Taxi 2000. But early excitement for the project, which had the potential to make Smith a wealthy man, faded when Raytheon bought out the project and reengineered it, adding massive architectural supports that made the project too expensive and too inflexible for construction by cities, such as Chicago, that were considering it. A model for the project was built on Raytheon's property in Marlboro, Massachusetts, but never went any further. Meanwhile, Ira—whose top salary never exceeded $64,000 a year—would come home from work and find Barbara waiting for him to go out and pick up or deliver more goods. "I'd see this look in her eyes," he said.

It was not long before the couple became recognizable figures. Children in the nearby working-class town of Maynard sometimes ran after the Smiths, shouting items of furniture that their parents needed. Exasperated landlords in low-income housing, tired of the expense of removing furniture left in the street by families that had skipped town or were evicted, also began to call on the Smiths to help them out by removing goods at no expense.

When Ira awoke the morning after he retired from engineering in 1995, Barbara was waiting for him—a schedule of pickups and drop-offs in hand. At 170 pounds, he represented the duo's brawn. Barbara weighed 108 pounds soaking wet. The sight of the couple arriving to remove a refrigerator or a stove would often leave donors baffled. One day, an area psychiatrist called for their help because he and his wife were moving from their house to a smaller apartment in Cambridge and had to downsize. It was a broiling hot day, and the Smiths were struggling to finish and get everything into their truck.

"Ira, let's go home," Barbara said.

"No, damn it, we're not leaving until we've taken it all," Ira shot back.

The psychiatrist spoke up. "You know, you're both positively certifiable."

They relish telling the story, but swear by the physical and psychological benefits of the work they've done for the last two decades.

Other than a period a couple of years ago when Ira suffered a flare-up of a rigidifying psoriatic arthritis, the Smiths say that lifting and moving furniture and appliances has helped maintain them in the best physical and mental shape of their lives.

To accomplish the feat of lifting heavy things, such as a stove or a sofa bed, "we learned first to think and stay focused," Ira said. "We stand on either side, use our legs, and keep our backs straight. Actually, the sofa bed feels lighter when picked up in the middle, and then we don't have to twist our bodies getting it onto the truck."

All too frequently, they have had to warn off younger men, who don't know how to lift but whose masculine egos are threatened by the sight of Barbara and Ira carrying off a stove. Once when they arrived to collect a refrigerator from a house, the donor became upset when she saw the two of them alone. She begged them to leave before her husband saw them at work. "He's just had a heart attack, but if he sees the two of you, he'll never let you do this alone, and it'll kill him," she said.

Erica Gauthie's expression was subdued when the tall thirty-four-year-old woman with long brown hair, who was wearing a University of Massachusetts sweatshirt, entered the HGRM warehouse one morning. She had recently graduated from a drug rehabilitation program in nearby Lowell. After several months living in a halfway house, she was testing the waters of full sobriety and moving into an apartment of her own with her seventeen-year-old daughter and her daughter's boyfriend. She had no furniture. Her mother, an uncle, and another recovering addict had come along to help her gather and carry whatever she needed. While the others dispersed across the warehouse with the excitement of game show contestants, an overwhelmed Erica stood frozen still.

Ira Smith, who has a wise, grandfatherly smile, recognized her reaction. He had seen it often enough before. He went to Eric's rescue, gently introducing himself and handing her a batch of name tags to attach to whatever she selected. "Go get your mattresses first. The good ones go quickly," he told her.

Erica nodded appreciatively and headed to the "Mattress Room." Before she got there, she spotted a couple of headboards she liked and was about to tag them when a watchful Ira rushed over. "A bunch of people are coming in soon; you should pick your mattresses first," he said. "The good ones go quickly," he repeated.

Erica's helpers were moving fast. They picked out a pumpkin-colored convertible couch, a pair of upholstered chairs, and a lamp for her living room. Erica's mother tagged a coffee table. Her uncle took a bookcase. And they kept filling a rented U-Haul truck with all manner of things, including an espresso machine, a microwave, a bagel toaster, and a popcorn maker. "Do they have teakettles?" Erica called across the warehouse to her mother. "You know I like to drink tea instead of coffee during the day."

Later, as Erica and her family rushed to conclude their two-hour harvest, her mother ran to the front of the warehouse holding a framed picture. "You've got to have a Jesus," she shouted. Barbara smiled, recorded the picture in the computer log, and instructed lightly, "Just take care of Him." Just as some people may mistake Barbara's sinewy shape for frailty, so some may mistake her enthusiastic warmth for weakness. But mistake it would be. Barbara can be steely stern. Indeed, when Erica's mother began to leave the warehouse with a second floor lamp from a new shipment of hotel lamps, Barbara stopped her and, without visible annoyance, told her to put the second lamp back. "There's a limit of one per family on those," she said, leaving no room for debate. "We want to have some left for others."

By then, Erica was reaching for her final item, a yellow ceramic cookie jar. She took a deep breath. "The people who donate all these things don't really know what they're doing for a person like me. I can't believe how much they've helped me. Two days ago, I thought that I'd be sleeping on the floor of an empty apartment. I didn't have the money to do anything, and now I've just walked in and took away everything I need." She took another breath and began to sob, "I'm overwhelmed. I can't speak."

When I related the conversation to Ira, he, too, grew teary-eyed. "Every day, I am rewarded here," he said. "Every day, I still ask myself, *Is this really happening?*"

Barbara Kelly and Ira Smith met in the fall of 1949 when they were sophomores in college in Potsdam, New York, north of the Adirondacks. Ira was studying engineering at the then all-male Clarkson College of Technology. Barbara was a student at what was then Potsdam State Teachers College (now part of the State University of New York system). The first time they saw each other, Barbara was dressed up for a sorority Halloween party in a cowgirl outfit with toy pistols. But they did not date until two years later, when Ira returned from ROTC sporting a buzz cut in the fall of their senior year. "The one and only night I think I ever went out on a weekday night, one of the girls I was with saw him and asked, 'Didn't that used to be Ira Smith?' I was sitting at the end of the booth, so I said I would go ask." In less than four months, they were engaged. "It was the only way I could get a date with her. She had a couple of other guys after her," Ira said.

Barbara almost didn't go to college, though she graduated as valedictorian of her class of twelve at Heuvelton High School. Even the state college tuition of $900 a year was prohibitively expensive for Barbara's family. Her father, Edward "Bert" Kelly, was a well-respected farmer with an eighth-grade education. He owned a small dairy. Her mother, Corrinne Gilbert, worked as a domestic for the wealthy in and around Ogdensburg. Together they barely made enough to keep their family afloat. Born into the teeth of the Great Depression in 1931, Barbara was the youngest of ten children.

During the summer of 1948, she received a letter notifying her that she had won a New York State scholarship. It asked her to indicate to which college the money should be sent. She scurried around to find a college that would accept her at that late date. Her father scraped together the additional $300 needed to pay the first year's tuition. "It was a stretch for him, but he did it," Barbara said.

There seems little doubt that the old-fashioned values of helping others that existed in the communal life of a farm have influenced Barbara's devotion to HGRM. Despite the size of her family, her parents kept an open house and were forever taking in others who needed a place to stay and work, a tradition that Barbara and Ira would later continue. Moreover, Barbara developed the habit of letting nothing go to waste. "We used everything. I learned to squeeze a nickel, as they used to say, until the Indian was riding the buffalo."

Ira was the only child of a mother who also did domestic work for wealthy families, and a gas station owner and truck driver who eventually became highway superintendent of Westport, New York, on Lake Champlain. The family was comfortable but thrifty. Ira had no real ambition when he graduated from high school. But in the post–World War II climate, there was much talk of engineering as the profession of the future. And mostly with that as his rationale, he signed up to study electrical engineering at Clarkson. He wasn't well-suited for engineering, he later realized, and fared little better than average in his course work.

Barbara and Ira were married in 1954 soon after he returned from serving in the army in Korea after the armistice was signed. He went to work as an engineer at the Rome Air Development Center (RADC), an important Cold War research and development lab that the Air Force had opened a year earlier at Griffiss Air Force Base in Rome, New York, not far from where Barbara grew up. Credited for the time he served in Korea, Ira was made a first lieutenant and assigned to a unit developing technical navigation systems for the nascent missile defense program. Being able to write more clearly than other engineers—not a great accomplishment, Ira jokes—he moved up the ranks quickly.

In 1960, he was appointed chief engineer of the Pincushion Project, a radar system that was meant to analyze incoming missiles, decoys, and their data. "Back in those days, you could get money for all sorts of ideas, whether they were well thought out or not. The government was spending money like crazy. Pincushion was one of those programs that, for technical reasons, never should have been started. But we didn't know that. Two years later, it went belly-up."

By then, Ira had had enough of working in an isolated military outpost. With a burgeoning family of five children, ranging in age from one to six, and another child on the way, he was anxious to move to the private sector. He landed a job with Raytheon in Bedford, Massachusetts, and moved from hands-on engineering to managing others who were writing specifications for test programs. For a period of time—when he was part of a Raytheon team that won a contract to produce Patriot missiles—Ira was actually happy at work. But when his involvement with the Patriot program ended, work became unsatisfying.

For years, Barbara was more than fully employed raising the Smiths' brood. She cooked, cleaned, checked homework, and worked hard to stretch the family budget and still put savings aside for investment. "Ira let me take care of the money, and it was the only thing that kept me from going out of my mind," she said.

While the Smiths' children all found initial academic success, the college years did not go smoothly for some of them. Their two oldest sons, Rick and David, dropped out of Tufts and Princeton, respectively, and joined The Way, a self-described Christian biblical teaching fellowship. Critics, including Barbara and Ira, considered it a cult. "It was exceedingly painful for me," Barbara said. "We had major philosophical disagreements with The Way. And the boys were very upset with us because we didn't agree."

Eventually, the Smiths made their peace with their sons' religious paths. But it wasn't easy. Rick Smith had been a National Honor Society student and a track star in high school. After his involvement in The Way subsided, he returned home, worked at a series of low-level jobs, and lived with his parents for ten years. He later moved to Princeton, where he got a job in a warehouse, and lived with David, by then a successful contractor, and his family.

The Smiths' children say they were intensely aware of their father's unhappiness at work, though they had little idea what he actually did. "The man you meet now is not the man I grew up with as my father," said daughter Elizabeth Otterbein, a research chemist for a pharmaceutical company. "The father I grew up with came home every night and had a drink. Then, with six kids sitting at the dinner table, he tuned out and didn't say a word."

After dinner, he dropped into the BarcaLounger and nodded off for the evening. Saturdays were often even more unpleasant. Ira barked orders at his children to do work around the house, Otterbein recalled. "My mother was always vacuuming the carpets, doing laundry, making the beds, and cleaning the bathrooms. We grew up with a lot of tension." Only Sundays brought respite. Ira would take the children to bowl or to hike, and Barbara would relish the vice of shopping for groceries and family needs by herself. Popcorn with dinner was the family treat.

While the children began to see their father's spirits lift in the years following his retirement and often came home to find that their parents were using the extra bedrooms to give refuge to someone in need, nothing prepared them for their parents' commitment to the Household Goods Recycling Ministry. In fact, they were skeptical about their obsessive immersion in it. They worried, too, that their parents, already in their sixties, might injure themselves with all the lifting they were doing. It was also disconcerting to return home for visits and find the driveway and the family's volleyball court filled with sofas, refrigerators, and stoves. "For the first few years, everyone was under the impression that my mother was crazy. It was as if she was trying to earn her way to heaven," David said. "Then, over the years, we came to see that she was changing a lot of lives."

In time, even the Smiths' driveway, lawn, and house were not enough to hold all the donated goods. So the Smiths acquired permission to use storage space in the basement of a local Methodist church, an unused carriage house, and a large, privately owned garage. Then they acquired the use of a century-old barn. It didn't have concrete floors, electric lights, toilets, or heat. When it rained, the odors of its former life as a barn were awakened. One day when the temperature inside the barn hit five below, Ira recalled, "We looked at each other and said, 'This is it! Either we quit with the big furniture or we get into the fund-raising business and get a big place of our own.'"

They had little trouble finding community members willing to serve on a board of directors. Soon, the Smiths were sharing their operation with a swelling cadre of volunteers—who pick up furniture, repair it and all kinds of electronics, assist clients in finding what they need, raise funds, schedule clients' appointments, keep the financial books, update the agency database and contacts, and work on publicity.

Jill Henderson, a former art and antiques dealer, helped the Smiths raise the capital to rent a legitimate warehouse. She first met them several years earlier when she needed to dispose of thousands of dollars' worth of brand-new items from an estate sale she was handling. "When I drove up to their house, there were fourteen sofas in the driveway under tarps. At the back door, there was a blue-and-white sign that just said, 'Think Prayer.' And then these two warm, smiling saints came down the stairs. The hairs on my arms stood up on end. We bonded, and I've been working with them ever since."

Henderson helped the Smiths send out their first flyers, with Ira and Barbara's pictures on the front. The response was staggering. "People are beyond generous when they understand what our mission is. And because Barbara and Ira exude calm, serenity, and dignity, people like to be near them," Henderson said.

For a long time, the Smiths did not recognize how valued they were by their own community. A decade ago, they went to the venerable Concord-Carlyle Community Chest and apologetically asked for a $25,000 grant to rent the warehouse where HGRM is still housed. "We promise, we won't come back to you for more money next year," Ira told Community Chest director Astrid Williams.

"No, please do come back," Williams said as she assured Ira and Barbara that as long as the Household Goods Recycling Ministry continued to serve as many people locally as it did, the Community Chest would support its efforts. And each year since 1999, the Community Chest has given HGRM $10,000. The Smiths have remained humble and appreciative, Williams said, and their organization has continued to serve as a model of volunteerism and community assistance.

"They give without interrogating. People come to them for help and leave with their dignity intact. They have a well-run organization in which their volunteers convey the empathy Ira and Barbara transmit. It is one of our favorite organizations. So many times, it's hard to measure the impact an organization really has. But when you go to HGRM, you really see people's lives transformed in the space of three hours," she said.

Without trying, Ira and Barbara inspire others. "They set a high standard of what you can do with this life," said board member Joseph Chappell, a successful forty-seven-year-old software company consultant and former CEO of several software companies, including one that sold for $240 million a few years ago. "They created an environment that motivates people and brings out the best, just by how they treat people. You look at them and you wonder how it can be work, if they're having such a good time." Chappell himself now drives one of HGRM's trucks to make pickups three days a week. "It's tiring, but I'm happy to be a part of it. Barb and Ira have a spirit that infects other people and makes you want to emulate them."

Often the very people HGRM helps return to volunteer. A decade after he was ordered to do community service at HGRM by a local court, Bob Zink, a forty-year-old mason, continues to volunteer and supervise pickups three days a week. "Every once in a while, they'd give me a call, and I'd go help pick up a sofa, a bed, or a washing machine. Now, it's nonstop. But if they need anything, all they have to do is holler and I'll do it for them."

Despite the wish to keep the organization all volunteer, by 2008 its growth demanded change. To avoid haphazard training, eliminate confusion, and maximize output, HGRM hired its first paid employee, a coordinator of volunteers. She is paid $43,000 out of a total annual budget of $228,000. One-third of that budget comes from the sale of high-quality goods volunteers discover amid the goods collected. (They count, in particular, on Bob Zink's savvy eyes to find the gems.) The bulk of the budget goes for rent and to operate HGRM's trucks.

Those who work closely with the couple are astonished by how well the Smiths get along, considering the grueling hours they have spent working together over the last twenty years. Their complementary styles, they say, make Barbara and Ira particularly effective: she is strategic and detail- and business-minded; he is, first and foremost, an emotional man who easily turns the personal connections he makes to the advantage of HGRM's larger mission. Where Barbara thinks things through to their logical conclusion before attempting them, Ira experiments.

In late 2007, the U.S. Department of Veterans Affairs flew Barbara and Ira to San Diego to present them with the Secretary's Award for outstanding achievement by a community organization in the service of homeless veterans. "This organization epitomizes the true spirit of charity and reciprocity in the original sense of the word," Mary Fardy, the VA coordinator for homeless services in Bedford, Massachusetts, said of HGRM in her nominating letter. It "sustains the veterans we serve in both concrete and spiritual ways. The help is holistic. Those veterans that have been referred come back and tell us it is rare in their experience and circumstance to be treated as well as they have been at HGRM. They say that the compassion and support they receive from people in this agency is palpable and that they are awed by being seen as worthy human beings."

In February 2009, HGRM was recognized, too, by Pine-Sol, which awarded it the annual $10,000 Powerful Difference Award grand prize.

At seventy-nine, the Smiths still go to work at the warehouse six days a week, fifty weeks a year. They take off only one week after Christmas when HGRM is closed and one week in July for Barbara's family's annual reunion. "I try to stay away from the counter and putter around in the back," Ira said. For him, puttering entails working much of the day and often until 10 P.M. at home on HGRM's database, which includes some 1,200 agency representatives. Barbara, too, has tried to restrain herself from shadowing the daily managers. But the truth is that the volunteers show great deference to both Barbara and Ira and, when they are present, depend on them. Barbara is the only one who knows which bed frame goes with which bed, one manager said, explaining why volunteers are constantly calling out to her. "Yes, I have that essential knowledge," Barbara joked. "And I don't pass it on. That makes me indispensable."

It is impossible to doubt Ira or Barbara when they say they feel blessed that they have had the good fortune to do the work they have done for others. They radiate something as old-fashioned as niceness. It is rare that a client tries to take advantage of HGRM's generosity. Barbara and Ira prefer to remember the day two women who were victims of severe domestic violence and had remained in a shelter for nearly two years arrived at the warehouse. They were with a social worker, helping them on her day off. "They timidly chose furniture and all the household goods they needed to furnish their two new apartments. By the time they had crammed everything into a rental van, they were talking excitedly and almost dancing," Ira said. "We realized that life for them would change from that day on."

While they are conscious of their advancing age, Barbara and Ira are convinced that the daily surprises of their activity, the demands of its labor, and the appreciative interactions with a loving and diverse chunk of humanity—volunteers and clients alike—reward them with physical, cognitive, and spiritual health. One hundred-seventy years ago, Ralph Waldo Emerson identified the phenomenon when he wrote: "It is one of the most beautiful compensations in life that no man can sincerely try to help another without helping himself." In recent years, scientific studies have suggested that the Smiths' intuition is correct: doing good and helping others strengthens the immune system and lengthens lives. A five-year study of 423 older couples by psychologist Stephanie Brown of the University of Michigan found that those who provided significant support to others were more than twice as likely to have remained alive during the study.

"Creating and realizing HGRM's success means that I can pass from this life knowing that I have made a difference. But when I reflect on the fruits of my labors, I feel young in body, mind, and spirit," Ira said. What began with a request to help furnish one apartment has become proof of the saying that a life lived for others is a life well-lived. And that's the life the Smiths plan on living "as long as we can get out of bed in the morning," Barbara said.

Living Color

"Despite my ambiguous skin color . . .
I have lived the black experience."

After the phone rang at five-thirty, there was no way Betty Reid Soskin could return to sleep: Even though the sky over Washington, D.C., was gray and the mercury stood at seventeen. Even though she had timed it and knew precisely how long it would take to walk to the Capitol. And even though she had only to cut through little Lincoln Park, pass the Emancipation Statue paid for by newly freed slaves at the end of the Civil War, nod good morning to the bust of educator and civil rights advocate Mary McLeod Bethune, and walk twelve blocks with the thousands of others funneling through the street.

She showered and slipped into a pair of new long johns. In the cold, the fine-boned, five-foot-five-inch woman would need them. She pulled on her forest-green trousers and a black cashmere turtleneck sweater, over which she put on her government-issued gray long-sleeve shirt. She affixed the gold name bar on her right breast pocket. Proudly, she pinned a gold badge over her heart. She regretted not having remembered the flag pin for her lapel. "It was optional, except for this day, when I would have given anything to have it," she said.

She caught a glimpse of her late mother, Lottie, in her own reflection in the mirror, and grinned. *Where on earth has Betty gone?*

She parted her black hair down the middle, pulled it back, and bound it in a clip. She penciled arching brows above her dark, deep-set eyes. She brushed blush on her lightly complected cheekbones, and touched her lips with gloss. Betty put on her hip-length, regulation raincoat and stuck extra tissues in the pockets. Then she picked up a small black-and-white photograph and tucked it in her breast pocket. It was of "Mammá," her great-grandmother, Leontine Breaux Allen, a slave in Louisiana until she was freed at nineteen. She died, at 101, in 1948, when Betty was twenty-seven. "Slavery, you see, is no abstraction for me. Mammá would share this day with me. It was, after all, as much for her as for myself that I was there at all," she said.

Finally, Betty put on her Smokey the Bear hat. At eighty-seven, America's oldest National Park Service ranger was ready to celebrate.

After all, Betty had long fought for civil rights and civility. She had lived the long arc of moral history and, as Martin Luther King Jr. had promised, had finally seen it bend toward justice. Betty was approaching sixty when she set out to rescue a legendary family record store in Berkeley, California, a one-time mecca for black music on the West Coast, and she ended up saving a drug-infested neighborhood. She had started in her late seventies to work as a legislative aide in the East Bay, and by her eighties was responsible for persuading the National Park Service to rethink its approach to the Rosie the Riveter/World War II Home Front National Historical Park in Richmond, California, and to present an unvarnished history of the complex race relations on the home front.

Throughout her journey, Betty never surrendered her uplifting smile, her keen intellect, or her hope that one day America would embrace its diversity. There was no way she was going to be late for the inauguration of Barack Obama as the forty-fourth president of the United States.

Born Betty Charbonnet in New Orleans in 1921, her early life intersected with another seminal event in the racial history of the United States, one of the nation's most devastating natural disasters, the great Mississippi flood of 1927. She had not thought about it much until 2005, when the images of Hurricane Katrina jarred loose long-buried memories. Among them, she remembered the water rising in her family's house on Touro Street, not far from where Katrina first breached the levee. "I was in my bed, which was stacked on orange crates, and water was lapping around it. My father was building a boat. And my sister, who was nine, and I went outside with cousins to bail water because my father hadn't caulked it yet," Betty recalled.

The 1927 deluge inundated a million acres of land, from Illinois to Louisiana. It killed one thousand people and displaced some nine hundred thousand Southerners. The odor of fetid river muck that coated everything was nothing compared to the stench of racism the flood released. As John M. Barry detailed in *Rising Tide: The Great Mississippi Flood of 1927 and How It Changed America,* the flood "shattered the myth of a quasi-feudal bond between Delta blacks and southern aristocracy." And it unleashed the great migration of African-Americans out of the South, setting in motion a demographic change that would alter American cities, politics, and culture forever.

It also destroyed Betty's family's property and prospects in New Orleans and "catapulted my mother and her three little girls on a train bound for California with all their possessions in a cardboard suitcase," Betty said. "She had little more than the hope of survival in a strange place" where Betty's grandfather had already settled. Her father would follow after the destruction was tallied.

It was a traumatic upheaval that wrenched the Charbonnets from a place where their ancestors, natives of Thiers, France, had settled before the United States made the Louisiana Purchase. Her line of people became a proud, accomplished, mixed-race Creole family. Her paternal grandfather, Louis Charbonnet Sr., an engineer and a millwright, and his sons designed and built several important buildings in New Orleans, including a convent for the first order of black nuns in the United States. At home, in the hallway of her condominium in Richmond, California, Betty still keeps a collection of her grandfather's leather-bound engineering texts. Nearby, there is a gallery of historical family photographs, including a portrait of her debonair-looking father, Dorson Louis Charbonnet, wearing a three-piece suit and a pale Stetson. Blond and hazel-eyed as a child, her father was a tall, fair-skinned, and formal man who resembled the actor Paul Newman.

On Betty's mother's side, the Breauxes trace themselves to feudal France, near Loudun. By 1661, they had settled in Nova Scotia as fur-trading Acadians. They were chased out by the British and eventually invited by Spain to settle in Louisiana. They became planters in St. James Parish, next to the Mississippi River. One of Betty's Cajun ancestors owned sixty-three slaves, and one of his heirs fell in love with a mulatto slave named Celestine. He married her one month after Lincoln signed the Emancipation Proclamation, seventeen years after she gave birth to their child, Betty's great-grandmother Leontine.

Mammá Leontine, who became the family matriarch, spoke only French, rarely wore shoes, and, having grown up a slave, never had the privilege of learning to read or write. "She was the midwife in her village. There was a white doctor who was a circuit rider, who came through on horseback every three months. And it was her job to go out and drop a white towel over the gatepost wherever he was needed," said Betty, who has done extensive research of her family tree and has, since 2003, written an engrossing blog documenting her family and life. "And this is what blew my mind when I learned that. I realized that I, too, had spent my whole life dropping white towels over fences. I never ran for public office. I never sought a position anyplace I've been. I was always going around showing people where things needed to be changed. I spent my life doing that, and I'm still doing it."

Betty grew up in East Oakland, California, with little conscious awareness of race. There were then fewer than twenty thousand African-Americans living between Sacramento and Monterey, and only about fifteen black families in the East Bay, most of whom were Betty's cousins. "We thought we were together because we liked the company. My life was surrounded by Creole pride and Catholicism," said Betty, who knew next to nothing then about African-American culture.

During her youth, the only experience she had with racism occurred when an English teacher told Betty that, though she deserved it, she could not give her the lead part in a play because the other students' parents would never allow it. "For the first time, I understood for a fact that I wasn't white," she said. Besides her light skin color, one of the reasons she never thought of herself as any different from her white classmates was that her father, whom she adored, never considered himself black. He spoke of African-Americans as "American Negroes" and, without apology, treated dark-skinned people as underlings. As well, her parents, who spoke French patois at home in their ethnically mixed and working-class neighborhood, worried mostly that Betty would "marry black." No one considered what she might do with her life other than marry, and, she said, "My mother set the bar pretty low. She mostly wanted her daughters to marry handsome men and to get married before they became pregnant."

A date in 1940 with a former UCLA gridiron star named Jackie Robinson, seven years before the future Hall of Famer broke Major League baseball's color line, sparked her racial awareness as had nothing before. Betty's father was peeking from a doorway when Robinson, wearing a tuxedo and carrying a corsage, arrived to escort the beautiful and sought-after nineteen-year-old to a postgame party at the International House, on the University of California Berkeley campus. "The look of horror on my father's face was enough to ruin my evening," Betty said, adding, with a smile, "But I braved it out." Still, her father's behavior prompted her to cut off communications with him for a while and planted the seeds of a powerful consciousness about race.

Her alienation from her family ended when Betty married Mel Reid on May 24, 1942. Her parents considered the chisel-faced, café-au-lait star athlete at San Francisco State "a good catch." He was, after all, the descendant of a pioneering African-American family that arrived in California before the Civil War. In a wedding photograph, taken in Betty's parents' backyard, the slim-waisted bride and the dimple-chinned groom looked like fashion models. Six months after the bombing of Pearl Harbor, it betrays nothing of the ways World War II was about to change the context of their lives.

Like millions of other women who answered the call to "make history, working for victory" by replacing men who were joining the fight, Betty took a job. Hers was as a filing clerk in the basement of the Civil Service Commission in San Francisco. The job was monotonous and incomprehensible, until years later when she figured out that the pink and blue cards she was filing indicated to the FBI who was suspect as a Nazi or communist sympathizer and who was okay. She transferred to a job with the air force in an Oakland office building. Not long after, she began to run into an acquaintance. Instead of acting warmly, the woman ducked out of sight every time she saw Betty. Her reaction was confounding until one day the two women met in a restaurant. "What are you passing for?" Betty's friend asked. "What am I passing for?" Betty said. "I'm not passing for anything."

"Oh, you must be," her friend said, "because they don't hire any colored folks here."

Betty became self-conscious and panicky, and she realized that the only other African-American people working in the office were employed in the canteen or as janitors. Not long after, the lieutenant in charge of the food section asked the woman who worked next to Betty to come to the front of the office to speak with him. "She kept nodding her head and was very animated. Her face got redder and redder," Betty said. "When she came back to her desk, I asked, 'What was that?' She didn't want to answer. 'Was that about me?'"

The embarrassed woman admitted to Betty that the officer wanted to know if she knew that Betty was "colored." "He thought I should know because I've been spending a lot of time with you," she said. Betty leaped up from her desk and strode to the lieutenant's desk. "Who told you that I was *not* colored?" she said. "Don't worry, Betty, I've spoken with your supervisor and your friend," he said. "It's okay, your work is fine. Everyone's willing to work with you."

"But are they willing to work under me?" Betty asked. "What happens when I get an upgrade?" The lieutenant assured her that she would get paid accordingly. Betty turned around, picked up her things, and walked out. She was shocked to be treated as a second-class citizen and she was not going to tolerate it. "That's when I fired the government."

That evening Betty received a telegram from Mel with the cryptic message: "It didn't work out." After dropping out of college to enlist, he had left home three days earlier for Seattle and his induction into the navy. When he returned home to Oakland, he told Betty how he had been segregated with other young black men and told he was being shipped to Michigan for training in the Messmen's Corps. Mel had wanted to fight for his country, and he refused to accept being told that the only job for which he was fit was working in a kitchen. The navy gave him a psychological exam, issued him a check for forty-five dollars, and mustered him out of the service with an honorable discharge. "And for this, he'd left college!" Betty said.

After leaving her air force office job, Betty went to work in Richmond, which had become the center of the wartime shipyard business, spearheaded by contractor Henry Kaiser. Overnight, everything about the East Bay changed. Nowhere was that more true than in Richmond. Until then, it had been a sleepy town of twenty-four thousand residents, almost all white. The exceptions were a handful of Japanese greenhouse owners, who would soon be sent to internment camps, a few original Mexican families, and 270 African-Americans. Her experience was hardly the stuff of Norman Rockwell's iconic can-do, sleeves-rolled-up woman riveter. Chronic labor shortages in the Bay Area had helped white women, the so-called "Rosies" (actually Wendy Welders in Richmond), get skilled jobs in the shipyards. But blacks, mostly recruited by Kaiser from the Deep South, who eventually made up nearly 20 percent of a shipyard workforce that rapidly swelled to 100,000, faced blatant discrimination.

Once again, she was hired to do filing. This time it was for the Boilermakers Union, Auxiliary 36. Black women did not get a chance to work industrial jobs in the shipyard until the final months of the war. Black shipyard workers were classified as "trainees" and relegated to powerless Jim Crow union auxiliaries, including the one where Betty was hired. They paid dues, but were not given the right to be trained for skilled jobs, a strategy meant to ensure that black workers would not be able to compete for jobs with white labor when the war ended. "It was hoped they would return to the cotton fields and tenant farms from where they'd come," Betty said.

Mel, who worked part-time in the shipyards as a "chipper," and Betty had by then moved into their own house, a duplex on Sacramento Street in a then-integrated neighborhood of Southwest Berkeley which they had bought from an Italian-American named Aldo Musso. When Mel had expressed an interest in getting into business for himself, Musso, who had a jukebox route, agreed to show Mel the ropes. While working for him, changing records in jukeboxes and making collections, Mel noticed how difficult it was to find so-called race music for the black bars, clubs, restaurants, and sandwich shops springing up in the Bay Area.

Soon, he and Betty were selling 78s out of their garage. When Mel was working his other jobs or off playing football (he was an MVP quarterback for the Oakland Giants in the pre-NFL Pacific Coast League), Betty ran the store. She did so while tending to Rick, the infant boy she and Mel adopted in March 1945, after she failed to conceive during the first three years of marriage. To stimulate the new business, the couple bought radio time on a local station, WKRE. In those days, radio stations had no black disc jockeys but some of the hipper deejays picked up on what the Reids promoted. One day, after the Reids played "Around the Clock," a slightly risqué recording by blues shouter Wynonie Harris, other deejays kept replaying it and droves of customers began scouring the neighborhood for the Reids' garage. "We sold out of it that day," Betty said.

By the start of the next decade, the record business was lucrative enough for the Reids to buy a half-acre lot Mel had seen one day driving through the suburb of Walnut Creek. In 1950, Betty had given birth to the first of three children. To accommodate their growing family, the couple began designing a four-bedroom redwood house, inspired by pictures of homes in *House Beautiful* and *Sunset* magazines. They were shocked when they were confronted by racially motivated threats. "We didn't know we were moving into a hornet's nest," Betty said. "But pretty soon, we began to get letters from neighbors warning that if we tried to stack lumber to build our house, they would burn it."

No overt acts of violence ever occurred, but unbeknownst to Betty and Mel, their adopted son Rick, the first black student in the elementary school, was regularly bullied with impunity. On one occasion, Betty learned that the Parkmead Elementary School was holding a minstrel show for a PTA fund-raiser. Betty was appalled by the vision of white people in blackface and kinky wigs, and summoned the courage to confront the principal. She went to his office unannounced. He wasn't there, but his costume of baggy pants and polka-dot shirt was hanging on the door. "I could feel my chest tighten," she recalled. "I knew this was terribly wrong, but I still didn't know why I was so offended."

When the principal returned, his face reddened. Betty asked if it was true that the school was having a minstrel show. He said it was, but he wanted her to know there was no intent to insult anyone. "We're doing this to show how happy black people were," he said.

"Do I look happy?" Betty said. When he acknowledged that she did not, instead of demanding that the show be canceled, she asked only that the principal inform the participants of how she felt and that she would be sitting in the front row for their performance. "It was a miserable night from which little was gained," she said. "There was as much anger and resentment stirred by my act as there was enlightenment."

Her metamorphosis into the person she calls "Betty the Defender" had its genesis in the mid-1950s, when she read about an improvement association at a newly built housing development in nearby Pleasant Hill that was trying to prevent a young African-American couple, a truck driver and a nurse, from moving into a home they bought. The association was distributing pamphlets warning the community that the couple endangered its health, safety, and property values, and it had scheduled a meeting to air its concerns at a local school.

Dressed carefully to avoid calling attention to herself, Betty slipped into the school auditorium unnoticed. She listened as, one after another, residents stood and spoke against *The Invasion of the Undesirables!*" She was lost in ironic reflection that for all her "undesirability," no one had noticed the blackest woman in Walnut Creek when her attention was called back by a shrill voice: "If we can't get the niggers out any other way, we can use the health department because of the filthy diseases they'll bring in!"

Now Betty rose from her seat. She walked to the front of the auditorium and turned to face the crowd. "I'm Betty Reid and I'm one of the *undesirables* you're speaking about," she said. The audience stared at her in disbelief. "The words threatened to dry up mid-throat! I spoke nonstop for ten minutes," she said. She talked about her family's experience in Walnut Creek. She said that she knew that members of her community had every right under the Constitution to *feel* that resentment. "But I said that that same Constitution guaranteed my family and the new neighbors in Pleasant Hill the right to house our families as we wished. I told members of the homeowners association that they would survive, just as we had."

When she finished speaking, she walked straight down the aisle to the main door and into the menacingly dark parking lot. "My mouth was bone-dry and panic was taking over my body as I heard chairs scraping against the floor of the auditorium and feet scuffling." As she reached her car, Betty heard footsteps rushing behind her. She was crying in terror as she struggled to put her key into the door lock. At last, she heard a young reporter's voice reassuring her. He only wanted her address and phone number. She was momentarily relieved. But as the reporter retreated, Betty felt a strong hand on her shoulder. "It's all right, I'm David," a man soothed. He was a lawyer, David Bortin, who had read Betty's recent letter to the editor in the newspaper denouncing the homeowners' association's racism and called to offer his support. When she had told him she was going to speak at the meeting that night, he had expressed his concern for her welfare and promised to be present at the meeting.

The following day, the *Contra Costa Times* reported on Betty's appearance at the last known meeting of the Gregory Gardens Improvement Association and on the night that was a turning point in Betty's life. Not only had she dared to speak as never before, but Bortin's support gave her hope in humanity that she desperately needed. He also invited Betty to the fledgling Mt. Diablo Unitarian Fellowship. She went, and the congregation's embrace was additionally healing and empowering. "It gave me permission I didn't have from any other place," she said. "Here was a community of people who were content to search together, who did not need to agree on answers." She became an active and adored member. "Betty just had this delicate, shimmering quality and a warmth that put everyone at ease," said Bortin's widow, Beverly.

But Betty's newfound courage put her on a psychological collision course with her upbringing, her religion, and the racially hostile community where she lived. In addition, she was contending with the painful stress of knowing that her adopted teenage son, Rick, was homosexual—long before gay liberation—and that her toddler daughter, Dorian, was brain-damaged and would need support for the rest of her life. Making matters worse, Mel was unwilling to discuss any of the issues with Betty. Instead, he retreated into longer hours at the store and affairs with other women.

As a result, she grew depressed and suicidal. One afternoon, she nearly killed herself after suffering a panic attack while driving across the San Francisco Bay Bridge and becoming unconscious with fear at the wheel. When she came to, she drove her car into a hillside. After her release from the hospital, Betty stayed at home for three years while being treated for severe depression by a Jungian psychiatrist. Betty's full recovery set the stage for the next phase of her life. "Looking into the seductive face of suicide can be the catalyst for monumental changes—for those of us who survive the temptation to use this permanent answer to temporary change," she told me.

And change monumentally she did, mentored by minister Aaron Gilmartin, the agnostic socialist leader of the Mt. Diablo church. At first, she became active in the civil rights movement and then, gingerly, in the Black Revolution. She cautiously participated in protests and, with Gilmartin driving her into Haight-Ashbury in San Francisco in his Volkswagen bus, occasionally delivered money raised by the mostly white church members for support of Eldridge Cleaver and the Black Panthers. "I was a well-dressed, station-wagon-driving dilettante," Betty appraised. "I didn't really know anyone in the Panthers but served as a conduit, the vessel through which the congregation could express its activism."

Betty's political development was hastened by the race riots in Detroit and Newark in 1967, when disenfranchised African-American communities reacted violently to acts of police brutality. In the aftermath, a major rift developed in the Unitarian church. Some black intellectual leaders, supported by whites, including Gilmartin, called on black Unitarians to forge their own agenda and abandon the immediate goal of racial integration. "Gil" urged Betty to enter the debate and represent Walnut Creek's Unitarians when African-American Unitarians held their first national black caucus in Chicago. With no college degree and no real job experience, Betty felt ill equipped and went reluctantly. But there, she met and mixed with people like Carl Stokes, the mayor of Cleveland; poet Gwendolyn Brooks; the Reverend Jesse Jackson; and historian and editor Lerone Bennett Jr. She became particularly close with Henry Hampton, who would one day make the definitive PBS documentary on the civil rights movement, *Eyes on the Prize*. Initially excited by the brilliant black intellectuals she met in the Black Movement, she grew disillusioned by the reverse racism, the increasingly violent rhetoric, and the sexist hypocrisy she witnessed over the next couple of years. She walked out of her third and last black Unitarian conference in Cleveland. "On the way home, I kept thinking, *It's not about race. It's not about color. Something else is going on here.* When I lived in suburbia, I was not quite white enough. When I went into the Black Movement, I was not quite black enough. I had the sense of being nothing until I realized I was ahead of everybody else. I was everything." She decided she would affirm her blackness, but in a multiracial perspective. On the plane ride back to California, she penned a song with the lyrics, "And someday, it shall be the blackness and the white of us/ are just the day and night of us." It was one of several of her own poetic and political songs she began to sing at college concerts with unique and captivating folk jazz phrasing. She briefly considered offers to make a career of singing.

She ultimately rejected the idea and, at fifty-one, found herself back in Walnut Creek, alone. By then, Rick had his own place in Berkeley, Bob was becoming a professional folksinger, and David, still in high school, was traveling in Europe. Dorian was in a boarding school several hours away. "Here I am, in this four-bedroom house with a senile black rabbit, a fifteen-year-old turtle, and three cats," she said.

Politics rescued her from despair and bolstered her ego. She was elected—in the same white community that had threatened her two decades earlier—to serve as a George McGovern delegate at the 1972 Democratic National Convention in Miami. It was a bizarre convention, but a heady time for Betty. Actors Shirley MacLaine, Leonard Nimoy, and Marlo Thomas, and activist Dolores Huerta of the Farm Workers Union, were among the other California delegates, and, after rubbing shoulders with them, Betty's self-esteem continued to grow.

At home and flying on adrenaline from the experience, she applied for her first job since World War II, as an administrator for a start-up research study known as Project Community. Led by noted social psychologist William Soskin, a professor at UC Berkeley, the study was meant to examine addiction in the wake of rampant drug use in Haight-Ashbury and elsewhere in the sixties. After an initial interview, Soskin asked Betty for lunch. Ostensibly, Soskin—a former member of Lyndon Johnson's Great Society brain trust—wanted to hear Betty's account of the Democratic Convention. He was smitten, hired Betty, and six months later they were dating. She was fifty-five when they married in 1976.

"We had a good and very Berkeley marriage," Betty said. Soskin was a tall, pipe-smoking, cashmere-sweater-wearing social scientist. "I was his trophy wife. He got to look much more sophisticated than he really was because he had this exotic, pretty, youngish-looking wife. And I got ten years of travel, unbelievable exposure, and was a faculty wife," she added. After more than thirty-five years of struggle and racial tension, life with Bill leveled the playing field. The Soskin's living room became a meeting place for leaders in the new

Human Potential Movement and friends who, like Soskin, were serious Tibetan Buddhists, including psychologist and LSD advocate Timothy Leary, science fiction writer Isaac Asimov, and social psychologist and futurist Don Michaels. "After years of making oatmeal, wiping noses, kissing boo-boos, I found myself as curious as a twelve-year-old—with a thirst for knowing what I was only dimly aware of until that time," she said. "I got my Ph.D. at the breakfast table."

In 1978, grittier realities intruded into Betty's idyllic Berkeley existence and pulled her back to Sacramento Street, galvanizing her, once and for all, as an advocate for public good.

Her son Rick had arrived for work at Reid's Records one morning and found Mel in a coma in the back room, where he had been living for months. The neighborhood, in decline for years, had gotten drastically worse; there had been so many break-ins that Mel had taken to sleeping there with a rifle at his side. Betty rushed to her ex-husband. He had, it turned out, been diagnosed as diabetic but told no one. His body was so ravaged that after years of not having seen him, Betty barely recognized him. His decline was mirrored by the descent of the street. Drug dealers ruled the neighborhood, cruised the sidewalks, and conducted their business on benches outside the store and at crack dens and bordellos across the street. Given Mel's desperate medical condition, Betty had barely noticed the street that day. At the hospital, Bill Soskin stood next to her at Mel's bedside as the former athlete woke from anesthesia and was told his right leg had been amputated.

Betty left the drug research project. While she had become Soskin's full-fledged partner, writing grants, editing research, and working as a co–drug therapist at schools where the program was run, her list of responsibilities had grown too overwhelming. Not only did it include tracking Dorian's care and visiting her regularly at a boarding school; caring for her aging, ninety-plus-year-old father, blind and bedridden, and her mother; and shopping for Mel and chauffeuring him to medical appointments, she was about to add running Reid's Records. She had once hoped the store would provide a financial legacy for her children. In the sixties, Mel's uncle, Paul Reid, a successful insurance businessman and popular gospel deejay, had joined him in the record business. Together, they transformed Reid's Records into one of the biggest outlets for gospel music on the West Coast. They staged major gospel concerts with the likes of James Cleveland, Shirley Caesar, and the Blind Boys. But after Paul died, the business tanked and Mel began to gamble. Sadly, the business Betty took over was a shambles. "It had found its way to the street level. Sacramento Street had become the sin capital of Berkeley," she said.

The store's counters were stocked with water pipes, rolling papers, and drug paraphernalia. Black light posters of nudes hung on the walls. The store's annual gross sales had plummeted from $300,000 to next to nothing. The Internal Revenue Service had seized the duplex where Betty and Mel had lived as newlyweds. And the store itself was in foreclosure. Its only remaining value was the two-story stucco commercial building itself.

"I remember standing there, knowing little about how to save the business, and saying to myself, *Okay, Betty, you can only manage five hundred feet. And everything in my five hundred feet has to be right,*" she recalled.

Of all the many turning points in her life, her determination to act now, to reclaim the dream of the store and a patch of the street, would be the bravest and the most transformative. Though the culture of the street and the times were stacked against her, she was compelled to challenge her world with action. In other words, it was one of those defining moments in Betty's life and in the lives of the other subjects of this book, that personality, history, and an event combined to cause personal perception to shift tectonically and courage to be activated. Suddenly, Betty knew what she had to do with the rest of her life if it was going to have meaning.

"The successful iconoclast learns to see things clearly for what they are and is not influenced by other people's opinions," neuroscientist Gregory Berns wrote in *Iconoclast,* a book examining how innovative thinkers break through barriers. Referring to the part of the brain responsible for the processing and memory of emotion, Berns continued, "He keeps his amygdala in check and doesn't let fear rule his decisions. And he expertly navigates the complicated waters of social networking so that other people eventually come to see things the way he does."

One of Betty's first steps was quite simple. She put a can of paint under the counter and whenever she saw a mark of graffiti on her building, "I would get my little can and go paint over it." After a while, "the little drug dealers who stood at the bus stop across the street wouldn't let anyone put a mark on it, either. And at night, when I was in the store alone, if they saw anyone suspicious enter, they would wander in to make sure I was all right."

Betty got her first practical lesson in local politics when she came to suspect her upstairs tenant, a professed businessman, of being a major drug dealer in the neighborhood. When she tried to push him out, he pushed back with lightly veiled threats. Betty assumed political connections could help, and through a well-heeled friend of Soskin's, she secured a meeting with Shirley Dean, a former mayor who was running for the city council. Dean declined to help. Instead, she told Betty that she considered the tenant an important community leader and was counting on him to bring out the vote for her ticket.

Livid, Betty got in her car and drove directly to the opposing Democratic mayoral candidate's headquarters. Without knowing anything about political newcomer Gus Newport, Betty took home as many campaign posters as she could carry. She plastered her store windows with them and got all the merchants in a three-block radius to do the same. The next day, when she drove down from affluent Grizzly Peak to Southwest Berkeley, she found that all of her posters were turned around and replaced by Dean's posters. Her tenant had harassed the store owners after she had visited them. None cared enough about politics to resist. But she was not about to be intimidated. She went to work knocking on doors and registering voters. She even got the young drug dealers who had befriended her to put on shirts and ties and help her. "It was a wonderful experiment in democracy," she said, tickled by the memory. Her candidate won, and Dean's ticket was defeated. "For the first time I saw how I could move politically. I flexed my political muscles and something happened."

With chain record stores opening in the area, Betty soon realized that Reid's Records would never do the kind of business it once did. But she saw an opportunity to use the store as a social platform that might be able to save Sacramento Street. She conceived of a strategy by which she would be "pretty little Dr. Soskin's wife when that was convenient" to make some political inroads, and "slip into being my angry black merchant from Sacramento Street when I needed" to make others. To improve her political position, Betty got herself hired as an aide to a Berkeley council member, Don Jelinek. He had been her lawyer when she divorced Mel. Before moving to Berkeley, the native New Yorker had served as a civil rights lawyer for Martin Luther King Jr. in Mississippi. Betty began attending city council meetings and preparing information packets for Jelinek, and soon became City Hall savvy. It was not long before Mayor Newport appointed her to serve on a committee to select sites for low-income housing in the city. She soon had an arsenal of information with which to create the Sacramento Street Housing Development Corporation and push for the redevelopment of the blighted street. "I learned to set myself short-term, achievable goals, and to be satisfied with the fulfillment of them," she said.

For seven years, Betty worked behind the scenes, convincing city officials that the shooting galleries, houses of prostitution, and other derelict buildings were a cancer in the South Berkeley community and had to be removed. She came up against those in government who believed in a kind of appeasement policy, allowing the illicit activity to continue on Sacramento Street to keep it from arising elsewhere. On the street, there were many who distrusted Betty's motives, fearing her efforts to clean up the block were a self-motivated ploy for gentrification.

Finally, one day in 1985, she was working in the record store when she heard the sound of large construction trucks on the move. "We rushed to the front of the store to stare out the windows at the sight of that humongous claw machine chewing its way through that infamous house across the street," she said. As a crowd gathered, Betty thought about all the people who had told her she would never succeed and of all the time she'd been plodding along, identifying steps, making moves, and drawing others along, despite their protests." "And here it was, happening before our eyes," she said. The following week, the street rejoiced, a band played in the newly cleared lot, and children flew kites over Sacramento Street. "It was like an exorcism."

Not long after, the then-sixty-five-year-old Betty held a ceremonial shovel, along with Mayor Lonnie Hancock, and broke ground for the \$8.5 million construction of forty-one units of affordable housing that would resuscitate the neighborhood.

Surely Betty deserved some respite, a time to savor her success. But for the next decade, her life was consumed with painful personal upheaval. Her marriage to Soskin ended in as Berkeley-like a way as it began: he left for India to become a lama. "When Bill went off, I still loved him very much. Mel was my best friend, but Bill was my great adventure, my great love." Then, within a two-year span, the three most significant men in Betty's life died: Mel, at seventy, after a decade of decline; her father, Dorson Louis Charbonnet, at ninety-five; and Bill Soskin, in 1988, of cancer. They were followed by her son, Rick, who died an alcoholic, at age fifty, in 1991. Four years later, Betty's mother died, at 101.

In addition to those emotional trials, in her seventies, Betty had to devote considerable time and energy to settling her now middle-aged daughter, Dorian, into an independent life in her own apartment in the community, monitoring it and occasionally, for Dorian's safety and welfare, bringing her home to live with her. "Since she has little awareness of what the risks are, she does better than I do," said Betty, who even now continues to oversee Dorian's daily life. "My Dorian will live her life like the bird with a broken wing, designed to fly but unable to fulfill her promise for reasons beyond her control or mine."

As heartbreaking as the deaths of so many important men in her life were, according to her sons, they also released Betty into yet another new stage of growth. She became even more confident, self-directed, and independent. "She had always deferred to men. She was articulate, but she wasn't confident. She didn't have her own constituency," her son Bob told me. "Now, she seemed a force in her own right." As if to put an exclamation mark on that, the California Women's Legislative Caucus named her the 1995 "Woman of the Year" for her work fostering the redevelopment of South Berkeley.

Betty, reflecting with characteristic modesty on the recognition, says only, "I follow what's in front of me to be done and I do it. I'm often doing things I don't know how to do. I just find a hole and I fill it."

Wisdom, of course, has long been considered the primary virtue of old age, surely one that Betty possessed in amplitude by her late seventies. Which is why Dion Aroner, a state assemblywoman, hired her at seventy-eight, in 1999, to work as her outreach representative in west Contra Costa County. Such jobs are generally reserved for twenty-somethings who exchange energy and passion for political experience and mentoring. When Betty assumed the role, she instantly became the oldest legislative aide in California. "Betty and my relationship wasn't like that," Aroner laughed. "Betty wasn't learning from me, I was learning from Betty." She had impeccable intuition that was grounded in formidable knowledge, Aroner added. "Her eyes were critical to our success."

Left to find her own way in Richmond, San Pablo, El Cerrito, and other cities in the assembly district, Betty got involved with the Rosie the Riveter/World War II National Home Front Historic Park in 2000 after President Clinton signed legislation giving the national park the go-ahead. Its goal was to honor the six million women who labored in the shipyards and in industrial jobs across the United States, challenged traditional notions of women's capabilities, and ensured American wartime productivity during World War II. As Betty listened to planning specialists bat around their visions of the park, she became perturbed. "The whole thing was preposterous. If they tried to tell the story as designated, they were going to tell a white story in an overwhelmingly minority city," she said. "If they wanted to make this entire city into a park, they damn well couldn't do it that way. They had to allow for the multiple stories."

The project manager for the Rosie the Riveter Memorial, cultural historian Donna Graves, was also hoping to create a more inclusive history. She asked Betty to give an oral history as a "Rosie the Riveter" for one of eight bay trail markers—eighteen-foot-tall metal stanchions meant to suggest the prow of a ship—that contain old photos and quotations from people who worked in the wartime shipyards. Once she became convinced that she would not be seen as a "Rosie" ("That's a white woman's story"), Betty obliged. "The war shed light on America's promise," her quote says in part, on a marker with the theme Divided We Live.

As Betty drove me around Richmond, she pointed out the churches, movie theaters, union halls, and housing from which blacks and other minorities were excluded during World War II. More problematic was showing where minorities had lived, worked, and enjoyed themselves. Those homes and buildings were demolished in just weeks after the war ended in a failed attempt to get African-Americans to return to the southern states from which they had come. Richmond today has a population that is 44 percent black. With another 12 percent Asian and Pacific Islander, Betty believed passionately that the national park there needed to have a wider palette of voices than originally seemed likely.

Because 75 percent of the shipyard workforce during World War II was white, some historians and site planners were concerned that Betty's vision of the park would "overrepresent" the African-American story. Officially, that restraint disappeared when the National Park Service brought in Superintendent Martha Lee from Yosemite National Park in 2005 to take charge of the World War II Home Front park and three other national parks in California. "For us to thrive here we needed to demonstrate that our history is this rich, diverse fabric, interwoven with these stories that have never been told in our schools or university classes, stories like the ones Betty had started to turn over stones to uncover," Lee said, referring to a documentary, *Lost Conversations,* that Betty wrote and narrated for the park service to help start a dialogue on the subject with visitors.

In 2006, thanks to Lee's nomination, Betty was honored by the National Women's History Project in Washington, D.C., as one of the nation's "builders of communities and dreams sustained."

But because she believed that Betty had still more to contribute— that the park service, in fact, needed Betty's peerless ability to identify who to contact in the community and how to best approach them—the following year Lee offered the eighty-six-year-old a new wardrobe, Smokey the Bear hat included. Betty put a side her reservations, and accepted. After a brief period feeling awkward about it, Betty now wears her government uniform with pride and rarely goes out into the community dressed otherwise. She loves the look in little girls' faces when they see her, and she imagines that they are seeing another possibility of what they could become. There is, too, another aspect. "Life has placed a soapbox under my feet. And as the number of female home-front workers grows smaller each year, I feel a growing responsibility to a generation that helped save the world from Nazi imperialism—the same generation for whom my right to a place in the workforce was questionable at best."

To meet the challenge of that paradox, Betty created an innovative bus tour to introduce visitors to the national park as a place critical to both the Allied victory and the history of civil rights in America. On the tour, after a park ranger discusses the importance of a particular site, an older African-American, incognito until then, speaks up and says something like, "Ah, honey, that was for the white folks. Colored folk weren't allowed to go in there." Unfailingly, people on the tours begin to share stories. "We're having conversations that weren't possible ten years ago," Betty said. "Henry Kaiser was not a social reformer, but, when he built the shipyards in Richmond, he brought together white privilege and black expectation, and together those forces changed the whole nation. Another story of emancipation was born."

Betty's amazing journey speaks not only about the evolution of the nation's attitudes toward race, it also demonstrates how far we have come and how we can continue to grow and develop beyond anything we once imagined. As her story and the others in this book testify, with passion and purpose, we can, at any age, empower ourselves to do things that change the world and change history in ways subtle and significant.

So it was that Betty came to sit in the audience on January 21, 2009, as President Obama was sworn into office, the nation's first African-American commander in chief. As he spoke of how his father might not have been served in a restaurant sixty years earlier, tears came to her eyes. "And the kinship with power rained down. I recognized that he was one of us because he had lived the black experience," she said. Despite her ambiguous skin coloring, she, too, had lived the black experience and surmounted its hardship. "That can never be erased, no matter how long I live," she said. "My children and grandchildren will confront their own time in their own ways. I pray that I've provided them a model of how that might be done and that, however they identify, it will be with pride and dignity." Betty reached for her cell phone and called their numbers, as if by some magic she might extend her feeling of power across the continent to them. And then she touched the little picture in the pocket next to her heart, and hoped that her great-grandmother Mammá Leontine Breaux Allen might feel it, too.

Notes

Introduction

1 *"that hulking milestone of mortality"*: William Styron, *Darkness Visible: A Memoir of Madness* (New York: Random House, 1990), 78.

1 *In recent years, neuroscientists have been providing news*: *The Brain That Changes Itself* by Norman Doidge, M.D. (New York: Penguin, 2007), provided a fascinating introduction to neuroplasticity and the scientific pioneers who discovered and mapped the ways in which the structure of the brain changes to meet its challenges. Dr. Doidge's book captured my imagination and underscored themes that I considered as I gathered my subjects' stories.

2 *79 percent of boomers between fifty and fifty-nine did not intend to voluntarily retire from full-time work at the traditional age*: The MetLife Foundation/Civic Ventures Encore Career Survey was directed by Phyllis N. Segal of Civic Ventures and conducted by Peter D. Hart Research Associates, Inc., from February to April 2008. It involved 1,063 phone interviews and 2,522 online interviews. By 2008, boomers had rapidly advanced into encore careers without much help from institutions or policy makers, the survey found. Those pursuing encore careers were hardly

unusual, amounting to somewhere between 6 and 9.5 percent of those forty-four to seventy years old, or between 5.3 and 8.4 million men and women.

2 *encore careers*: In Marc Freedman's *Encore: Finding Work That Matters in the Second Half of Life* (Philadelphia: PublicAffairs, 2007), the founder and CEO of Civic Ventures notes that 25 percent of all U.S. residents will be sixty or older by 2030. In arguing for second careers, Freedman was looking beyond the need for baby boomers to earn money to defray the costs of living longer lives to how they could best use their accumulated knowledge and skills for the greater good, solving society's largest problems.

3 *three pounds of protoplasm*: I don't remember precisely when I first heard Marian C. Diamond, Ph.D., one of the world's leading neuroanatomists and a professor at the University of California at Berkeley, use this phrase to refer to the brain. But she owns it. She has used it often in her writings and university lectures on anatomy, and she used it in a 2009 telephone interview. For forty years, Diamond and her colleagues studied the brain development of rats in enriched and impoverished environments. To create enriched environments, toys were placed in the cages of some rats. Those rats were found to have more connections in their brains than rats that were kept in empty cages. After discovering during a visit to Japan that lab rats there lived much longer than those in her labs, she discovered that touching and holding rats, rather than leaving them untouched in their cages, significantly extended their lifespans.

Surrounding "ourselves with a rich amount of stimuli to fulfill a useful life can mean living a full one hundred years," Diamond said. She likes to enumerate five commonsense elements to promote ongoing neurological development as we age: diet (particularly protein, vitamin B_6, and antioxidants); exercise (an hour a day, she says, is optimal, including balancing on one leg at a time for at least one minute); challenge (because the brain gets bored); novelty (new ideas and activities); and love (a warm, nonsexual touch). At eighty-two, still teaching neuroanatomy at Berkeley, she travels to Cambodia each winter to work with children in a neural development program at an impoverished orphanage run by Buddhist monks. She also continues to swim laps five days a week, at 5:45 a.m., in Berkeley's Hearst Pool, "where the air is freezing but the water delicious."

3 *the more likely it is to shrink*: Numerous skill acquisition studies have found functional enlargement of regions that underlie particular skills. An MRI study by the Wellcome Department of Imaging Neuroscience at the Institute of Neurology in London showed that the left angular gyrus—an important language center of the brain—contains more gray matter in bilinguals than in people who speak